Europeanization and the European Economic Area

This book examines Europeanization in the European Economic Area (EEA), exploring whether non-member states can have an input into EU decision-making and whether the EU can successfully export its policies within the framework of the EEA.

Iceland, Norway and Liechtenstein, while not EU member states, are members of the European Free Trade Association (EFTA) and signatories of the EEA Agreement. The Agreement allows participation in the EU's internal market but also requires extensive and continuous adaptation to EU rules. Whilst existing literature is limited mainly to the EU's impact on its own member states or neighbours to the east, this book extends the study of Europeanization to the EEA, exploring whether Iceland, as a non-member state, can have an input into EU decision-making and, conversely, whether the EU can ensure that its policies are adhered to outside its borders. The author argues that, although the EEA Agreement is not without its challenges, it has proved considerably more resilient than originally expected. This raises the question of whether the EEA provides a realistic alternative to EU membership for other states with close ties to the EU.

Delving into the largely unknown intersection between the EU and the EEA and providing important new insights into the Europeanization process, *Europeanization and the European Economic Area* will be of strong interest to students and scholars of European Union politics and policy-making, European Union Enlargement, Nordic politics and comparative politics.

Johanna Jonsdottir completed her doctorate in European Studies at the University of Cambridge. She is currently a policy officer at the EFTA Secretariat in Brussels.

Routledge / UACES Contemporary European Studies

Edited by Federica Bicchi, London School of Economics and Political Science, Tanja Börzel, Free University of Berlin, and Mark Pollack, Temple University, on behalf of the University Association for Contemporary European Studies
Editorial Board: Grainne De Búrca, European University Institute and Columbia University; Andreas Føllesdal, Norwegian Centre for Human Rights, University of Oslo; Peter Holmes, University of Sussex; Liesbet Hooghe, University of North Carolina at Chapel Hill and Vrije Universiteit Amsterdam; David Phinnemore, Queen's University Belfast; Ben Rosamond, University of Warwick; Vivien Ann Schmidt, University of Boston; Jo Shaw, University of Edinburgh; Mike Smith, University of Loughborough and Loukas Tsoukalis, ELIAMEP, University of Athens and European University Institute.

The primary objective of the new Contemporary European Studies series is to provide a research outlet for scholars of European Studies from all disciplines. The series publishes important scholarly works and aims to forge for itself an international reputation.

1. The EU and Conflict Resolution
Promoting peace in the backyard
Nathalie Tocci

2. Central Banking Governance in the European Union
A comparative analysis
Lucia Quaglia

3. New Security Issues in Northern Europe
The Nordic and Baltic states and the ESDP
Edited by Clive Archer

4. The European Union and International Development
The politics of foreign aid
Maurizio Carbone

5. The End of European Integration
Anti-Europeanism examined
Paul Taylor

6. The European Union and the Asia-Pacific
Media, public and elite perceptions of the EU
Edited by Natalia Chaban and Martin Holland

7. The History of the European Union
Origins of a trans- and supranational polity 1950–72
Edited by Wolfram Kaiser, Brigitte Leucht and Morten Rasmussen

8. International Actors, Democratization and the Rule of Law
Anchoring democracy?
Edited by Amichai Magen and Leonardo Morlino

9. Minority Nationalist Parties and European Integration
A comparative study
Anwen Elias

10. **European Union Intergovernmental Conferences**
Domestic preference formation, transgovernmental networks and the dynamics of compromise
Paul W. Thurner and
Franz Urban Pappi

11. **The Political Economy of State-Business Relations in Europe**
Interest mediation, capitalism and EU policy making
Rainer Eising

12. **Governing Financial Services in the European Union**
Banking, securities and post-trading
Lucia Quaglia

13. **European Union Governance**
Efficiency and legitimacy in European Commission committees
Karen Heard-Lauréote

14. **European Governmentality**
The liberal drift of multilevel governance
Richard Münch

15. **The European Union as a Leader in International Climate Change Politics**
Edited by Rüdiger K. W. Wurzel and James Connelly

16. **Diversity in Europe**
Dilemmas of differential treatment in theory and practice
Edited by Gideon Calder and Emanuela Ceva

17. **EU Conflict Prevention and Crisis Management**
Roles, institutions and policies
Edited by Eva Gross and
Ana E. Juncos

18. **The European Parliament's Committees**
National party influence and legislative empowerment
Richard Whitaker

19. **The European Union, Civil Society and Conflict**
Nathalie Tocci

20. **European Foreign Policy and the Challenges of Balkan Accession**
Sovereignty contested
Gergana Noutcheva

21. **The European Union and South East Europe**
The dynamics of Europeanization and multilevel governance
Andrew Taylor, Andrew Geddes and Charles Lees

22. **Bureaucrats as Law-Makers**
Committee decision-making in the EU Council of Ministers
Frank M. Häge

23. **Europeanization and the European Economic Area**
Iceland's participation in the EU's policy process
Johanna Jonsdottir

Europeanization and the European Economic Area

Iceland's participation in the EU's policy process

Johanna Jonsdottir

LONDON AND NEW YORK

First published 2013
by Routledge
2 Park Square, Milton Park, Abingdon, Oxfordshire OX14 4RN

Simultaneously published in the USA and Canada
by Routledge
711 Third Avenue, New York, NY 10017

First issued in paperback 2014

Routledge is an imprint of the Taylor & Francis Group, an informa business

© 2013 Johanna Jonsdottir

The right of Johanna Jonsdottir to be identified as author of this work has been asserted in accordance with sections 77 and 78 of the Copyright, Designs and Patents Act 1988.

All rights reserved. No part of this book may be reprinted or reproduced or utilised in any form or by any electronic, mechanical, or other means, now known or hereafter invented, including photocopying and recording, or in any information storage or retrieval system, without permission in writing from the publishers.

Trademark notice: Product or corporate names may be trademarks or registered trademarks, and are used only for identification and explanation without intent to infringe.

British Library Cataloguing in Publication Data
A catalogue record for this book is available from the British Library

Library of Congress Cataloging in Publication Data
Jonsdottir, Johanna, 1981-
Europeanization and the European economic area : Iceland's participation in the EU's policy process / Johanna Jonsdottir.
  p. cm. – (Routledge/UACES contemporary European studies ; 23)
Includes bibliographical references and index.
  1. European Union–Iceland. 2. European Union countries–Foreign economic relations–Iceland. 3. Iceland–Foreign economic relations–European Union countries. 4. Iceland–Politics and government–21st century. 5. Iceland–Economic policy–21st century. I. Title.
  HC360.5.J66 2012
  337.1'42094912–dc23
                                  2012018175

ISBN 13: 978-0-415-50279-5 (hbk)
ISBN 13: 978-1-138-82994-7 (pbk)

Typeset in Times by
Taylor & Francis Books

This book is dedicated to my husband and to my family.
This work is founded on their love and support.

Contents

List of figures	xi
Preface	xii
Acknowledgements	xiv
List of abbreviations	xv
Introduction	1
1 Europeanization: An analytical framework	11
Europeanization in the context of the EEA 11	
Findings from other states 20	
Measuring Europeanization 27	
2 Uploading in the EEA	33
Limitations of a small administration 34	
The Commission as the main formal point of access 38	
Lobbying decision-making bodies from the outside 44	
Intra-EFTA collaboration 48	
Exemptions and adaptations 50	
Conclusions 53	
3 Downloading in the EEA	56
Domestic intervening variables 58	
External pressures 64	
How effective are these mechanisms? 71	
Conclusions 76	
4 Market competition in the electricity sector	78
Origins and objectives of the Electricity Directive 79	
Mismatch between the EU and national levels 81	
Attempts to gain an exemption as a small isolated system 83	

x *Contents*

    Transposition without exemption 86
    Over-implementation? 90
    Conclusions 94

5 European citizenship and free movement of persons   96

    Free movement as an integral part of EU citizenship 97
    EEA-relevance as a convenient excuse for non-adoption? 101
    Can the EFTA states say 'No'? 105
    Conclusions 110

6 The Emissions Trading Scheme   113

    What is the EU ETS? 114
    Incorporation of the ETS into the EEA Agreement 117
    Special recognition for ultra-peripheral regions? 120
    Implementation at the national level – or lack thereof? 126
    Conclusions 129

7 The Food Law Package   131

    Mismatch between the EU and national levels 132
    Incorporation of the Food Law Package into the EEA
        Agreement 135
    Adoption at the national level 137
    The national debate and content of the implementing legislation 140
    Conclusions and potential next steps 145

8 Review of key findings   145

    Analytical framework, research questions and hypotheses 147
    Is Iceland a decision-shaper? 151
    How likely is domestic adaptation in Iceland? 154

9 The EEA: Challenges and future scenarios   160

    Challenges in the EEA 162
    Future of the EEA 168

Notes	179
Appendix I: Interviews	198
Appendix II: Internal EFTA documents	201
Bibliography	202
Index	214

List of Figures

0.1	EFTA and the EU in 1960	4
0.2	EFTA and the EU in 2012	5
2.1	EEA decision-making	51
3.1	Two-pillar structure of the EEA	70

Preface

This book is based largely on doctoral research conducted at the University of Cambridge during the period 2006–10, although it has been substantially revised to take into account developments up until the beginning of 2012. I first embarked on a PhD with the idea of writing about Iceland's relations with the EU. After a great deal of brainstorming an interesting angle from which to approach the topic began to emerge, i.e. to study Europeanization in the context of the European Economic Area (EEA) Agreement. More specifically, the aim was to explore two interlinked questions which had been neglected. First, can a non-member state have an impact on EU decision-making? And, conversely, can the EU ensure that its policies are adhered to in a state which is outside its borders?

At the time, Iceland's economy was booming and the government seemed perfectly content with the EEA Agreement. It provided access to the internal market which was considered crucial to the economy while also allowing Iceland to maintain full control over its lucrative fisheries sector. However, the following years turned out to be a turbulent time in Iceland's history with the onset of global financial crisis and the collapse of its banking sector in the autumn of 2008. Public pressure led to the breakdown of the ruling coalition and the coming to power of a new, largely (though not wholly) pro-EU government. In July 2009 Iceland applied for EU membership and is, at the time of writing, officially an EU candidate country. Nonetheless, pending the results of its application, it also remains an active member of EFTA and party to the EEA Agreement.

Now, at the beginning of 2012, it is of course still uncertain whether Iceland will indeed join the EU. A public referendum will take place once negotiations have been concluded, and opinion polls indicate that feelings are mixed among the population. At the same time, the EU is experiencing a high degree of internal financial turmoil coupled with a severe case of enlargement fatigue. However, whether or not Iceland joins the EU, its membership application has highlighted certain questions about the future of the EEA which make the results of this study more relevant, particularly in light of increasingly loud calls for a multi-speed Europe. For example, does the Agreement provide a realistic alternative to EU membership? Could the

Agreement continue to function with Norway and Liechtenstein as its sole non-EU members? And is the EEA a model which should be considered for other states?

Having been in force for almost two decades, the EEA Agreement has proved considerably more resilient than was expected at the time of its inception. Furthermore, it appears to have functioned relatively well over the years and in many respects it has benefited its signatory states. Although it is not without its challenges, it is clear that this is an institutional framework which deserves attention.

Acknowledgements

First and foremost, I would like to thank my PhD supervisor, Dr Julie Smith, for her substantial contribution to this work. I could not have wished for better guidance while conducting my research. My secondary supervisor, Dr Baldur Thorhallsson, provided an important link to the academic debate in Iceland. I am also grateful to my PhD examiners, Dr Ulrich Sedelmeier and Dr Geoffrey Edwards, for their valuable insights and advice regarding the post-PhD publication process. The editors of the Routledge/UACES series and two anonymous reviewers also provided many useful suggestions for improvements.

Approximately 50 individuals kindly agreed to be interviewed for this study. My interview partners were, without fail, friendly, open and forthcoming: a blessing which cannot be understated in qualitative research. I am also much indebted to the staff at the EFTA Secretariat for their helpful comments and willingness to discuss and debate the ideas put forward in this book. Permissions were also granted to quote various internal EFTA documents which provided invaluable sources of information. The figures and illustrations used in this volume are also courtesy of the EFTA Secretariat.

I would like to thank the Chevening Fund, the Cambridge Overseas Trust, the Overseas Research Student Award Scheme, the Icelandic Centre for Research Graduate Research Fund (RANNIS) and Clare College for generous financial support which made this research possible.

While I am sincerely grateful to those who have contributed to this work, all errors and omissions remain my sole responsibility.

Abbreviations

ASI	Icelandic Confederation of Labour
BSRB	Confederation of State and Municipal Employees
CAP	Common Agricultural Policy
CEECs	Central and Eastern European Countries
CFP	Common Fisheries Policy
CFSP	Common Foreign and Security Policy
CJEU	Court of Justice of the European Union
CO_2	Carbon dioxide
COREPER	Committee of Permanent Representatives
DG	Directorate-General
DSO	Distribution system operator
EC	European Community
ECJ	European Court of Justice
EEA	European Economic Area
EEAS	European External Action Service
EEC	European Economic Community
EES	European Employment Strategy
EESC	European Economic and Social Committee
EFSA	European Food Safety Authority
EFTA	European Free Trade Association
EMCO	Employment Committee
EMU	Economic and Monetary Union
ENP	European Neighbourhood Policy
EP	European Parliament
ESA	EFTA Surveillance Authority
ETS	Emissions Trading Scheme
ETUC	European Trade Union Confederation
EU	European Union
GHG	Greenhouse gas
GWh	Gigawatt hour
JCD	Joint Committee Decision
LIU	Federation of Icelandic Fishing Vessel Owners
MEP	Member of the European Parliament

MP	Member of Parliament
MW	Megawatt
NAP	National Allocation Plan
NLF	New Legal Framework
OMC	Open Method of Coordination
QMV	Qualified Majority Voting
REACH	Registration, Evaluation, Authorisation and Restriction of Chemical Substances
RELEX	External Relations
SA	Confederation of Icelandic Employers
SI	Federation of Icelandic Industries
SV	Federation of Trade
SVTH	Federation of Trade and Services
TEC	Treaty establishing the European Community
TEU	Treaty on European Union
TFEU	Treaty on the Functioning of the European Union
TSO	Transmission system operator
UK	United Kingdom
US(A)	United States (of America)
UNFCCC	United Nations Framework Convention on Climate Change
WTO	World Trade Organization

Introduction

The European Union (EU)[1] is unique among international organizations in the extent to which it can compel national governments to adapt to its rules and requirements. As a comprehensive form of regional integration in which nation-states pool sovereignty, it has had an extensive impact on its member states. The EU's competences have expanded over the years and it now legislates in a wide range of policy domains. Accordingly, academic literature has increasingly focused on the EU's impact on the domestic sphere or the adaptation of national structures, behaviour and policies in response to the demands of the EU, a process which is frequently referred to as 'Europeanization' (Bache 2008: 10; Wong 2006: 15).

The EU's impact is not confined only to its member states; it is also felt in a range of non-member states within its sphere of influence. As the EU continues to expand its power and grow in size, the question of how it can effectively structure its relations with neighbouring states is becoming ever more important. Recent studies have drawn attention to the EU's impact on candidate countries which are subject to accession conditionality and states included in the European Neighbourhood Policy (ENP) (Featherstone and Kazamias 2001b; Grabbe 2001; Hughes *et al.* 2004; Kelley 2006; Schimmelfennig and Sedelmeier 2005c). Yet, while research on non-member states has tended to focus eastwards, the few remaining non-member states in Western Europe are in many ways the most closely linked to the Union and among those most heavily affected by the EU.

In particular, the members of the European Free Trade Association (EFTA) have a longer history of EU rule adoption and closer institutional contact with the EU than most other third countries. The current members of EFTA are Iceland, Liechtenstein, Norway and Switzerland. With the exception of Switzerland, the EFTA states are parties to the European Economic Area (EEA) Agreement. As such, they adopt a large bulk of EU legislation and are almost full participants in the internal market. In fact, it has been argued that the EEA Agreement entails a form of 'quasi-membership' of the EU (Lavenex 2004: 683), which can be compared and contrasted with the EU's relations both with its member states and with other non-member states such as candidate and ENP countries.

This book directs the lens towards Europe's north-westernmost boundaries, examining Iceland's participation in the EU's policy process through the EEA Agreement. A Europeanization approach is taken in order to explore two interlinked questions. First, can a non-member state have an impact on EU decision-making? And, conversely, can the EU ensure that its policies are adhered to in a state which is outside its borders? Although the focus is on Iceland, the aim is to generally examine the way in which the EEA Agreement works in practice and the extent to which a Europeanization approach can explain the EU's impact on quasi-member states such as the EFTAns.

Conventional wisdom maintains that associated states are unable to influence EU decision-making, while actively adopting EU legislation. If this is true, it brings us face to face with one of the paradoxes of quasi-membership status, i.e. the fact that states choose this form of association at least in part to maintain their sovereignty. However, it could perhaps be argued that they are in practice giving up more sovereignty than full member states. The findings of this book can shed some light on whether the EEA does indeed entail a form of 'taxation without representation'. If so, is this a situation which is sustainable in the long run? And can it be seen as a potential model for other states? These reflections must also take into account Iceland's application for EU membership. Before elaborating further on these questions and the way in which they will be addressed throughout the book, this introductory chapter gives a brief overview of the status of Iceland's relations with the EU as well as the history and content of the EEA Agreement.

Iceland has, in recent years, been the focus of much media attention due to the collapse of its banking system in October 2008 in the wake of the global financial crisis. Iceland's economic woes prompted the newly elected centre-left government to apply for EU membership in July 2009. The incentive of joining the Eurozone was a significant factor in this decision as the crisis led to a drastic devaluation of the Icelandic krona and the implementation of strict currency exchange restrictions. Adoption of the euro was therefore seen as an important step towards regaining economic stability (Foreign Affairs Committee of the Icelandic Parliament 2009). Nonetheless, at the time of writing the government was split on the issue of EU membership. Furthermore, opinion polls generally suggest that public support for EU membership is relatively low (usually just over 30 per cent).

The outcome of these polls might partly be explained by increasingly frequent reports of the EU's own economic difficulties. However, it is clear that decision-makers and the public in Iceland have traditionally been rather Eurosceptic. In general it can be said that, prior to the events of October 2008, Iceland was committed to remaining outside the Union. Until 2009 Iceland was the only Nordic state never to have applied for EU membership[2] and, at the time of writing, the Social Democratic Alliance was the only one out of the four major political parties to have adopted an unequivocally pro-EU policy.

Iceland's reluctance to join the EU may be traced to a variety of factors. Most commonly named is the desire to retain national control over the island's abundant fisheries resources. There is also a great deal of opposition towards the Common Agricultural Policy (CAP), particularly in rural areas. Furthermore, having only become a fully independent republic in 1944, Iceland is a relatively newly independent nation, at least by Western European standards. As such, nationalistic discourse is strong in Iceland and decision-makers have generally been unwilling to promote anything that could be seen as compromising the country's sovereignty (Thorhallsson 2004a: 191). Iceland's geographical isolation, its special security relationship with the United States of America (USA) during the Cold War years, the small size of its administration and the electoral system's bias in favour of rural areas are also sometimes named as potential causes for Iceland's cautious policy towards the EU (Thorhallsson 2004a: 190–200). Therefore, a Eurosceptic Icelandic population, coupled with a financially troubled and enlargement-weary EU, may mean that Iceland's road to EU membership will be a bumpy one.

Though Iceland is not a member of the EU, it has not been immune to its influence. As previously noted, it has been closely linked to the Union since 1994 through the EEA Agreement. Iceland's participation in the EEA may in fact be one of the most salient reasons for its lack of interest in full EU membership. Until the financial crisis, the EEA Agreement was generally thought to adequately serve the country's interests as it has enabled Iceland to participate in the internal market while remaining outside less attractive areas, chiefly the Common Fisheries Policy (CFP). Based on the results of recent opinion polls, which show a lukewarm attitude towards the EU, there appear to be many who continue to feel that the EEA Agreement provides a sufficient framework for Iceland's relations with the EU.

The history of the EEA goes hand in hand with the EU's plans to develop an internal market, which gained momentum in the 1980s. At the time, Western Europe was split into two blocks: the European Economic Community (EEC) and EFTA.[3] EFTA then included seven states – Austria, Finland, Sweden, Switzerland, Iceland, Norway and Liechtenstein[4] – representing some of the EU's most important trading partners. With the aim of allowing the EFTA states to participate in the internal market, Commission President Jacques Delors proposed, in a speech to the European Parliament (EP) in 1989, the formation of a 'European Economic Area' which would have structured arrangements in trade and common institutions (EFTA Secretariat 2006: 4).

Formal negotiations for the EEA began in June 1990. The EEA Agreement was signed in May 1992 by the seven EFTA states and the then 12 EU member states and came into effect on 1 January 1994. At the time of writing, however, the EFTA parties to the EEA Agreement include only Iceland, Liechtenstein and Norway (the EFTA-3).[5] Switzerland rejected membership of the EEA in a referendum on 6 December 1992 but remains a member of EFTA, while Austria, Finland and Sweden decided to join the EU, becoming full members in 1995, thereby leading to speculation that the Agreement's primary role would be to ease the EFTA states' transition to EU membership.

4 *Introduction*

Although the Agreement has proved considerably more resilient than was perhaps expected at the outset, the eastern enlargements of 2004 and 2007 have expanded the EU's membership to 27 states,[6] which has further accentuated the disparity between the EFTA and EU sides of the EEA. Figure 0.1 shows a map of EFTA and the EU at the time when EFTA was established in 1960, while Figure 0.2 shows EFTA and the EU in 2012.

In return for access to the internal market, the EEA Agreement requires a high degree of integration of EU *acquis*[7] into the national legal systems of the participating states. The EFTA states must adopt nearly all provisions relevant to the free movement of goods, services, capital and persons. In addition, the Agreement provides for the adoption of EU legislation in a variety of horizontal areas such as labour law, consumer protection, environmental policy, statistics and company law. As the EU's legal framework is in a state of continuous development, this includes not only legislation that was in place at the time the EEA Agreement came into effect but also all new legal acts that are passed in the relevant areas, which constitutes a large bulk of EU legislation. Furthermore, the EEA is not limited to the incorporation of relevant hard law into the Agreement. It also covers participation in a wide range of EU activities and programmes, for example in the areas of research and development, education, training and youth, enterprise policy, employment

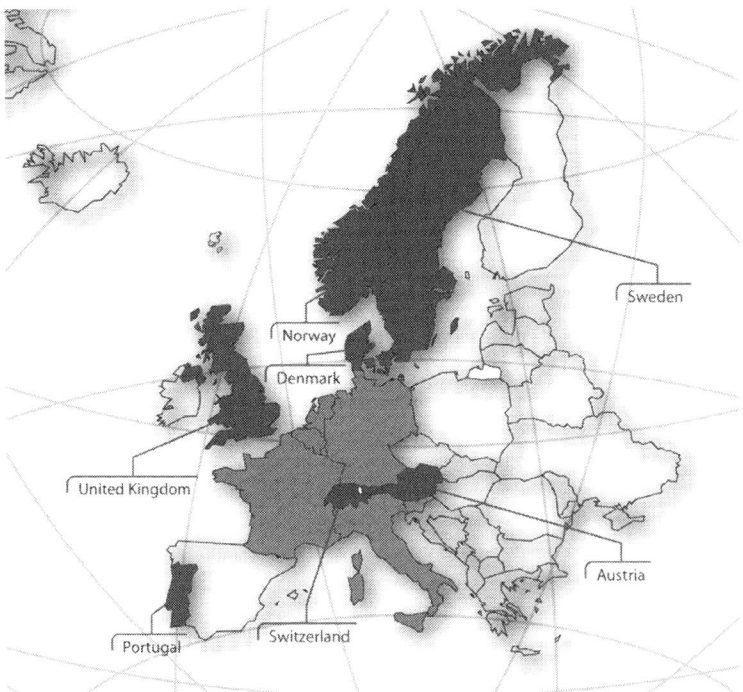

Figure 0.1 EFTA and the EU in 1960

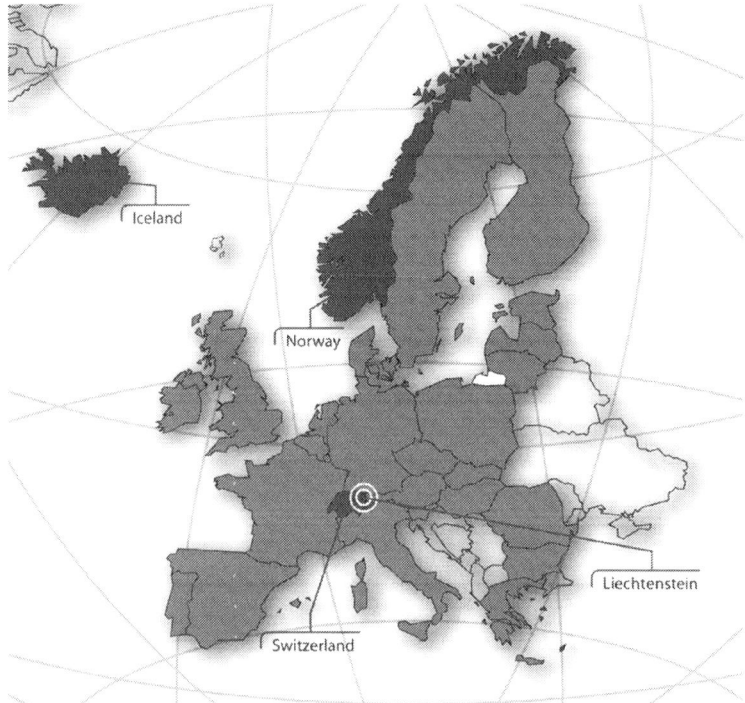

Figure 0.2 EFTA and the EU in 2012

and social policy, and civil protection. A number of substantial areas do fall outside the scope of the EEA, including the Common Agricultural and Fisheries Policies, Economic and Monetary Union (EMU), Customs Union, Common Trade Policy, Taxation, Common Foreign and Security Policy and Freedom, Security and Justice, although the EFTA states participate to a certain extent in some of these policy areas through other agreements.

The exact proportion of the EU legal framework which is covered by the EEA Agreement is difficult to measure. In 2010, the Norwegian Government commissioned a comprehensive review of Norway's agreements with the EU, the EEA being by far the most extensive. The results of this review, totalling 900 pages, were published in January 2012. The report estimates that, through its agreements with the EU, Norway has incorporated approximately three-quarters of all EU legislative acts into Norwegian legislation (EEA Review Committee 2012: 6). Iceland's membership talks with the EU are also sometimes cited as an indicator of the scope of the EEA. The Commission stated that, prior to commencing negotiations, Iceland had already fully implemented 10 and partially implemented a further 11 chapters out of a total of 33 policy chapters through the EEA Agreement (Ministry of Foreign Affairs 2012). Figures from the EFTA Secretariat show that at the end of 2010 approximately 8,300 legal acts had been incorporated into the EEA Agreement (Nordgaard 2011).

Despite the exclusion of certain fields, it is clear that the EEA Agreement is quite extensive, comprising most EU rules relevant to the four freedoms and a large number of horizontal and flanking areas. Few domestic policy sectors are thus unaffected by the EEA Agreement, and in some areas almost all national legislation adopted in the EFTA states originates in the EU (EFTA Secretariat 2002: 29). Indeed, the Norwegian report describes the 'extensive Europeanization of Norway over the last 20 years' noting that the EEA Agreement has affected far more sectors of society than was originally foreseen (EEA Review Committee 2012: 5).

The EEA Agreement has had a substantial impact not only on the content of public policy but also on the structure and behaviour of political and administrative organizations. A comparative survey conducted in the late 1990s of ministerial departments, central agencies and directorates in the Nordic countries showed that the central administrations of Iceland and Norway had undergone similar changes to those in their EU counterparts (Laergreid *et al.* 2004: 366). Furthermore, the impact of the EEA can be seen by increased transborder cooperation, the opening up of society and the transformation and diversification of the economy (Bergmann 2011).

This book aims to expand on previous findings and add new dimensions to the study of Europeanization through its focus on the EEA. As noted, Europeanization studies have generally settled around a common theme, i.e. domestic change brought about by engagement with the EU (Bache 2008: 9 and 15). However, most recent contributions exploring the impact of the EU on the domestic sphere have also recognized that there is complex interactive dynamic between member states and the Union in the sense that member states do not passively adapt to EU requirements but also actively 'upload' their preferences to the EU level (Bache 2008: 10). This study also takes an interactive view of Europeanization, looking at 'uploading', or Iceland's ability to project its preferences at the EU level and have an impact on EU decision-making, and 'downloading', i.e. the adoption of EU policy at the national level and the resulting domestic change.

Previous studies focusing on non-member states have concentrated almost exclusively on the downloading side of the Europeanization process, taking for granted that third countries could not have any impact on the policies they are required to adopt as they do not have access to the EU's decision-making institutions. The general perception is that uploading capacity is a phenomenon reserved solely for the fully-fledged members of the club and that others undergo a completely unilateral adjustment to EU policy requirements. In this way, studies on non-member states, such as candidate and ENP countries, appear to focus almost exclusively on how the state/s in question adapt/s to EU requirements, not the other way around (see for example Grabbe 2002; Hughes *et al.* 2004; Kelley 2006; Lavenex 2004; Schimmelfennig and Sedelmeier 2005c; Vachudova 2005). Indeed, non-member states such as candidate countries have been described as 'client states, with no say in decision-making' (Grabbe 2002: 266).

As the EEA Agreement has been in force for almost two decades, it is possible to determine whether Iceland has become little more than a helpless puppet of the EU, forced to submit to any policy regardless of detrimental effects, or whether it has, perhaps against the odds, developed an uploading capacity which has enabled it in some cases to have an impact on the legislation it is required to adopt. It is true that there is a price to pay for 'à la carte' relations with the EU, as the EEA Agreement grants the EFTA states very limited access to EU decision-making institutions, while requiring them to adopt all EU policies in the relevant areas. This inherent 'democratic deficit' is one of the main criticisms of the EEA. Despite this, Iceland has generally been satisfied with its cooperation with the EU through the EEA Agreement, and the majority of the EU legislation incorporated into the Agreement is uncontroversial.[8] Nevertheless, instances do come up in which EU policies go against its preferences. Therefore, the question of whether or not uploading is a possibility is important.

This study challenges the assumption that uploading capacity is only relevant for member states and that non-member states passively adapt to EU requirements no matter the cost. The first research question asks whether a non-member state such as Iceland can potentially develop machinery to have an input into EU policy-making as a result of prolonged structured relations with the EU through the EEA Agreement. Has Iceland developed capacity to upload its preferences, how effective is this and under what conditions can an associated third country influence EU policy-making? Through the years Iceland's administrative capacity to deal with EEA membership has increased. Furthermore, it has developed various tactics to make use of its formal and informal channels of access to the EU. Therefore, it is hypothesized that the case studies will show an interactive dynamic between Iceland and the EU. Nevertheless, there is also reason to believe that, because of its small size and lack of membership status, Iceland's ability to project its preferences will be significantly less developed than in the larger EU member states.

Iceland is also an attractive case for study with respect to the downloading side of the Europeanization process. Through the EEA, Iceland is required to implement much of the same legislation as EU member states, and many of the infringement mechanisms in the EEA Agreement are similar to those used in the EU. Therefore, the conditions shaping the EU's impact may in some respects be equally valid for Iceland as for the EU member states. By the same token, there may be similarities between Iceland and other non-member states adopting EU policy. However, there are also many important differences between Iceland and other states that make it an interesting case for further study. One is that Iceland has not wanted to join the EU, at least until the financial crisis hit. Past research has shown that the EU has successfully been able to induce domestic change among candidate countries through its policy of membership conditionality (Schimmelfennig and Sedelmeier 2005c; Vachudova 2005). In other words, for candidate countries the benefits of joining the EU and the threat of exclusion have generally provided strong enough incentives to meet EU requirements even if they conflict with other priorities. Other studies have shown that, although the ENP attempts to emulate membership conditionality, the EU's efforts at promoting compliance in the ENP countries, without offering them a membership perspective, have been significantly less successful (Kelley 2006; Lavenex 2004). Whether and how the EU can ensure domestic adaptation in non-member states without the carrot of membership thus become interesting questions which the Icelandic case in the context of the EEA Agreement can shed some light upon. Consequently, the second research question explores whether the tools provided for in the EEA are sufficient to ensure adaptation to EU requirements, particularly those deemed inconvenient, or whether pre-existing domestic institutions and practices are resilient to external incentives for change.

EU member states have formally submitted to supranationalism by which they pool their sovereignty and are required to adhere to EU legislation. This is not the case for the EFTA states. EU acts do not automatically become part of the EFTA states' legal orders and the EEA Agreement contains various clauses to formally protect them against loss of sovereignty. However, it is important to bear in mind that Iceland is extremely dependent on its access to the internal market and the relationship between the EU-27 and the EFTA-3 is undoubtedly highly asymmetrical. Furthermore, parts of the Agreement can be suspended if the contracting parties fail to adopt relevant acts. A similar logic of rule adoption could thus apply for the EFTA states as for candidate countries, if they are threatened with exclusion from the internal market. Thus, Iceland might in practice be more likely than the EU member states to adapt to the EU's requirements, as the latter do not risk suspension for non-compliance. The hypotheses that Iceland might be both less likely to be able to influence EU policy and more likely to adopt EU policy than EU member states could be considered slightly ironic, as one of the reasons Iceland has not joined the EU is most likely based on a reluctance to compromise its independence. The EEA Agreement could perhaps in some ways involve a greater loss of autonomy than EU membership. This paradox will be returned to throughout this volume.

Overall, there is considerable variation in the domestic impact of EU policy requirements between states (Wallace *et al.* 2005: 7). Each of the countries implementing EU policy has a different relationship with the EU; they all face varying degrees of policy incongruence and have different institutions or actors participating in the policy process (Borzel and Risse 2003: 73). It is thus difficult to generalize about the domestic impact of the EU (Ladrech 2004: 63). However, a focus on Iceland as a participant in the EEA that for many years rejected the idea of EU membership provides an interesting and new platform from which to examine the Europeanization process.

Comparisons will also be made between the EEA framework, EU membership and other forms of association.

The first chapter of this volume looks at the concept of Europeanization, including how the term will be defined for the purposes of this study as well as the driving forces behind the process of Europeanization, which have their theoretical underpinnings in new institutionalism. Chapter 1 also provides an overview of the main relevant findings of other Europeanization studies focusing on both EU member states and non-members. Finally, the methodology and key primary sources used in this book are specified.

Chapters 2 and 3 establish the framework in which the Europeanization process in Iceland takes place. They provide background analysis of how Iceland participates in the EU policy process in terms of both uploading and downloading. They also provide a degree of comparison between the EEA Agreement, EU membership and other forms of association with the EU. Specifically, Chapter 2 focuses on uploading, exploring the extent to which the framework of the EEA Agreement allows for Iceland to influence EU decision-making and how the EEA structure constrains the choices and strategies available to Icelandic actors in terms of getting their views across during policy formulation at the EU level. The key aim of the chapter is to give some insight into the larger question of whether an interactive model of Europeanization, which takes uploading into account, is indeed appropriate for non-member states. Chapter 3, on the other hand, explores the types of external pressure on Iceland to adopt EU policy in comparison to member and non-member states and domestic factors which are likely to facilitate or hamper the adoption of EU policy. The aim is to gauge how likely Iceland is to download the EU's policies effectively, even when they impose high adaptation costs and require considerable changes to pre-existing policies and administrative and political structures.

In the subsequent empirical case studies (Chapters 4–7), EU legislative initiatives in four areas, electricity, free movement of persons, environment and food law, are subjected to detailed examination. In each of the cases, Iceland's response to EU policy requirements is assessed, in terms of both uploading and downloading. The independent variable is taken to be pressure emanating from the EU in the form of specific policy requirements, while domestic responses to these initiatives are seen as the dependent variable, which can also be affected by a series of intervening variables, predominantly the institutional framework of the EEA Agreement.

The results of the four case studies are drawn together and analysed in Chapter 8, which gives an overview of the Europeanization process in the context of the EEA Agreement. Overall, the results show that the EEA Agreement provides rather limited opportunities for uploading, although in some cases uploading does occur. The structure of the Agreement also appears to give relatively strong incentives for Iceland to adapt to EU policy requirements even when they conflict with pre-existing domestic conditions. The processes of uploading and downloading do however need to be seen in conjunction with domestic political processes as well as the relatively small size of the Icelandic administration.

Of course, in light of Iceland's recent application for EU membership, it is possible that in the future its relations with the EU will no longer be structured through the EEA. Indeed, its application has highlighted some important questions regarding the future of the Agreement which are addressed in the 9th and final chapter of this volume. For example, is the EEA after all a mere stepping-stone towards EU membership? Can the Agreement continue to function with only two members on the EFTA side? Does the EEA provide any lessons for the EU's relations with other third countries?

As noted by Judge Thorgeir Orlygsson in his farewell speech to the EFTA Court, the EEA Agreement has long been a favourite subject of pessimists. Yet, almost 20 years down the road it still functions. The future of the EEA, however, remains uncertain. While Iceland negotiates EU membership, its EFTA partners are busy evaluating their relations with the Union. As noted, Norway has conducted an extensive review of the EEA Agreement and some media sources suggest that the majority of the population is sceptical not only of potential EU membership but also of the EEA, preferring a looser form of cooperation with the EU. At the same time, Switzerland is under considerable pressure from the EU to revise its current bilateral agreements and adopt a more dynamic EEA-like framework, although it remains uncertain that the Swiss people would back Switzerland's accession to the EEA. Liechtenstein has generally expressed satisfaction with the EEA and a desire to maintain the Agreement, although this is tempered by the knowledge that its future will, to a large extent, be dependent on the larger EFTA states (Frommelt and Gstohl 2011: 47–50).

Deliberations on the future of the EEA must also be seen in the context of the troubling economic situation within the EU as well as proposals to expand EEA membership to Western European micro-states such as Andorra, San Marino and Monaco and Eastern giants like the Ukraine. Following the UK's decision in December 2011 to veto a new EU Treaty designed to increase financial discipline, suggestions have even been raised as to whether the UK might better belong in the EFTA family rather than the EU. However, before expanding the EEA to any or all of these states it is necessary to examine fully how and why the Agreement works in practice. As the EU continues to grapple with economic difficulties as well as the dilemma of how best to organize relations with its neighbours, this book may offer some input into the debate of whether an EEA-type solution could be considered as a realistic or suitable alternative to EU membership. Therefore, an examination of the EEA Agreement is important not only in its own right but also in the broader context.

1 Europeanization
An analytical framework

Europeanization in the context of the EEA

This volume explores the Europeanization of a so-called quasi-member state, taking into consideration both uploading, or Iceland's ability to project its preferences at the European level, and downloading, or the adoption of EU policies at national level through the EEA Agreement. There have been numerous substantial academic contributions to the study of 'Europeanization', and the term has been applied across a wide variety of contexts with a range of different meanings attached to it. As a result, some would argue that it has almost been stretched beyond meaningful limits (Featherstone 2003: 5). Therefore, before engaging in a study of Europeanization, it is necessary to set clear boundaries to the definition that will be used and the theoretical and methodological approaches that will be applied (Featherstone and Papadimitriou 2008: 23). In particular, it is essential to specify how existing approaches can be used to explain and understand the impact of the EU on an EFTA state which participates in EU integration through the EEA Agreement. This section provides justification for the framework that is used in this book, taking into account the major debates in the field.

Europeanization defined as a two-way process

Although a standard definition remains elusive, significant trends can be observed in the Europeanization literature towards a common theme. In general, Europeanization studies focus on change within domestic political systems understood as a consequence of pressure from European-level institutions and policy requirements (J. P. Olsen 2002: 932). Ladrech (1994: 69) is widely cited has having offered the first such explicit definition of Europeanization in his examination of the EU and France, where Europeanization is defined as: 'A process reorienting the direction and shape of politics to the degree that EC political and economic dynamics become part of the organisational logic of national politics and policy-making.' Since Ladrech's study, considerable variations have developed within this framework.[1] However, in general, it is common to view Europeanization as a process of domestic adaptation to pressure from the EU (J. P. Olsen 2002: 932).

As the field of Europeanization research has expanded, empirical observation has revealed a more complex bidirectional dynamic between member states and the Union in the sense that member states do not passively adapt to EU requirements but also actively 'upload' their preferences to the EU level in order to avoid having to 'download' inconvenient policies (Bache 2008: 10; Borzel 2002: 193). Later contributions to the study of Europeanization have increasingly highlighted the interactive, rather than unidirectional, relationship between the EU and national political systems (Radaelli 2003: 34). Exponents of this view see Europeanization as a two-way process between states and the EU, where influence flows both down from the EU level to the national level and up from the domestic sphere to the EU. The interactive approach is generally thought to provide an accurate description of the way in which member states interact with the EU (Bache and Jordan 2006a: 22) and there is now widespread consensus that in the process of Europeanization two-way pressures operate (Bache 2006: 233).[2]

Useful terminology has been developed in previous studies for examining the top-down and bottom-up dimensions of Europeanization or how member states adapt to EU policies and shape them. Borzel (2002), for example, refers to these processes as 'uploading' and 'downloading'. Bulmer and Burch (2006) also see Europeanization as a two-way process in their study of central government in Britain. They maintain that domestic adjustment to the EU involves two institutional logics in the sense that institutions must both find suitable ways of processing and implementing EU policy and adapt their procedures to be able to make an effective contribution at the EU level. They call these two components of institutional response to EU policy requirements 'reception' and 'projection' (Bulmer and Burch 2006: 38). Although uploading and downloading (or reception and projection) can essentially be seen as separate processes, it is important to stress the interlinkage between the two. If states are successful at uploading, this may make downloading more palatable. Furthermore, knowledge of the likelihood of having to transpose difficult EU requirements may influence both the strategy and tactics of states during the uploading campaign.

In this volume such a two-way approach is adapted in order to study the process of Europeanization in a non- (or quasi-) member state. In line with these studies, the view is taken that it is essential to recognize the potentially interactive nature of the Europeanization process, even when investigating non-member states. As noted in the introductory chapter, the two key research questions posed in this volume relate to whether Iceland can upload its preferences to the EU level and in turn whether the EU can ensure that its requirements are downloaded at the national level. In general it has been assumed that the relationship between the EU and non-member states must be in the form of a top-down flow of influence whereby the EU impacts the state in question but not vice versa. Yet this view has not been formally substantiated. Therefore, it is necessary to test whether non-member states with close ties to the EU can in fact develop machinery to ensure their input into

EU policy-making, in addition to mechanisms to adapt to EU policy requirements. As such, this study examines the top-down impact of the EU, while also taking into account the two-way relationship between national actors and the EU, adopting the terminology of uploading and downloading or reception and projection throughout the book.

In order to capture the interactive nature of Europeanization, it is defined as 'the process whereby a state, in this case Iceland, becomes a participant in the EU's policy process both at the decision-shaping stage at the EU level and the implementation stage at the national level'. Through this involvement key actors learn the rules of the EU game and develop tactics and strategies for uploading their preferences and downloading EU requirements. The process of Europeanization can therefore have a substantial impact on states participating in the EU's policy process.

'Mismatch' as a trigger for Europeanization

Europeanization literature usually begins by looking at the degree of compatibility or 'goodness of fit' between EU requirements and domestic arrangements in the states under consideration in order to explain how and why the EU induces domestic change (Featherstone 2003: 14–15; Radaelli 2003: 40–41) or indeed why uploading takes place and why downloading can be problematic. The EU's policy competences have expanded over the years and it now makes legislation in a wide range of policy domains as well as issuing a large number of non-binding rules.[3] Incongruence between the national and EU spheres occurs because the EU policy process takes place on two different levels of governance: the national and the European. Policies are agreed at the EU level but transposed and implemented at the national level (Radaelli 2003: 40–41; Wessels *et al.* 2003: 3).

Mismatch[4] or incompatibility is generally seen as a necessary condition for domestic change (Borzel 2000; Borzel and Risse 2003: 58; Haverland 2003; Knill 2001). This is because there would be no need for domestic change if EU policy corresponded perfectly with domestic ways of doing things. For example, when EU regulations are compatible with existing national policies in a particular state, that state will not need to change its legal provisions and there is no redistribution of resources that impacts domestic actors (Borzel and Risse 2003: 61–62). Consequently, the state has no incentive to attempt to upload any preferences to the EU level, and downloading of EU policy at the national level will pose no challenges.

On the other hand, if an EU policy contrasts with existing national policy goals or regulatory standards, some degree of adaptation to legal and administrative institutions will be required in order to implement the policy (Borzel 2000; Borzel and Risse 2003: 61–62; Wessels *et al.* 2003: 14). As a result, a state will endeavour to upload its own policy preferences during the policy-formulation process so that it will have less trouble adapting to EU policy when it is implemented at the national level (Bache and Jordan 2006a:

19). This can involve attempting to push a certain policy that reflects its preferences onto the agenda, attempting to block a policy altogether or adapting a policy to its particular needs. If a state is unsuccessful or only partly successful in uploading, downloading EU policy can require significant domestic change and its implementation at the national level can entail considerable challenges for states (Wessels *et al.* 2003: 5).

This study adheres to the school that sees Europeanization as predominantly arising from a mismatch between the policies and practices of the EU and those of the state in question (Bulmer and Burch 2005: 863). Approaching Europeanization in this way highlights the preferences and strategies of states and the opportunity structures through which they attain their goals at the EU level (Mendez *et al.* 2006: 601; Wong 2006: 9), as well as the structure through which the EU exerts pressure on states to implement its policies and the domestic intervening variables that may determine the outcome of the downloading process. It could even be argued that mismatch is particularly important when looking at the EU's relations with associated states. This is because they are assumed to have limited uploading capacity, and so they might more frequently be faced with considerable mismatch between the EU and national levels when it comes to downloading EU requirements.

Dependent and intervening variables

During the Europeanization process, different components of domestic political systems can be impacted and, accordingly, studies of Europeanization look at different aspects of domestic change. Many emphasize formal, observable changes such as processes of domestic institutional adaptation and the adaptation of national policy and policy processes. Featherstone (2003: 7–11), for example, notes that institutional actors such as public administrative institutions, organized interest groups, political parties and non-governmental actors have adapted to pressure from the EU. Bache and Jordan (2006b) similarly divide their study on Europeanization in Britain into three sections: 'Polity', 'Politics' and 'Policies'. The polity section includes administrative institutions such as government, ministries and regional and local government. 'Politics' includes an examination of political parties, organized interest groups and non-governmental actors, while the policy section looks at the effects of the EU on the content of various policies such as foreign policy and environmental policy. Borzel and Risse (2003: 60) also use the distinction between policies, politics and polity to identify the three main observable dimensions along which the domestic impact of the EU can be analysed.

Radaelli (2003: 35–36), on the other hand, takes a broader approach which does not limit Europeanization to domestic changes in political and administrative structures or the content of national policy. Rather, cognitive and normative structures such as discourse, norms and values can also be impacted. Risse *et al.* (2001: 4–5), also take less-formal domestic changes into account, examining the effects of the EU on collective understandings of actors such as norms of citizenship or collective identities pertaining to the nation-state. On the whole, Europeanization can thus encompass wide-ranging structural and cognitive changes within domestic political systems due to pressures from the EU.

In this book, the Icelandic government is the key actor. Much like in studies focusing on EU member states, the independent variable is taken to be pressure emanating from the EU in the form of specific policy requirements, while domestic responses to these initiatives are seen as the dependent variable. The organization and behaviour of the Icelandic government administration is examined as it responds to EU policy requirements, both in terms of uploading and downloading. The extent to which the Icelandic government has been able to have a say in the content of EU policy is explored, as well as the degree to which EU policy has been transposed and implemented in Iceland. This can of course entail policy change, but also changes to political processes and institutional change.

The outcome of the dependent variable can be affected by a series of intervening variables, predominantly the institutional framework of the EEA Agreement which determines to a large extent the constraints and opportunities available to the Icelandic government during the uploading and downloading processes. Furthermore, the outcome can vary depending on the policy area in question and the specific conditions within the domestic system such as party politics, interest group mobilization, public opinion, the existence of veto points in the administrative structure or a particular culture which hinders or facilitates domestic adaptation. Furthermore, Iceland is smaller than any of the current EU member states in terms of population. Therefore, Iceland's small size and relatively limited administrative capacity need to be taken into consideration as important intervening variables when examining the Europeanization process. Due in particular to the small size of Icelandic society, interest groups often have very close and personal ties with the government and have actively participated in the policy process, and so their role should not be taken for granted.

Although this volume focuses particularly on the adaptation of policies, processes and institutions in Iceland to EU requirements, cognitive elements are also considered to be important. Accordingly this study aims to gauge the incentives behind the government's reactions as well as analysing the practical outcome of uploading and downloading. For example, whether government incentives relate primarily to material interests or social norms of appropriate behaviour. This incentive structure is closely linked to the theoretical underpinnings of the Europeanization process, as will be explored further in the following section.

Theoretical grounding in new institutionalism

It is important to note that Europeanization is not a theory in itself but has a broad agreement with the conceptual framework of 'new institutionalism'

(Bache 2008: 15; Bulmer and Burch 2005: 863; Featherstone and Papadimitriou 2008: 26; Vink and Graziano 2007: 13). In other words, an institutionalist understanding is frequently used to provide explanatory variables behind the Europeanization process. This view is particularly prominent among those who see Europeanization as arising from a mismatch or incongruence between the policies and practices of the EU and the domestic level (Bulmer and Burch 2005: 863). Therefore, an awareness of the new institutionalist literature is necessary for understanding how Europeanization works (Bache 2008: 13).

Different theories attach varying degrees of importance to the role of structure versus that of agency in political processes. Agents (or actors) are the entities capable of decisions and actions in any given context. Actors operate within a wider environment or structure that shapes the nature of their choices by setting limits to what is possible and by determining the nature of the problems which occur (Hill 2002: 26–27). From the 1950s to the 1970s, agency-centred theories were dominant in political science. However, in the 1980s and 1990s the so-called new institutionalism emerged, reflecting a gradual reintroduction of the importance of institutions (Pollack 2004: 137–38). New-institutionalist studies did not originate in the field of EU studies. However, given that the European Union is the most densely institutionalized international organization in the world, it is not surprising that this body of literature has been applied increasingly frequently to the study of the EU and its activities (Pollack 2004: 137–38).

New institutionalism does not constitute a single coherent theory (Knill 2001: 20). Three main strands of new institutionalism have emerged: rational choice and sociological and historical institutionalism. There are considerable differences between these different variants of the institutionalist framework regarding the way in which they define institutions and explain how they impact on actors' motivations, preferences and behaviour (Hix and Goetz 2001: 18). Their uniting point is that they each assume that institutions are important factors which can affect political behaviour (Knill 2001: 20). This study takes the middle ground, drawing mainly on historical institutionalism. However, as historical institutionalism includes elements of both rational choice and sociological institutionalism, it is necessary to give an account of all three strands.

Rational choice institutionalism has a fairly narrow interpretation of institutions as formal rules, operating procedures and organizations of government (Vink and Graziano 2007: 13). Actors are assumed to follow a 'logic of consequentialism'[5] in the sense that they engage in a rational pursuit of self-interest, evaluating the likely consequences of their actions and seeking to maximize exogenously fixed preferences within a given institutional setting (Eilstrup-Sangiovanni 2006: 396; March and Olsen 1998: 949–50). Institutions serve to structure the interactions or the bargaining game between actors, providing them with opportunities and constraints and determining the strategies they are able to adopt in pursuit of their interests (Featherstone and Papadimitriou 2008: 26–27; Rosamond 2000: 116). Thus, institutions are generally conceptualized as intervening variables as they can affect the cost/benefit calculations of the actors involved and the strategies they use to achieve their interests, but institutions have no impact on the formation of the said interests (Knill 2001: 24). A rationalist account would thus assume power to be zero sum and expect national actors to continue pursuing established goals, albeit in a changing environment (Bache 2008: 13).

With respect to EU-induced domestic change, rationalist accounts argue that domestic institutions put pressure on governments to maintain the status quo to avoid the material costs that changes to institutional structures would entail. In order for downloading to occur, when incongruence exists between the EU and national level, the institutional framework must be able to exert external pressure for change to counter the internal pressures for maintaining the status quo. As actors generally try to maximize their interests, national governments will comply with the EU's requirements only if the expected benefits of compliance exceed the potential gains of non-compliance (Eilstrup-Sangiovanni 2006: 396) or, inversely, if the potential costs of non-compliance exceed the costs of compliance. In the EU member states, domestic change can therefore be promoted by the Commission issuing infringement proceedings which can result in financial penalties in the form of a lump sum or a daily fine, depending on the scope and duration of the infringement as well as the capabilities of the member state (Borzel 2001: 806–08). So-called thin rationalist accounts, which border on recognizing a logic of appropriateness, also note that agents may pursue non-material goals and therefore argue that social sanctioning or shaming can also induce compliance. However, the choice mechanism is always a cost/benefit calculation (Checkel 2001: 558).

Rationalist approaches are undoubtedly conducive to parsimonious explanations. However, many would argue that a broader understanding of institutions is necessary to account for various cognitive and normative elements (Featherstone and Papadimitriou 2008: 27). Sociological institutionalism, which is grounded in constructivist literature, conceptualizes institutions more comprehensively, i.e. in addition to formal rules and procedures, they also encompass informal norms and conventions, symbols and cognitive beliefs which guide actors and shape the way in which they see the world (Pollack 2004: 139).

In the sociological approach, actors also have interests and preferences, but these can be shaped by the institutions themselves rather than taken as an external given, i.e. they are endogenous rather than exogenous (Hix and Goetz 2001: 20). Actors can internalize new norms through participation in institutions, and therefore institutions affect not only the strategic calculations of actors but also their basic preferences, beliefs, understandings and identities. As opposed to a logic of consequentialism, actors follow a 'logic of appropriateness' which sees action as being driven by 'rules of appropriate or exemplary behaviour' (March and Olsen 2004: 2). In other words, actors are less likely to pursue rational instincts than socially defined norms and therefore generally select the appropriate behaviour for a given institutional context (Featherstone and Papadimitriou 2008: 26; Rosamond 2000: 116). In contrast to rationalist institutionalism, a sociological perspective would assume power to be positive sum and expect actors to change their preferences through socialization in a changing environment (Bache 2008: 13).

During the process of Europeanization, domestic structures exert pressure on national governments to maintain the status quo because it represents the established way of doing things, to which actors have a long-standing commitment. However, a willingness to adopt EU policy can be promoted through high levels of social interaction at the EU level (Borzel and Risse 2003: 67–68; Checkel 2001: 561–62; Schimmelfennig and Sedelmeier 2005b: 6 and 9). Agents involved in the EU policy process undergo a gradual process of international socialization in which they are exposed to new rules and norms that can alter the way in which they perceive their preferences (Checkel 2001: 561–62; 2006: 414–15; Eilstrup-Sangiovanni 2006: 396; Schimmelfennig and Sedelmeier 2005b: 6 and 9). Furthermore, when actors interact with EU institutions they may acquire new interests through social learning which entails argumentation, deliberation and persuasion and they may, as a result, act in ways that cannot easily be explained by material incentives (Eilstrup-Sangiovanni 2006: 396).

This type of behaviour is based on a logic of appropriateness instead of a logic of consequentialism in the sense that actors do not always make decisions intended to maximize their objective rational interests but also try to 'do the right thing' by following socially defined rules and norms (Risse 2004: 162–63). Rules are then followed automatically and unconsciously once the actors have been socialized into their community (S. Berglund *et al.* 2006: 699). The outcome is sustained compliance based on the internalization of new norms, which is largely independent of material incentives or sanctions (Checkel 2005: 804). This does not mean compliance will necessarily always be perfect as we all 'occasionally run a red light even though we consider the rule valid' (Risse 2004: 163–64).

The third strand, historical institutionalism, incorporates both rationalist and sociological elements, but also emphasizes the importance of temporal dynamics or the effects of institutions over time. Therefore, this position is not a counterpoint to the rationalist or sociological schools, but a complement (Bache 2008: 14). According to historical institutionalism, institutions are generally thought to be characterized by 'stickiness' or resistance to change. This stickiness stems from the uncertainty associated with institutional designs and the significant transaction costs involved in changing the institutional framework. This can mean that actors have an incentive not to abandon existing institutions even though they are inefficient, but only adapt them incrementally to a changing political environment in order to avoid the cost of reversal (Pollack 2004: 139–40).

According to historical institutionalism, institutions are 'path dependent' in the sense that specific features of the institutional setting guide developments along a certain path, and institutions, once established, can influence and constrain the behaviour of those who established them, often in unintended ways (Featherstone and Papadimitriou 2008: 26; Pollack 2004: 139). The impact of the institutional setting can evolve over time into a more cultural form as actors become locked into it. Institutions can, therefore, be both an intervening and an independent variable, affecting actor preferences and interests in the short term and establishing distinct paths of development in the longer term (Featherstone and Papadimitriou 2008: 26).

It is often argued that rationalist and constructivist logics can occur simultaneously and that the logics need not be mutually exclusive but may be seen as part of a synthetic theoretical framework (Borzel and Risse 2003; Featherstone and Papadimitriou 2008: 27; Vink and Graziano 2007: 13). Therefore, it may be inaccurate to draw a broad distinction between the rationalist and constructivist mechanisms. The two approaches thus each have their legitimate place in the Europeanization debate and might apply within different domains, and they can complement rather than contradict each other (Beyers 2005: 932–33; Checkel 2001: 553–54; Eilstrup-Sangiovanni 2006: 398–99; Grabbe 2000: 937–39; 2005: 129; Lewis 2005: 937–39; Niemann 2004: 402; Risse 2004: 174–75). Historical institutionalism appears to be capable of accommodating the insights of the rival rationalist and sociological institutionalist research agendas (Pollack 2004: 139) as well as a temporal dimension to explaining actors' decisions within their institutional frameworks. Historical institutionalism has thus become a key component in Europeanization research and will also guide this study.

As noted above, EU requirements will be seen as the independent variable, while the institutional structure of the EEA Agreement is the intervening variable which restricts the preferences and choices of the Icelandic government. This generally corresponds to a rationalist institutionalist approach in the sense that it aims to determine how much room there is for the Iceland's preferences to be realized within the institutional framework of the EEA. In other words, how far does the EEA institutional setting constrain the choices and actions of the Icelandic government both when it comes to uploading and downloading their exogenously formed preferences? Nevertheless, it is important to accommodate both rationalist and sociological incentives, and the possibility is not discarded that a process of socialization may have occurred within the framework of the EEA which has been in place for nearly two decades. This may also serve to mould the preferences of key actors.

The EEA Agreement arguably provides a particularly relevant backdrop for a historical institutionalist account, as it has remained more or less unchanged despite significant transformations in its political surroundings. It was signed in 1992 and while the EU, its competences and policy style have evolved considerably since that time, the structure of the EEA has remained fairly static. The Agreement is fluid in the sense that all new legal acts in relevant areas are incorporated into the Agreement, yet the structures and processes through which this takes place have remained constant despite the evolving nature of the EU policy process. It is therefore a good example of the potential stickiness of an institutional framework and a historical institutionalist setting is arguably especially appropriate for this study.

Findings from other states

The EFTA parties to the EEA Agreement have been described as quasi-members of the EU which can be compared and contrasted with both EU member states and other non-members that are associated with the EU. This section outlines findings of Europeanization studies from other states with the aim of explaining how they can help us to draw inferences to the EEA context.

EU member states

In the previous section it was argued that Europeanization can be defined as a two-way interlinked process between states and the EU, where influence flows both up from the national to the EU level and down from the EU to the domestic sphere. These processes of uploading and downloading are generally triggered by a mismatch between EU policy requirements and pre-existing domestic conditions which gives states an incentive to project their preferences at the EU level and can also create hindrances to effective domestic adaptation to EU requirements.

In terms of uploading, it is clear that certain states are more adept at projecting their preferences than others. Borzel (2002) has, for example, distinguished between 'pacesetters', 'foot-draggers' and 'fence-sitters'. Large member states are more often likely to succeed in uploading their policy preferences because they have greater resources and carry the most weight in the two key legislative bodies of the EU. As evidence of the ability of large states to project their preferences, a number of initiatives have been successfully launched by the UK, notably market reform, economic competitiveness, defence, agricultural and rural policy (Bulmer and Burch 2006: 51). Nevertheless, a growing field of research has shown that the EU's policy agenda is no longer monopolized to the same extent by large states (Arter 2000: 695; Fairbass 2006: 151; Panke 2008; Thorhallsson and Wivel 2006). For example, the relatively small Nordic countries have repeatedly shaped EU environmental policy (Borzel 2002: 197). Various factors can impact a state's ability to upload its preferences, such as the level of expertise it has in a particular policy area, its administrative capacity and the ability it has to form coalitions with other states. Thus it is doubtful that the same group of actors will always be successful in promoting their preferences, and every state will at some point be faced with policy mismatch when it comes to downloading EU policy (Borzel and Risse 2003: 62).

As noted above, there are various so-called rationalist mechanisms designed to induce domestic adaptation in the EU's member states. For example, in areas of binding legislation, the Commission can issue infringement proceedings against a state for non-compliance which can culminate in the Court of Justice issuing a fine.[6] In areas within the competence of the member states such as employment and social protection, falling under the Open Method of Coordination (OMC),[7] social 'shaming' and peer pressure are the norm. These are, however, often considered relatively mild sanctions and therefore member states can in many instances 'rationally' afford to ignore EU legislation (Heritier 2005: 204–05).

In this context, it is important to note that member states are full participants in the EU's decision-making process which can, according to a sociological institutionalist model, serve to mould their preferences and legitimize the EU's policy output. The EU's decision-making is characterized by high levels of institutionalization, for example in the form of informal communication in working groups of the Council of Ministers or European-level policy networks centred on the Commission (Checkel 2006: 408–09; Niemann 2004: 380). In this environment, member states have a high degree of contact with their fellow member states, where they observe each other and are constantly reminded of their duties and obligations. It can therefore be argued that mutual solidarity can develop within the EU system of governance (Jachtenfuchs and Kohler-Koch 2004: 100).

Academic studies have found that pressures from the EU which are geared at tilting states' cost/benefit calculations are in many cases not sufficient to ensure domestic compliance or downloading in its member states when there is a high degree of domestic pressure for non-compliance. This appears to be the case even though this pressure is coupled with a process of social persuasion. Pressure from the EU may lead to domestic institutional change (Featherstone 2003: 14), but this is not automatic. In other words, adaptation pressure is seen as a necessary, but not a sufficient, condition for domestic change. Haverland (2003), for example, emphasizes the stickiness of national institutional arrangements and practices, arguing that domestic adaptation or downloading is unlikely if European policy requirements differ significantly from national arrangements and operating procedures (Haverland 2003: 209).

In his study of the Europeanization of national administrations in Britain and Germany, Knill (2001) also found that, in cases where EU policies challenge core institutional elements at the national level, domestic resistance to pressure from the EU should be expected and implementation is made difficult, if not impossible (Knill 2001: 4–5). Knill maintains that compliance is only likely in cases where EU policies require minimal institutional adjustments. In such cases it can either be facilitated by domestic actors who support the policy or obstructed due to lack of support (Knill 2001: 4–5). An example is Germany's implementation of the 'EMAS' Regulation (761/2001/EC), which allowed voluntary participation by organizations in a Community eco-management and audit scheme, appropriately both because national administrative traditions were relatively compatible with the EU policy and because it was supported by domestic environmental and industrial organizations. On the other hand, there was strong resistance in Germany to the

Access to Information Directive (90/313/EEC) and to Environmental Impact Assessment (EIA) (97/11/EC). Britain also resisted implementation in the case of EIA, while changes to comply with the Drinking Water Directive (98/83/EC) took place only after a delay of several years (Knill 2001: 3).

Borzel (2000) also argues that implementation failure can be expected when there are no domestic advocates that compel public authorities to comply with incongruent policies (Borzel 2000: 141). In her comparative study of the implementation of EU environmental policy in Germany and Spain, Borzel found that the two countries were generally reluctant to introduce the necessary legal and administrative changes in order to ensure correct transposition as well as practical application and enforcement of EU policy. However, mobilization by environmental groups, political parties, trade unions and local municipalities sometimes led them to implement various incongruent EU directives and regulations, thus initiating domestic change.

In general, the main problem with the EU's mechanisms to ensure adaptation in the member states appears to be lack of effective monitoring throughout all stages of the policy adoption process. In most cases of detected non-compliance, the EU has been able to force member states to adopt policies through its infringement proceedings. Sometimes simply opening infringement proceedings is enough to get states to comply. Other cases, where domestic resistance is strong, have to be taken before the ECJ (now CJEU), but even when countries are taken before the Court, non-compliance sometimes continues (Panke 2007: 850–51).

The effectiveness of the socialization mechanism is more difficult to pinpoint and measure than the more visible and operationalizable sanctioning mechanisms. Empirical evidence does suggest that socialization and social learning within European institutions can have an impact on member state compliance, although it usually works in parallel with a logic of consequentialism (Beyers 2005: 932–33; Grabbe 2005: 129; Lewis 2005: 937–39). In sum, it seems that EU incentives lead to domestic change in some cases but not others. This most likely depends on a variety of domestic intervening variables such as the level of misfit, mobilization in society in support of, or opposition to, the rule in question, the administrative capacity of the implementing state and to what extent a 'culture of compliance' exists within the domestic political system (Borzel *et al.* 2008; G. Falkner *et al.* 2005; Grabbe 2002; Haverland 2003; Knill 2001; Risse *et al.* 2001).

Non-members

The EU has a very different relationship with non-member states. In the wake of the formulation of accession conditionality and the launching of the European Neighbourhood Policy, the external dimension of Europeanization has become of ever-greater significance as countries on the periphery are increasingly impacted by the EU. Substantial differences exist in the institutional context between member states, candidates and neighbours. The cost/benefit calculations of compliance with EU policy vary considerably across different types of states, as do the opportunities for socialization. Therefore, the extent to which the EU is able to induce compliance depends to a large degree on its relationship with the implementing state. So, in addition to domestic factors, variation in compliance can also result from differing enforcement capacities at the European level (Sverdrup 2004: 25–26). Studies have thus expanded to include the domestic impact of the EU on various non-member states such as candidate states and ENP countries (Grabbe 2002; Hughes *et al.* 2004; Kelley 2006; Lavenex 2004; Schimmelfennig and Sedelmeier 2005c; Vachudova 2005).

As noted, work on non-member state uploading capacity is virtually non-existent. However, when it comes to the downloading of EU policies, research has shown that the Union has been able to exert a high degree of leverage over candidate countries[8] (Vachudova 2005: 259) and to a lesser extent the countries included in the Neighbourhood Policy. The EU has generally based its relations with non-member states on a system of reinforcement by reward and sanctions, i.e. offering the government of a 'target' state incentives such as aid or membership on the condition that it adopts and complies with the Union's norms and rules (Checkel 2005: 809). For example, the primary tool exercised by the EU to secure compliance in candidate countries with desired policy outcomes is accession conditionality (Hughes *et al.* 2004: 525), whereby the EU sets the adoption of the 80,000-page *acquis communautaire* as a condition that candidates must fulfil in order to receive benefits such as trade and cooperation agreements and, eventually, full membership.

Candidate countries generally consider membership of the EU to be an important goal. Furthermore, the EU's monitoring and sanctioning mechanisms are very strong with respect to the candidate countries. The EU monitored the progress of the candidate countries for the 2004 accession carefully[9] in annual reports which were used to decide whether to admit each country to further stages of the accession process (Bretherton and Vogler 2006: 141; Grabbe 2002: 256–57 and 62). This is much more extensive monitoring and control than the member states are subjected to (Heritier 2005: 208–09). So, perhaps not surprisingly, membership conditionality has proved highly effective in ensuring transposition of EU legislation. Before the EU spelled out its accession conditionality in the mid-1990s, some EU rules had been adopted in the Central and Eastern European countries (CEECs). Examples include the adoption of command and control rules against air pollution in the Czech Republic, moves towards regionalization in Hungary and elements of health policies in Hungary and the Czech Republic, although this was patchy and selective (Schimmelfennig and Sedelmeier 2005a: 217–18).

After the explicit formulation of conditionality, vast improvements in rule adoption were observed (Schimmelfennig *et al.* 2005: 50; Vachudova 2005: 181–82). In general, the political, economic and social benefits[10] of joining the EU and the potential threat of exclusion from membership provided a strong enough incentive to meet EU requirements even where these demands conflicted with other domestic priorities, although adoption of EU rules did appear to be slower when domestic adaptation costs were high (Grabbe 2001: 1015; Jachtenfuchs and Kohler-Koch 2004: 110; Schimmelfennig and Sedelmeier 2004: 672). Even in the more illiberal states of Central and Eastern Europe, such as Slovakia, Bulgaria and Romania, the EU's leverage proved successful in undermining rent-seeking elites and stimulating political and economic reform (Vachudova 2005: 138–39).

In sum, there are substantial differences in the institutional context between member states and candidate countries regarding their relationship with the EU. Studies have found that the EU's leverage is quite strong with respect to candidate countries in comparison to its member states, though it may be interesting to examine whether this leverage has decreased in light of the EU's internal financial turmoil. Regarding the member states, the EU can only issue infringement proceedings in response to non-compliance but cannot threaten them with exclusion from the membership process so, according to a logic of consequentialism, candidate countries should generally be more likely than existing member states to implement EU policies. Nevertheless, EU member states also undergo a process of socialization. For candidates, on the other hand, it is likely that socialization plays a limited role in the policy-adoption process as they are generally not given any access to the EU's decision-making process and so opportunities for preference change through social learning are limited, as actors are not exposed to the context in which preferences are formed.

As noted by Sedelmeier (2008a: 2), in the candidate countries, pre-accession conditionality depends primarily on the conditional incentive of membership, rather than processes of persuasion and social learning. During recent accession negotiations, the EU did provide a range of policy advice to CEECs through technical assistance offered through the Phare and the Twinning programmes that was aimed at helping them adapt their administrative and democratic institutions to comply with membership requirements by learning from member state experiences of framing the legislation and building the organizational capacity necessary to implement the existing legislation and policies of the EU (Grabbe 2002: 261). The presence of EU-centred networks of experts and officials and interactions between CEEC officials and experts from EU counterparts may have facilitated social learning to some degree (Schimmelfennig and Sedelmeier 2004: 674). However, the fact that the candidate countries were not treated as equal partners and had no say in EU decision-making was found to undermine the effectiveness of social learning and any EU rule was likely to pose legitimacy problems and have the stigma of foreign imposition (Schimmelfennig and Sedelmeier 2005b: 18–19).

The EU is generally thought to have exerted tremendous leverage over the domestic political systems of candidate countries during the accession process (Kelley 2006), and past studies, as outlined above, have highlighted the effectiveness of membership conditionality in inducing rule adoption in candidate countries. This is in contrast to studies focusing on EU member states which often illustrate lack of domestic adaptation. These findings would seem to highlight the importance of the EU being able to exert sufficient leverage to tilt a state's cost/benefit mechanisms in the EU policy-adoption process. Nonetheless, there has been considerable reluctance to dismiss the significance of socialization pressures. For example, it has been argued that EU rule adoption in the candidate countries may, in many cases, have consisted mainly of formal transposition without full and effective implementation (Schimmelfennig and Sedelmeier 2005a: 226). Evidence suggests that the candidate countries prefer a form of adoption that minimizes their domestic costs unless they are subject to continuous and effective monitoring. For example, the CEECs knew that the Commission and the member states monitored adoption of Schengen rules particularly closely, while, in other areas such as social policy, superficial rule adoption would not present an obstacle to concluding accession negotiations (Schimmelfennig and Sedelmeier 2005a: 217). The candidates thus adopted Schengen rules particularly carefully, despite high adaptation costs, because of the weight the EU and its member states attached to this policy area (Grabbe 2005).

Full implementation is more difficult to monitor than transposition, and furthermore the CEECs were still at a very early stage of the adoption process when they were admitted to the EU. Therefore, during the accession process it was primarily the formal, legislative adoption that could be observed rather the implementation (Schimmelfennig and Sedelmeier 2005a: 224). Once candidates have joined the EU and are reaping the benefits of membership, the external incentives of EU conditionality no longer apply and rule adoption might slow down, stop or be reversed, and domestic adaptation costs, which were eclipsed under the pressure of conditionality, may increase in relevance (Schimmelfennig and Sedelmeier 2004: 676). Nonetheless, the absence of conditionality does not necessarily result in the complete stagnation or breakdown of compliance. Upon accession new member states are subject to the same infringement procedures as the member states. As members, they also participate fully in the EU's decision-making processes and so socialization might begin to play a greater role in creating incentives for rule adoption. Furthermore, the Commission has introduced special instruments to monitor compliance in the new member states, such as the publication of annual 'scoreboards' on implementation records with internal market legislation, and new policy instruments such as the OMC are also available (Schimmelfennig and Sedelmeier 2005a: 227).

Indeed, research on the application of EU rules in the new member states has not shown a heavy decline in rule adoption. For example, empirical evidence from a comparative project on transposition, enforcement and application of EU legislation in the Czech Republic, Hungary, Slovakia and Slovenia post-accession shows that the new member states have not decreased their compliance efforts in the sense that their transposition records are still good, although there have been some obstacles to practical application of the law (Falkner and Treib 2008: 293 and 307–08). Sedelmeier (2008b) also found that data on infringements of EU law in 2004–08 showed that the new member states outperformed the old member states during the first four years of membership. According to Sedelmeier, potential explanations for this could be that during the accession process the candidates had invested heavily in institutional infrastructure to increase their legislative capacity, which could allow them to correctly transpose EU law in a timely manner. Furthermore, because of their pre-accession experience the new member states could be more susceptible to shaming and more likely to consider good compliance as appropriate behaviour.

It is important to note that a system of reinforcement by reward, such as membership conditionality, is only likely to work if the relevant government expects the rewards to be greater than the costs of compliance (Checkel 2005: 809). The EU has attempted to extend the concept of conditionality to neighbouring states through the ENP,[11] but without offering them the prospect of membership. This policy is also largely based on a rationalist logic of increasing the benefits of compliance by offering states aid, trade and other economic benefits. It includes strategically adapted enlargement policies such as action plans, regular reports and negotiations (Kelley 2006: 29). Nevertheless, unlike the prospect of EU membership, the benefits included in the ENP have in many cases not been considered sufficient to offset the costs of unpopular policies (Grabbe 2002: 256–57; Lavenex 2004: 694–95). For example, in Ukraine, despite comprehensive frameworks and significant assistance, the practical impact of the ENP can be considered extremely limited (O'Donnell 2006). In sum, the carrot of increased association with the EU does not generally seem to outweigh other considerations regarding the domestic adaptation to EU policy in the ENP countries.

The EEA Agreement is based largely on a logic of increasing the costs of non-compliance embodied in the threat of exclusion from the internal market. Like the EU's relations with other non-member states, the relationship between the EFTA states and the EU is clearly asymmetrical. The EFTA states are highly dependent on their access to the internal market, while the EU depends relatively little on them. Furthermore, the EEA Agreement contains a clause threatening a suspension of the affected part of the Agreement should the EFTA states fail to incorporate a relevant act. The asymmetrical power relationship between Iceland and the EU and the potential cost of exclusion from the internal market could thus mean that domestic actors in Iceland are less likely to oppose or delay the implementation of EU legislation than EU member states, even though it is incompatible with domestic arrangements. However, it is also important to bear in mind that Iceland is less exposed to the EU's rules, norms, practices and structures than the member states and thus perhaps less likely to be socialized into the EU ways of doing things. The two logics of consequentialism and appropriateness might therefore be expected to yield diverging outcomes for Iceland. In comparison to EU member states, adaptation pressure gives stronger incentives for domestic actors in Iceland to comply with EU policy requirements according to the logic of consequentialism, but weaker incentive following the logic of appropriateness. Intervening factors such as domestic mobilization in support of or opposition to EU policy, administrative capacity and the extent to which a 'compliance culture' exists in Iceland might also play an important role in the process of change. These debates will be explored further in the subsequent chapters of this book, where the process of domestic adaptation to EU requirements in Iceland will be assessed, as well as Iceland's ability to have an impact on the policies it is required to adopt, but first the structure and methodology of this volume will be outlined.

Measuring Europeanization

This study offers a theoretically informed, empirical analysis of the interaction between EU adaptation pressure and domestic organizations and institutions in Iceland, moderated through the framework of the EEA Agreement. Taking a qualitative case study approach, it identifies the mechanisms for domestic change in response to EU policy requirements, providing an evaluation of the process of Europeanization in Iceland. Out of the three EFTA parties to the EEA Agreement, Iceland was selected for analysis. The three EFTA partners share the common framework of the EEA Agreement, as well as certain common characteristics such as relatively high levels of socio-economic development and education, yet there are important differences between them, particularly with respect to population size. In this respect, Iceland represents a middle ground, with a population of almost 320,000. Norway is by far the largest of the three, with a population of approximately 5 million. Liechtenstein, on the other hand, has just over 36,000 inhabitants.

As outlined in the previous section, a vast amount of Europeanization literature is available. These studies base their findings on different types of methodology, which each have their respective advantages and disadvantages. Quantitative studies in this field rely predominantly on the Commission's Internal Market Scoreboard, which is published twice a year and examines how quickly the member states transpose directives into national law and also highlights the number of infringement proceedings that are underway against each member state. These figures are often taken as indicators of the level of compliance or domestic adjustment to EU requirements (Borzel 2001: 803).

The advantage of quantitative studies is that they can compare a wide range of policy areas and countries. However, as Borzel (2001) notes, the drawbacks are that transposition rates say nothing about the quality of the legislation being transposed and infringement proceedings only cover cases which have been detected by the Commission. The Commission is not able to systematically monitor implementation of Community law and many cases of non-compliance might thus occur without being caught and/or recorded. It is difficult to estimate the cases of hidden non-compliance. In many cases, even if a piece of legislation is said to have been transposed, it may not have been properly or correctly transposed or implemented, which severely curtails its effectiveness and also the impact it has at the domestic level. The detection rate is in all likelihood rather high for complete failure to transpose legislation, but the chances of discovery significantly decrease when it comes to complete and correct transposition, practical application and enforcement (Borzel 2001: 808–09). Furthermore, large-N studies might be able to establish causal relationships by correlating policy inputs with policy outcomes, but they are not able to identify the relevant mechanisms behind these correlations (Haverland 2003: 217). Finally, quantitative studies have hitherto not been able to successfully look at the process of uploading and thus they do not take into account the interactive nature of the Europeanization process.

Unlike large-N studies, which either include all instances of a class of events or a representative sample of that universe, small-n studies with relatively few cases, such as this one, are not representative of the universe. Therefore, the data obtained cannot be used to generalize about the causal relationship between the dependent and independent variable nor can they provide a completely infallible confirmation or invalidation of the hypothesis (Burnham *et al*. 2004: 54–54; George 1979). Although small-n studies can make only tentative conclusions about how much a particular variable affects outcomes (George and Bennett 2004: 25), this research design has considerable advantages. First, it is able to pinpoint the incentives and motivations behind the Europeanization process, which is of vital significance in a historical institutionalist account. Furthermore, in small-n studies data on a wide range of variables can be collected and a relatively complete account of the phenomenon can thus be achieved, which enables the formulation of a convincing argument about the causal relationship between variables (Burnham *et al*. 2004: 53–54). Only an intensive research design is able to identify the processes and underlying forces by which change occurs and rule out other explanations (Radaelli 2003). As noted by Vink and Graziano (2007: 17), qualitative analysis allows for a detailed description, which is necessary to point out the critical junctures in European and national policy or institutional change.

A qualitative research design thus permits an in-depth look at the processes of both uploading and downloading, where downloading is taken to entail not only transposition of EU requirements into the national legal framework but also the practical application of these requirements. This is important as both the transposition and the implementation of EU measures at the national level should correspond with the objectives defined by the EU (Knill 2001: 17) in order for a policy to be fully downloaded and have a lasting impact on a domestic political system. For these reasons, an intensive research design was chosen which focuses in-depth on four cases. Although a qualitative approach was deemed the most appropriate for the purposes of this study, it may also have the potential to pave the way for future studies, possibly quantitative large-N studies, that might allow for further generalization.

As policy mismatch has been identified as a necessary condition for domestic change, only EU legislation that diverges from pre-existing national ways of doing things was chosen for analysis. Policy mismatch is identifiable where there is a clear EU requirement or model with regulations setting out principles in the domestic arena (Bache 2008: 16). It can be measured by comparing an EU proposal with the corresponding national policy with respect to the compatibility of their problem solving approaches, policy instruments and/or policy standards (Borzel 2000: 148). Regarding case selection based on mismatch, it is important to bear in mind that the majority of legislation which is incorporated into the EEA Agreement is non-controversial. Indeed, in many cases EU acts are considered beneficial by the EFTA states. The cases selected are therefore in no way representative of the entire universe of cases, i.e. all legislative acts adopted into the EEA Agreement. This inevitably skews the results and paints an excessively conflictual picture of Iceland's relations with the EU through the EEA Agreement. However, using mismatch as criteria was arguably necessary in order to fully trigger the Europeanization processes and shed light on the two research questions, i.e. whether a non-member state can influence EU decision-making and whether the EU can ensure that its rules are adhered to beyond its boarders. The main aim of this study is therefore to highlight the conditions under which specified outcomes occur and the mechanisms through which they occur, but not the frequency with which they occur, which, as noted by George and Bennet (2004: 31), is generally the goal of case study research.

Four EU policies in the areas of electricity, free movement of persons, environmental policy and food law were thus chosen for analysis. EU obligations in each of these areas were in conflict with existing preferences and prescribed a new model to which domestic arrangements must be adjusted (Featherstone 2003: 14; Knill 2001: 36–37). The first three cases were selected through pilot interviews, where officials were asked if they remembered particular instances of mismatch between EU policy requirements and domestic preferences. The last case, involving food law, was discovered through the author's work at the EFTA Secretariat. For each of the cases, the outcome of the dependent variable was however largely unknown at the outset.

The key goal of the Electricity Directive was to create a single market for electricity in Europe and it prescribed a separation between generation, transmission and distribution of electricity. The Icelandic electricity market is very small and isolated from the rest of Europe and prior to the adoption of the Directive there was no separation between generation, transmission and distribution activities. Therefore, it was argued that the measures proposed by the Directive required extensive changes which were unsuitable for Icelandic conditions. Nonetheless, this case shows that domestic change can occur despite a high degree of mismatch, if EU policy corresponds with the general preferences of domestic political elites.

The Citizenship Directive (2004/38/EC) was controversial, as Iceland and Liechtenstein believed that it overstepped the boundaries of the EEA Agreement and that various aspects of should not be considered EEA-relevant. For a long time they refused to incorporate it into the EEA Agreement, running the risk of the relevant Annex to the Agreement being suspended. This case demonstrates the leverage of the EU when it comes to incorporating acts into the EEA Agreement. It also shows that lack of mobilization in society in opposition to EU requirements may mean that the government is more prepared to adapt to the EU's demands at the national level.

The Emissions Trading Scheme (ETS) (2003/87/EC) establishes a system for greenhouse gas emission-allowance trading. The aim is to help the EU member states attain their Kyoto obligations. As Iceland negotiated a separate agreement at Kyoto, the Icelandic government believed that adopting the Directive infringed on its right to negotiate international agreements independently of the EU. Furthermore, revisions of the Directive extended its scope to include air travel which, because of Iceland's isolated location, would have a considerable impact on Iceland. In addition to drawing particular attention to Iceland's uploading strategies, this case highlights the significance of domestic party politics and the impact of governmental change during the downloading process.

Finally, the Food Law Package incorporated legislation in the area of general food law, hygiene and control in food production and animal by-products into the EEA Agreement and revoked Iceland's exemption in this area, making all EU legislation concerning animal products applicable to Iceland. The implications were that Iceland would become part of the internal market with respect to trade in animal products: a situation which Icelandic authorities wished to avoid in order to protect Icelandic farmers from external competition. This case shows that the process of downloading can be severely delayed and thwarted when there is strong mobilization within civil society in opposition to EU demands. Indeed, the close ties between government and civil society may be particularly marked in a small society such as Iceland.

As noted, these particular cases share important characteristics which make them suitable for the purposes of this study. They represent areas of positive integration where the impact of the EU is direct and pronounced in the sense that it is aimed at replacing existing domestic regulatory arrangements with parallel provisions defined by the EU (Knill 2001: 36–37). EU obligations in these areas thus prescribe a model to which domestic arrangements must be adjusted (Featherstone 2003: 14). In each of the areas explored, EU policy is in conflict with existing Icelandic policies and institutions and thus potentially can have a deep impact on the domestic sphere (Knill 2001: 36–37). Yet, each case also has specific, unique characteristics, and the Europeanization process has yielded diverging results. The different cases thus draw attention to specific explanatory factors that can potentially lead to differing outcomes such as the level of support/opposition within government and civil society and changes in the domestic political scene. The cases can thus help to gauge the impact of different intervening variables and shed light on the conditions under which a non-member state such as Iceland can influence EU decision-making and the EU can elicit compliance beyond its borders.

Each of the case study chapters is organized along similar lines. First, they explore whether Iceland attempted to upload its preferences to the EU level, which strategies it used and how successful it was. Increased activities of domestic actors at the EU level as well as improved structures and resources can be seen as a projective response to EU-induced change. Uploading success is notoriously difficult to measure. However, in each case Iceland was working to secure specific adaptations or prevent legislation from becoming part of the EEA Agreement, rather than moulding the overall shape of the EU's legislative framework. This makes it rather easier to determine the extent of its success.

Next, the degree to which each of the EU directives has been downloaded is established. Downloading is usually operationalized as the domestic transposition and implementation or practical application of EU policies (Vink and Graziano 2007: 3–4). A policy can thus be considered to be effectively downloaded if it is fully and correctly transposed into national law, conflicting national provisions have been amended or revoked, the necessary administrative infrastructure and resources have been provided to put the objective of the policy into practice and the competent authorities have obliged others to comply with the legislation by monitoring, imposing sanctions and compulsory corrective measures (Borzel 2000: 149; Cini 2003: 352–53). In this study, an important aspect of downloading also involves the initial incorporation of the relevant legislation into the EEA Agreement.

The degree of domestic change resulting from participation in the EU policy process is then evaluated and grouped according to one of three potential categories based on a taxonomy developed by Radaelli (2003). First, inertia, or lack of change, may take the form of lack of participation at the formulation stage at the EU level, lags and delays in the transposition of directives and sheer resistance to EU-induced change. Second, accommodation can be said to have occurred when domestic institutions and organizations show a mixture of resiliency and flexibility. They absorb certain non-fundamental changes but maintain their core. Institutions and organizations accommodate policy requirements by incorporating EU policies and adapting existing processes, policies and structures without substantial modification or changes in the logic of political behaviour. Finally, transformation has arguably occurred when the fundamental logic of political behaviour changes. Existing policies, processes and institutions have been replaced by new substantially different ones or altered to the extent that their essential features are fundamentally changed (Borzel and Risse 2003: 69–70; Radaelli 2003: 38). Once the level of change caused by each of the policies has been established, it is determined whether adaptation pressure alone was sufficient to cause domestic administrative change or whether pressure from existing structures and support or opposition of domestic actors also made a difference. Furthermore, did the mechanisms of change work through a logic of consequentialism or a logic of appropriateness? In other words, why did change/lack of change occur?

The study builds on a variety of primary written sources such as the European Economic Area (EEA) Agreement, EU and national legislation, EFTA publications, policy documents, newspaper articles and press releases. Various internal EFTA documents were also used including meeting reports and memos, subject to permission from the delegations of the EEA EFTA states.[12] Some of the information in this volume is also based on personal observations of the author having worked at the EFTA Secretariat. However, the bulk of the data used for qualitative analysis was collected via in-depth semi-structured interviews. Interviews were conducted with relevant individuals such as government officials, members of specialist agencies and administrative authorities responsible for each policy area, and officials at the EFTA Secretariat and Surveillance Authority, as well as politicians, academics and members of interest groups and non-governmental organizations. Furthermore, representatives from the Commission were interviewed in order to triangulate the statements of national actors against the EU view.[13]

As this is a historical institutionalist account, which takes into consideration both rationalist and sociological mechanisms for change as well as a temporal dimension, motivations for change, i.e. why change occurred/failed to occur, are important. Therefore, the focus of the interviews was to establish how/whether domestic actors perceived that the proposed EU legislation would have an impact; whether/why the government supported or opposed the legislation; whether it tried to influence the outcome of the proposal and, if so, how; which measures were taken to implement or thwart the implementation of the relevant initiative after it had been adopted; and which changes occurred in domestic structures following its implementation. Actors' views and motivations at each stage of the process were also taken into account. The interviews were conducted during the period from November 2007 to February 2012, although a large majority were conducted in the year 2008. Most of them were tape-recorded and transcribed before being subjected to qualitative analysis. Each of the individuals interviewed was given a chance to comment on the references made based on his/her evidence. Many of the interviews were conducted in Icelandic. Quotations that appear from these interviews throughout the book have been translated by the author into English.

The outcomes of the four cases are explored fully in Chapters 4–7 and drawn together and analysed in Chapter 8 of this volume, which provides a base to look at the EEA framework in a broader context and as a potential model for other states in the concluding chapter of the volume. However, before moving on to the empirical cases, it is necessary to establish the institutional framework within which the Europeanization process in Iceland takes place. That is the focus of the next two chapters, which provide background analysis of Iceland's participation in the EU policy process in terms of both uploading and downloading.

2 Uploading in the EEA

Uploading involves making systematic use of resources, strategies and opportunities in order to exert influence and advance national preferences at the EU level (Bulmer and Burch 2005: 867; McGowan 2005: 996). Research has shown that actors actively engage in uploading in order to avoid having to download undesirable policies, and so uploading is now seen as an important aspect of the Europeanization process. Therefore, it is necessary to assess Iceland's uploading capacity in the context of the EEA Agreement, which relates to the first research question posed in this volume: can a non-member state such as Iceland develop uploading capacity? In other words, is it correct to assume that third countries undergo a completely unilateral adjustment to EU policy requirements, with uploading capacity a phenomenon unique to EU member states, or do domestic institutions and organizations in non-member states develop mechanisms and strategies to ensure their input into EU policy-making as a result of prolonged structured relations with the EU? Although the majority of the EU legislation that the EFTAns are required to adopt is uncontroversial, instances do come up in which EU policies go against their preferences.[1] This question is therefore an important one.

It is clear that the EEA Agreement encompasses considerable asymmetries in the power of actors and their access to the policy-making process. Iceland, Norway and Liechtenstein are allowed to participate in the EU's internal market and, in return, they adopt the relevant *acquis*. The EEA Agreement does not, however, grant the EFTAns much formal access to EU decision-making institutions and does not accord the parties to the Agreement equal rights as regards the evolution of EEA law. Some have even gone so far as to characterize the EEA as 'legalized hegemony' (Pederson 1994: 70–71), highlighting the dominance of the EU pillar of the Agreement at the expense of the EFTA pillar.[2] As one Commission official noted: 'It is strange to take over so much legislation without access to decision-making.'[3] Yet the EFTA states frequently put a positive spin on their participation in the EU policy process, referring to their contribution as 'decision-shaping' as opposed to decision-making (EFTA Secretariat 2009). Although the term decision-shaping is not specifically referred to in the EEA Agreement, it has been coined so frequently by the EFTA states that an Internet search yields almost exclusively articles related to the EEA. According to a special bulletin on decision-shaping published by the EFTA Secretariat, the term refers to 'the process of contributing to and influencing policy proposals up until they are formally adopted' (EFTA Secretariat 2009: 20). But is Iceland really an effective decision-shaper?

In addition to non-member status, Iceland's small size may also hamper its ability to make its voice heard effectively at the EU level. Larger states have more resources to develop capacity to project their preferences. It is therefore hypothesized that Iceland's participatory and contact networks may be less developed than in the EU member states, particularly the larger ones. The first section of this chapter explores the structural features of the Icelandic administration, taking into account the hurdles faced by small states in their attempts to influence EU policy. The following sections focus on Iceland's non-member status, discussing the framework of the EEA Agreement in terms of uploading. Iceland's formal access points to EU institutions are identified as well as more informal channels and strategies that may have been developed over the years to enable it to project its preferences at the EU level.

The Commission is the main formal point of access granted through the EEA Agreement. However, in recent years the Council and particularly the Parliament have begun to play an increasingly important role in the European policy process, and so the EFTA states have had to adapt their strategies to take these developments into account. The EFTA-3 also rely on internal collaboration to gather information and promote their views. Finally, the EEA framework sometimes allows for the negotiation of adaptations and exemptions for the EFTA states before acts are incorporated into the Agreement. Each of these potential uploading points will be explored in the following sections. While this chapter refers to various specific examples of uploading attempts, the practical application of Iceland's mechanisms and strategies is tested in greater detail in the case studies in Chapters 4 to 7. This chapter, along with the case studies, thus aims to give some insight into the larger question of whether an interactive model of Europeanization, which takes uploading into account, is indeed appropriate for non-member states such as Iceland.

Limitations of a small administration

Even among the EU's member states, there are substantial discrepancies between small and large states with respect to their impact on EU policy. National preferences are generally expected to be projected to the EU level by the larger, more powerful member states. Take, for example, the case of the CAP for France and that of industrial competition for Germany (Wong 2006: 15). Small EU member states on the other hand face various disadvantages in uploading their policy preferences to the EU level. One of the most obvious reasons is that they have fewer votes in the Council and therefore less bargaining power (Panke 2008: 1). Studies have, for example, found that, even though qualified majority voting (QMV) over-represents the number of citizens in smaller states, larger member states are more than twice as likely to be part of a winning coalition than the smaller ones (Hix 2005: 84).

The EU's decision-making process is based on compromise and votes are only called in a small minority of instances. Therefore, although lack of votes matters, it is perhaps not the primary obstacle faced by small states. Powerful, typically large, member states are also more likely to succeed in uploading their policy preferences at the EU level because they have more resources to deal with each policy. Effective uploading generally requires a well-staffed administration with high levels of policy expertise to allow states to present a coherent position and persuade others of the value of a particular argument. Smaller states have fewer financial and administrative resources which are necessary to exert influence and they are therefore less likely to be successful in projecting their views (Panke 2008: 1 and 6). This is not to say that small states cannot be successful, but they are at a considerable disadvantage.

Iceland is smaller than any of the current EU member states, including Luxembourg and Malta. With approximately 320,000 inhabitants it could even be classified as a micro-state. Accordingly, the size of the national administration is much smaller than that of most EU states (Thorhallsson and Vignisson 2004: 164). Due to its small size, Icelandic departments have to handle a much broader range of issues than their counterparts in other countries (Laergreid *et al.* 2004: 364–65). The administration has lacked staff and expertise to deal with the EEA Agreement, which has undoubtedly prevented the administration from engaging as actively in European affairs as it would have liked (Thorhallsson 2005: 130). As one official noted: 'I haven't been able to follow things well enough, but that is just because I'm drowning in work. Everyone is drowning. We are clearly too few ... we need more people, that would make a difference.'[4]

Despite significant limitations, Iceland's capacity and ability to engage in European policy-making has increased as a result of its participation in the EEA (Thorhallsson and Vignisson 2004: 180–81). In fact, a survey from 2004 found that government departments in Iceland and Norway were just as focused on involvement in EU rule-making as those in the other Nordic countries despite being non-members (Laergreid *et al.* 2005: 33). After the EEA Agreement came into effect, the size of the central administration, and particularly the Ministry of Foreign Affairs, grew considerably, which is important as the Foreign Ministry is responsible for the coordination of EU matters in Iceland as in most states (Thorhallsson 2004b: 163, 2005: 130). Up until the 1990s only a handful of officials dealt with EU matters within the Icelandic administration at any given time; indeed in the 1970s only 53 people worked in the entire Foreign Service (Thorhallsson 2004b: 166). By 2001, this number had increased considerably to 150, although still small compared to 206 in Luxembourg, 1,150 in Norway and 9,800 in France (Thorhallsson and Vignisson 2004: 164).[5] The Foreign Service continued to grow in the early 2000s. However, in light of the financial crisis, it has faced substantial budgetary cuts in recent years.[6] As a result, the number of staff posted abroad has decreased, although locally recruited personnel have been hired to a greater extent to partially fill this gap (Utanrikisraduneytid 2012). According to data from the Ministry of Foreign Affairs, in 2010 there were 54 individuals posted in Iceland's diplomatic missions abroad. In comparison, Luxembourg had 62, Malta had 75, Belgium had 448, Denmark had 539 and Iceland's EFTA partner Norway had 630 (Utanrikisraduneytid 2012).

In addition to its inherently small size, reductions in government expenditure prompted by the financial crisis are likely to place some constraints on Iceland's uploading capacity. Nonetheless, the Icelandic administration has adopted many specific features found in other European states that are designed to enhance relations with the EU and its member states. For example, all ministries now employ EU specialists (Thorhallsson and Ellertsdottir 2004: 101). The Directorate of External Trade and Economic Affairs within the Ministry of Foreign Affairs has a special EEA Department which is in charge of promoting Iceland's interests in relation to the EEA Agreement and dealing with the running and development of the Agreement in close collaboration with the Icelandic Mission to the EU in Brussels and the EFTA Secretariat.

Iceland's Mission to the EU in Brussels plays an important role in coordinating Iceland's participation in the EEA Agreement. Indeed, its functions are in many ways similar to those of the permanent representations of EU member states, monitoring EU policy developments and defending Icelandic interests both vis-à-vis EU institutions and other states. However, due to recent financial constraints, the number of staff at the Mission has not been increased, despite greater pressure on its resources in view of Iceland's accession negotiations with the EU. In 2007, the Mission had representatives (counsellors) from each of the government ministries, except for the Prime Minister's Office, who were charged with looking after Iceland's interests in their designated areas (Forsaetisraduneytid 2007: 36). In the wake of the financial crisis some ministries have decided not to post counsellors at the Mission.

In addition to the Mission in Brussels, Iceland has embassies in nine EU/EEA member states. Its embassies in Helsinki and Vienna were set up after the EEA Agreement came into force.[7] Nevertheless, it does not have representations in important EU member states, including Spain and the Netherlands, or any of the new member states, including Poland. Seven EU/EEA member states, i.e. Denmark, Finland, Norway, Sweden, the UK, Germany and France, have embassies in Iceland. Furthermore, when Iceland applied for EU membership, the EU set up a representation in Iceland; previously, the EU representation in Oslo also served Iceland. Representations are important structural features, particularly as 'intra-EU diplomacy' has become increasingly important in an EU of 27, where every Council vote counts. They can serve a key function when it comes to monitoring and influencing other states' positions. Iceland has far fewer representations than most of the larger EU states, which have representations throughout the Union. Furthermore, due to budgetary cuts Iceland closed two of its European representations, in Strasbourg and Rome, in 2010.

One method of counterbalancing the limitations of a small administration has been through extensive collaboration with interest groups (Thorhallsson and Vignisson 2004: 179). The Icelandic government works in close contact with Icelandic interest groups in various areas that are active at the EU level, and often relies on them to gather information and increase awareness of Icelandic concerns in Brussels. This does not mean to imply that all Icelandic actors have the same concerns or interests or that they always coincide with those of the government. However, the Icelandic government and interest groups do share certain nationally based common interests, for example to avoid policies that would have a detrimental effect on the Icelandic economy as a whole or certain sectors or groups in Icelandic society.

Many Icelandic interest groups have taken part in European umbrella organizations[8] and so provide an important link to the EU level. Some Icelandic organizations even have representatives based in Brussels. The social partners are particularly active as they participate in the social dialogue and have direct access to the policy-formulation process. According to representatives from both Icelandic labour and management organizations who have participated in the social dialogue, it does not matter that the EFTA states are not members of the EU. Their opinions are taken into consideration like everyone else's. Iceland has, for example, emphasized issues relating to parental leave and part-time employment which representatives felt had been well received.[9]

In addition to participating in the social dialogue, Icelandic labour and management organizations are also members of the EEA Consultative Committee, which is an advisory body that represents workers, employers and other organizations in the EEA countries and includes representatives of the European Economic and Social Committee (EESC) as well the social partners from the EFTA states[10] (EFTA Secretariat 2006: 9). An Icelandic Labour representative in this committee noted that, although it was a rather weak venue in terms of influence, it was important for information-gathering purposes.[11] Other Icelandic interest groups also follow the EU legislative procedure closely, for example the Association of Local Authorities, the Farmers Association and the Federation of Icelandic Fishing Vessel Owners (LIU). The Icelandic Chamber of Commerce is a member of EUROCHAMBERS, and the Federation of Trade and Services (SVTH) and the Federation of Icelandic Trade (SV) are members of EUROCOMMERCE.

Interview evidence suggests that Icelandic interest groups play a larger role in terms of information-gathering and strategizing than actually influencing EU policy, except in areas covered by the social dialogue.[12] When they become aware of something in the pipeline which might affect their interests they usually alert the Icelandic government and ask it to take action. For example, the Icelandic government learned of a Commission proposal to ban fishmeal and fish oil in animal feed through a representative of the Association of Fishmeal Manufacturers. The government was then able to take action which resulted in a partial exemption for fishmeal from the overall ban on processed animal protein in animal feed (Thorhallsson and Ellertsdottir 2004). In general, relations with interest groups have been an important platform for the Icelandic government to connect with the EU policy process and have served to augment its limited resources.

Overall, Iceland's small size and lack of administrative capacity, which has been accentuated even further by the financial crisis, is likely to pose certain restrictions on its ability to upload preferences to the European level. Despite various drawbacks, it is important to note that there are also some advantages of a small administration. Officials generally have more autonomy and flexibility to deal with EU issues, which means that things can often get done more quickly than in countries with larger, more laborious bureaucracies (Laergreid *et al.* 2004: 364–65). Finally, previous research has shown that small EU member states have been able to engage in various strategies such as prioritization of issues and coalition-building in order to further their interests (Panke 2008; Thorhallsson 2006). However, in addition to small size, Iceland is at a further disadvantage compared to EU member states in that it does not have equal access to the EU's decision-making institutions. The following sections outline Iceland's formal and informal channels of access to the EU decision-making process within the EEA framework.

The Commission as the main formal point of access

The EU institution to which the EFTA states have the most access is undoubtedly the Commission. According to the EEA Agreement, the Commission 'shall informally seek advice from experts of the EEA EFTA States in the same way as it seeks advices from experts of the EC Member States in the elaboration of its proposals'. In this way the EFTA states have participated in a variety of Commission expert groups which play an important role in the formulation of legislative proposals and policy initiatives. In addition, the EEA Agreement grants access to comitology committees, which assist the Commission in exercising its executive powers, as well as other advisory bodies. Finally the EFTA states participate in a number of EU programmes and have access to the committees which assist the Commission in the management of the relevant activities under these programmes. This section focuses primarily on expert groups and comitology committees due to their importance in the EU legislative process.

Expert groups

The Commission is generally responsible for the formulation of legislative proposals. Member states thus regularly try to induce the Commission to come up with certain initiatives (Princen 2007: 22–23). In principle Commissioners and staff within the Commission are meant to be independent, but because of their previous occupations, contacts, future aims and national media scrutiny, they do tend to have considerable links with domestic politics and often defend the interests of their own member state (Hix 2005: 44 and 47–49). The EFTAns are at a disadvantage compared to the EU member states, as they do not have Commissioners or staff within the DGs, although seconded national experts from the EFTA states are allowed to work in the Commission. Generally, however, if the EFTAns want the Commission to initiate a legislative proposal of particular importance to them, they must lobby it from the outside. This is not common, and Iceland has very seldom tried to initiate a piece of legislation.[13] As noted, uploading can entail trying to initiate or block a particular policy or adapting a proposal to suit specific needs. It is fairly safe to say that Iceland is not generally an 'agenda setter' in the EU policy process.

The EEA Agreement does, however, allow for the participation of EEA EFTA experts in the Commission's expert groups during the formulation of legislative proposals, and EFTA experts have the same formal status within these groups as EU delegates.[14] They therefore have some possibility of shaping EU legislation at the preparatory stage of the decision-making process. In theory, the Commission invites experts to participate in expert groups based on their professional qualifications. They are not considered representatives of individual states and their contributions are not necessarily meant to reflect their government's official position. Rather, they are expected to provide input based on scientific, ethical, practical, judicial or sector considerations. However, in practice, experts often convey their government's views (EFTA Secretariat 2002: 12). A high-level EFTA official observed that, although the impact of participation in expert groups was difficult to measure, attending these meetings was important as it provided a platform to raise awareness of any foreseen problems with the legislation, although it was important to emphasize these issues from an expert perspective, not a political one.[15]

In 2005 the EFTA states had access to 179 of the Commission's expert groups (Forsaetisraduneytid 2007: 43). This is a relatively small proportion of the total number of expert groups registered by the Commission; in 2007 the Commission had 1,261 functioning expert groups (European Commission 2007). This can in part be explained by the fact that EFTA experts do not have access to expert groups in policy areas that are not included in the EEA Agreement, such as Agriculture or External Relations. However, in some cases EFTA experts also feel that civil servants in Brussels are not granting the EEA countries as much access as they are entitled to or are forgetting to consult EFTA specialists (Einarsson 2003: 103–05). It has sometimes been suggested that the Lisbon Treaty might have an impact in this respect, as the legal basis of new EU proposals and their location within the pillar system has been used as an indication as to whether legislation falls under the scope of the EEA and accordingly whether the EFTA states are allowed to participate in the relevant expert groups. The elimination of the pillar structure and increased uncertainty surrounding EEA-relevance could therefore affect the participation of the EFTA states in the Commission's expert groups, although this effect appears to have been minimal so far.

In any case, Iceland participates in relatively few of the groups to which it has access. In 2005 Icelandic representatives participated in only 77, or less than half, of the expert group meetings that it could have attended (Forsaetisraduneytid 2007: 44–45). This limited participation is probably due mainly to the small size of Iceland's administration.[16] National ministries, their institutions and surveillance authorities do not have enough funds or experts to attend all meetings within the Commission (Thorhallsson and Ellertsdottir 2004: 101). Instead the Icelandic administration has prioritized certain key areas such as energy and environmental policy, and maritime and marine policy (Utanrikisraduneytid 2007: 34) and therefore has not regularly attended meetings in some areas.

Prioritization is not necessarily negative or unique to Iceland. Rather, the working procedures of small administrations in dealing with the EU decision-making system are generally characterized by prioritization (Thorhallsson 2000). Selective engagement allows small states to concentrate their limited capacities on important issues and not spend too much time, personnel and administrative and financial resources on policies that have little impact on them (Panke 2008: 9). Prioritization can therefore be an effective strategy to compensate for the limitations of a small administration. As one EFTA official noted:

> It is important to know when to participate. There are hundreds of expert groups, and a small administration must decide which meetings are absolutely necessary. A lot of the issues being discussed are highly technical and perhaps will not have such a big impact. Furthermore, the EFTA states often work together. If a Norwegian official participates in a meeting he will generally let his EFTA colleagues know at our working group meetings, where we exchange information in a particular policy area and often also get Commission officials to attend. This means Iceland will often know what is going on, even though it hasn't participated in a particular meeting.[17]

It is, however, clear that more extensive expert participation would be desirable. Due to small size, lack of resources and distance from mainland Europe, Iceland is heavily dependent on the counsellors at its Mission to the EU to attend expert group meetings. These counsellors are expected to cover broad policy areas and therefore often lack the highly specialized knowledge required to make an effective contribution within expert groups. This can be contrasted to Norway's approach. There are examples of large delegations arriving from Oslo to participate in a group while the sole representative on Iceland's side is the Mission counsellor (Thorhallsson 2001: 43). One official said the following:

> In my opinion the Icelandic civil service is just so small and over-worked that people are barely able to go to the meetings that they are entitled to

go to. No one has the time to follow what is going on in Brussels during the formulation stages. Of course there are issues where there are high interests at stake when it would be good to send a representative but that is an exception and only in extreme cases.[18]

The significance of Iceland's participation in the Commission's expert groups can be called into question for various other reasons. There may be (unofficial) limits placed on participation by non-EU member states as their participation might not be well regarded by the Commission or the EU member states. Representing a non-member state could also have a psychological impact to the extent that EFTA officials suppress their views in deference to representatives from 'fully-fledged' EU member states (EFTA Secretariat 2002: 14 and 32).

Yet, interview evidence suggests that Icelandic representatives generally felt that their views were taken as seriously as those of the EU member states as long as they had something worthwhile to say. A frequent comment was that the Commission did not care from where it got good advice.[19] One official noted that, although the Commission did not really mind where a good proposal came from, it was generally critical of input from experts and defended its own views staunchly.[20] Another said that it depended to some extent on the DG as some DGs were more open than others.[21] It is likely that the extent to which the EFTA states are taken note of depends on their degree of expertise on the subject and the extent to which they have a clear interest in the area. For example, regarding the development of the maritime strategy, the Commission sought close cooperation with Iceland and Norway (EFTA Secretariat 2009: 10). This may not be the case in other areas.

Another reason for calling into question the impact of expert group participation is that the Commission's policy formulation has changed since the entry into force of the EEA Agreement. It has become much more open to outside input, which arguably means that the privileged position of the EFTA states has been diminished to some extent. As one EFTA official explained:

> Today the Commission has a much broader process where everyone can get involved. They publish green papers and invite interest groups, regional authorities and anyone who is interested to submit comments. It is a completely open process. This means that our access at the expert level, which was so exclusive before, is not so anymore. I mean regional entities and interest groups in Norway submit comments on Commission proposals just like the Norwegian government. This means our status is no longer so special. Our exclusivity has been watered down.[22]

It is also important to note that in some areas the Commission relies less on expert groups than in others which means that the EFTA states must act like any other lobby group if they wish to have an impact.[23] Finally, expert groups are purely advisory and do not take binding decisions or vote. Thus, ultimately it is up to the Commission both whom it asks for advice and whether or not it takes it. Unlike the EU member states, the EFTA states are not able to vote on legislative proposals in the Council or Parliament. This is important, as the Council and, particularly, the EP have become more assertive in the EU policy process in recent years, at the expense of the Commission, and proposals often change considerably in their hands. Therefore, although expert consultation is one of the main formal channels of EEA EFTA participation in the policy-making process, the impact of this alone might be considered fairly limited, particularly when the entire decision-making process is examined.

Comitology committees

The EFTA states also have access to the Commission's comitology committees through the EEA Agreement. While major policy decisions are sent to the Council and the EP for approval, technical implementing legislation within particular areas has been developed through the comitology procedure. This includes the majority of legal acts of the EU, and hence of the EEA. In comitology, the Commission is subject to the supervision, and in some cases the approval, of committees composed of national civil servants appointed by the Council, through which member states' interests are represented (Steiner *et al.* 2006: 31–32).

Under Article 100 of the EEA Agreement, the EEA-3 have observer status in the working groups of comitology committees and are thus also able to provide some input into the outcome of legislation in this procedure (EFTA Secretariat 2006: 14). A Declaration of the European Communities attached to the Final Act of the EEA Agreement further clarifies the nature of EEA EFTA participation, stating, among other things, that EFTA experts 'will be involved on an equal footing together with national experts from the EC member states in the work preparatory to the convening of the EC committees relevant to the *acquis* in question'.

There was some degree of concern among the EFTA states regarding the impact of the Lisbon Treaty on their participation in comitology. The Treaty distinguishes between delegated acts and implementing acts.[24] Prior to Lisbon, both were subject to comitology but, post-Lisbon, the comitology system only applies to implementing acts. The EFTA states followed these developments attentively and, in conjunction with the EFTA Secretariat, they were in close contact with the Commission in order to avoid any potential negative impact on EEA EFTA participation, particularly with respect to delegated acts, as they are no longer subject to the comitology procedures. Although, at the time of writing, there was limited experience with the new system, the Commission's guidelines on delegated acts contain specific references to the EEA EFTA states, stating that they should be allowed to attend meetings as observers where they have a direct interest in the *acquis* in question.[25]

Unlike expert groups which are purely advisory, comitology committees have a formal role in the Community decision-making process and there are limitations on the role of EFTA representatives. They do not have voting rights within the committees and representation is often limited to working groups, which carry out the committees' preparatory work. In these sessions, representatives of the EFTA states have the opportunity to contribute to deliberations. However, when comitology committees take a vote, practices vary depending on the policy area in question. In some committees, the chairman allows EFTA experts to be present during voting proceedings, but in others they are barred from participating once the proposal has reached this stage (EFTA Secretariat 2002: 31). As they do not have voting rights, it is important for representatives from the EFTA states to identify potential problematic issues early in the deliberative stage of the comitology procedure, and certainly before the committee takes a vote, if they want to be able to influence the process (EFTA Secretariat 2009: 23).

Their non-voting status may deter representatives from the EFTA states from speaking when they are entitled to do so. A representative who had participated in the Banking Advisory Committee and the Insurance Committee noted that, due to his observer status, he felt he must restrict his speaking time to a minimum and only speak if he had something of substance to contribute (EFTA Secretariat 2002: 18). The Head of Energy Policy at the Icelandic Ministry of Industry, Energy and Tourism also noted that participating in comitology committees felt different as he was not representing a member state and that he had always been asked to leave when it came time to vote. However, he also observed significant differences between the large and small EU member states. The larger states like Britain and Germany had an opinion on everything and the resources to prepare for all matters. Luxembourg, on the other hand, did not say much unless it was a real matter of national interest.[26] Therefore, Iceland's small size may be as much of an impediment as its non-member status when it comes to participation in the comitology process.

There is a general feeling among EFTA representatives that awareness of the EEA Agreement has decreased through the years, particularly in light of the recent enlargements of the EU. One official complained that enlargement had had a negative impact on EFTA participation in comitology:

> At first people showed us some courtesy, especially if we had a reliable expert, but with the enlargement there were a lot of committees that began to question the participation of the EFTAns. In many cases there was an inner circle and an outer circle. When we went into the meetings and there were no placings for the EFTA states, we had to ask for them specially and were told to go sit somewhere at the back. But this also depends on the area. If the EU has an interest in involving Norway, for example, then we had more say. It is in the nature of the EU to listen to those that have interests and expertise in a particular area.[27]

At the end of 2009 there were a total of 266 functioning comitology committees in the EU and 158 of these committees had a legal base in the EEA

Agreement.[28] However, this number does not indicate actual participation of EFTA experts and there is reason to believe that this may be more limited. For example, earlier figures from 2005 show that Iceland participated in just 38 of the 108 comitology committees to which it had access (Forsaetisraduneytid 2007: 44–45). Again, this can most likely be traced to the limitations of a small administration and the necessity to prioritize.

Although delegation to the Commission is permissible only in matters of implementation rather than determining general policy (Steiner *et al.* 2006: 55), legislation adopted through comitology can be controversial and large-scale commercial interests are often at stake (Corbett *et al.* 2000: 255–56). Therefore, the importance of participation in comitology committees should not be underestimated. For example, Iceland's access to the relevant committee proved vital in preventing a ban on fishmeal in animal feed. In this case, the Icelandic Ambassador attended the meeting and was able to convince the members of the committee that fishmeal was not dangerous to animals and was easily distinguishable from other types of animalmeal (Thorhallsson and Ellertsdottir 2004: 114).

Nevertheless, as noted, it is likely that their non-EU status places Icelandic officials at a disadvantage in influencing the outcome of proceedings in comparison to the EU member states. Furthermore, proposals that do not gain a qualified majority in the committee are passed to the Council and Parliament, where the EFTA states have no inside role. Moreover, despite having access to the Commission through expert groups and comitology committees, it sometimes happens in the context of the EEA that legislation has been passed to the Council and EP for approval before Iceland becomes aware of it.[29] In these cases Icelandic officials must try their best to influence the decision-making institutions from the outside in order to upload their preferences.

Lobbying decision-making bodies from the outside

The Council

The EEA Agreement does not grant the EFTA states any representation in the Council or access to its working groups or committees (EFTA Secretariat 2002: 31). It is true that Iceland is a small country and would not have a large proportion of the vote in QMV. Nonetheless, the fact that its voice is absent from discussions during the working groups, COREPER (Committee of Permanent Representatives) and Council meetings means that, unlike the EU member states, it is unable to influence from within any changes to Commission proposals, once they have reached this stage of the policy process. This is a significant limitation as the Council bodies are the main forums where national governments voice their concerns and promote their preferences. The governments of the EFTA states thus lack an important institutional link to the Council, which makes it difficult to follow and influence important processes (EFTA Secretariat 2002: 33).

Icelandic officials complain about not being able to follow through on their preferences at the decision-making stage.[30] Often, they say, the difficulty is not knowing what is happening inside the Council, as sometimes proposals stay there for months or even years, and then all of a sudden a new piece of legislation emerges which looks completely different from the original proposal.[31] As a former Icelandic Minister of Foreign Affairs once noted:

> One of the important advantages of the EEA Agreement is that it gives the EFTA states access to hundreds of Commission committees and working groups. It would of course have been more interesting to gain access also to the Council and its working groups where the real debate on policy issues takes place but that was not to be. ... We therefore have to make the most of what we have.
> (EFTA Secretariat 2002: 7–8)

Although the Council is generally a fairly closed institution, the country which holds the Presidency has sometimes invited ministers from the EFTA states to participate in informal ministerial meetings where they have been able to express their views. Participation in these meetings can be important as their outcome can often develop into legislative proposals. Therefore, visits of EFTA ministers to Brussels and meetings with Council representatives can increase awareness of their interests within the EU (Forsaetisraduneytid 2007: 47) and could potentially be a forum for them to collaborate with countries with similar interests.

It is likely that, in some cases, the EFTA states are invited to these informal meetings as they are expected to be able to contribute substantially to the policy area in question. For example, the EU was keen to ensure the involvement of Iceland and Norway in the development of its Integrated Maritime Policy and so they were invited to an informal meeting of ministers coordinating maritime matters held in Lisbon in October 2007 (EFTA Secretariat 2009: 11). The EFTA states also have a good reputation in other areas such as social and equality policy, energy matters and environmental affairs. As noted by one official: 'We don't sit at the Council table but if the EU believes we have something to add to the discussion they show us a lot of attention and invite us to meetings.'[32]

The EFTA states have also participated informally in the work of some of the Treaty-based committees which contribute to the preparation of Council proceedings in different areas. For example, although the OMC as such is not covered by the EEA Agreement, EFTA representatives have regularly been invited to attend informal meetings of the Employment Committee (EMCO), which plays an important role in the development of the European Employment Strategy (EES). At these biannual meetings the EFTA experts provide information about their respective labour market situations and exchange views and best practices with the EU member states on employment-related topics.[33]

Iceland also maintains an informal link to the Council through its Nordic counterparts. The Nordic countries have a long history of cooperation in various policy areas which has been institutionalized in the form of the Nordic Council and the Nordic Council of Ministers.[34] Denmark, Finland and Sweden have often enhanced their bargaining and voting power in the Council via the Nordic cooperation which also includes Norway and Iceland (Panke 2008: 13). Iceland and Norway frequently have so-called pre-meetings with the other Nordic, and sometimes also the Baltic, states before Council meetings in order to discuss the items on the Council's agenda (Forsaetisraduneytid 2007: 47).

Through the Nordic cooperation, Icelandic and Norwegian representatives try to get messages across to the EU member states and then hope that they will make their opinions known within the Council, but this is quite an informal process. The Nordic countries are not necessarily always on the same side and always looking out for each other, but they do often have similar interests.[35] One official recalled that Nordic cooperation had been particularly useful when discussing deportation issues.[36] Another noted that this had proved to be a constructive venue for cooperation with respect to the REACH Regulation.[37] In the fishmeal case, the Icelandic Minister of Foreign Affairs was in particularly close contact with the Danish Minister for agriculture and fisheries as a ban on the use of fishmeal in animal feed would also have affected the Danish industry (Thorhallsson and Ellertsdottir 2004: 108–09 and 20).

As the EU continues to grow, EU decision-making entails a greater need for coalition-building, and no single member state is able to systematically shape the EU agenda on its own (Borzel 2002: 200). Particularly with the recent enlargements and increased use of QMV, even large EU member states have recognized the growing need for closer engagement with other member states (Bulmer and Burch 2005: 877). Strategic partnerships and regional cooperation are thus relatively common strategies among EU states to enhance their bargaining positions (Panke 2008: 8). Although it does not have a seat at the table, Iceland also participates in this strategy through the Nordic cooperation and in some cases also by exploring whether any other countries have similar interests.[38] Nonetheless, not being able to follow the decision-making process from within the Council is clearly a significant disadvantage when it comes to uploading.

The European Parliament

One of the key changes to the EU policy process that have occurred since the EEA Agreement came into effect is the more prominent role of the European Parliament. The EP's powers have been gradually increasing since the introduction of direct elections in 1979, and it is now a major force in the EU decision-making process across a wide range of policy domains. Its role has been even further strengthened by the Lisbon Treaty by extending the co-decision (now called the 'ordinary legislative') procedure to more areas. Although members of the EP (MEPs) sit in pan-European party groups rather than along national lines, the national delegations have remained powerful within the Parliament and often, when MEPs are torn between their national interests and their EP group, they vote according to their national allegiance (Hix 2005: 93). Therefore, having MEPs can be important for member state governments in the uploading process, although if Iceland were a member of the EU it would only have six MEPs which is the minimum number under the Lisbon Treaty. As one official observed: 'Some governments are probably in contact with their MEPs but small countries can't block anything in the EP anyway.'[39]

As is the case with the Council, the EEA Agreement does not grant the EFTA parties any formal access to the EP's committees. Icelandic officials have complained that they felt their overall influence was decreasing because of changes in the EU decision-making process, particularly the more powerful role of the European Parliament, where Iceland doesn't have any access. In relation to the Parliament, Iceland is just like any other interest group.[40] Traditionally, Iceland has spent fairly little time lobbying the EP.[41] However, many people in the Icelandic administration have begun to realize that their efforts should be aimed to a greater extent at the EP, and some changes can be seen in this direction.[42] As the EP is a relatively open institution, Iceland has had some opportunities to gather information and informally participate in discussions within the Parliament. The counsellor for transport at the Icelandic Mission noted it was much easier to get into the Parliament than the Council and that he had been to the Parliament to present Iceland's views when they were asking for input from interested parties on particular policies.[43] Icelandic Members of Parliament (MPs) have also been invited to participate in EP committee meetings as experts in matters regarding the EU Common Fisheries Policy. There they have been able to express their opinions and give advice on the future of the policy (Forsaetisraduneytid 2007: 48).

MPs from the EFTA states do have a formal link with the European Parliament through the EEA Joint Parliamentary Committee, which meets twice a year and is made up of MPs from the EFTA states and MEPs.[44] Its key task is to discuss the functioning of the EEA Agreement and contribute to a better understanding between the EU and EFTA sides in the fields covered by the Agreement (EFTA Secretariat 2008a). The MPs that represent the EFTA states in the Joint Parliamentary Committee also meet separately from the EU in the EFTA Parliamentary Committee. According to a former leader of the Icelandic delegation to the EFTA Parliamentary Committee, it may be possible to have some impact on EU policy through the Joint Parliamentary Committee, although this is difficult to measure. In her view, this platform does, however, serve to increase awareness among MEPs of the EEA Agreement and the EFTA states, which is important.[45] Another official who participated in the Committee in the early 1990s noted that it was a useful forum of cooperation as it allowed the EFTA states to follow the EU debate and perhaps even have a small impact.[46] It is important to note that the focus of the Joint Parliamentary Committee has evolved over time. In the early years, its deliberations were mainly devoted to commenting on past developments. However, it has increasingly begun to concentrate on new proposals which could become EEA-relevant in areas such as health services, energy and environmental issues (EFTA Secretariat 2012). Therefore, it may now play a more significant role in the uploading process.

Iceland's relations with the EP have further increased as a result of its application for EU membership. A Joint Parliamentary Committee between Iceland and the EU was set up in 2010 which is made up of nine Icelandic MPs and nine MEPs. Each of Iceland's representatives in the EFTA Parliamentary Committee also has a seat in Iceland's Joint Committee with the EU. According to the rules of procedure of the Committee, its role is to consider all aspects of relations between the EU and Iceland, particularly those related to the accession process, and it may make recommendations to the EU institutions and the Icelandic government. In sum, therefore, Iceland's awareness of and collaboration with the EP appears to have increased considerably since the EEA Agreement first came into effect, which is important in light of the institution's ever-more prominent role in the EU's policy process. Nonetheless, lack of formal access does pose a serious obstacle.

Intra-EFTA collaboration

In its attempts at decision-shaping, intra-EFTA collaboration has been very important for Iceland. The EFTA Secretariat plays a key role in monitoring developments on the EU side, pointing out issues that might be of importance to the EFTA states, ensuring that the Commission grants them access to its committees and coordinating positions between the EFTAns (Magnusdottir 2008; Thorhallsson 2001: 41). This is particularly important for the smaller states, Iceland and Liechtenstein, as Norway is relatively self-sufficient when it comes to information gathering at the EU level. As one Icelandic official noted: 'We use EFTA a lot as we don't have many people. The Norwegians have a lot more resources than we do and so often have more information, and so EFTA has been our lifeline.'[47] Experts in Liechtenstein also consider direct contacts with their counterparts from the other EFTA states and the EFTA Secretariat to be very important for their work (Frommelt and Gstohl 2011: 31).

The EFTA working groups provide a forum for the EFTA states to exchange information and coordinate their positions in different policy areas. Some of them meet more frequently than others. For example, the working group on energy matters meets approximately five or six times per year as it is a very active sector which has a high degree of relevance for the EFTA states. At these meetings they generally discuss matters amongst themselves, before having a joint meeting with Commission representatives where they go over relevant issues and are informed of new developments in the field.[48]

The EEA Agreement also gives the EFTA states the right to make the EU aware of their views on forthcoming legislation through the submission of comments in response to initiatives from the Commission which are relevant to the EEA Agreement (EFTA Secretariat 2006: 14). Comments may be sent individually by each EFTA state, but they are generally thought to be more effective if they are coordinated at the EFTA level. Joint EEA EFTA comments are sometimes sent after a formal legislative proposal has been presented by the Commission to the Council and the Parliament and so they can be a way for the EFTA states to provide input into emerging EU policy, once the opportunity to contribute at the formulation stage has passed. Nevertheless, it is considered best practice to submit comments as early as possible in the decision-making process to increase the likelihood of having an impact.[49] Ideally they should be submitted before the draft proposal is discussed in the responsible committee of the Parliament or before the Council has agreed on a common position (EFTA Secretariat 2009: 25).

More than 100 such EEA EFTA comments have been submitted on Commission initiatives, usually about five to ten per year. The comments are sent to the relevant services in the Commission, EP and Council (EFTA Secretariat 2009: 24). The Commission is obliged to transmit comments to the EU member states, but is not bound by their content. It may be that the Commission is not a very committed advocate, except when its own views coincide with those of EFTA (Thorhallsson and Ellertsdottir 2004: 100). Some comments are of a more political nature than others. In some cases, comments are submitted in order to voice particular support for a proposal. These are usually fairly uncontroversial.

Other comments voice opposition to Commission proposals, such as the comments on a proposal for a regulation on the accelerated phasing-in of the double-hull or equivalent design requirements for single-hull oil tankers (Standing Committee of the EFTA States 2006). These particular comments do not seem to have had much impact on the final outcome of the legislation, which was passed by the Council and the EP. Other EFTA comments appear to have had more success. For example, EFTA submitted comments regarding the New Legal Framework (NLF) for marketing products, consisting of two regulations and one decision, which was adopted by the EU in July 2008. Many of the amendments advocated by EFTA were adopted and most parts of the Commission proposals that were explicitly defended by EFTA were retained. The final NLF was therefore deemed a successful end result for EFTA (Thomassen 2008).

Much like other uploading strategies, just submitting comments to the institutions is usually not enough, as they have to be acted upon. This is especially true given the increased use of public consultations by the Commission, which usually generate a large number of responses from stakeholders throughout Europe. For example, in the case of the REACH Regulation, EEA EFTA comments were supplemented with high-level meetings with Commissioners, MEPs and relevant ministers from the member states. One of the main points for the EFTA states was to ensure that dangerous substances were substituted with less dangerous substances wherever possible. These requirements were included in Articles 55, 60 and 61 of the Regulation (EFTA Secretariat 2009: 26). Despite apparent success in some of these cases, it is important to note that the impact of EFTA comments is quite difficult to measure.[50] As one official explained:

> We commented on protection on children in advertising but we don't know which other states had the same views. In all likelihood other states agreed so it is difficult to measure the exact effect of our comments. Also we usually do something else in parallel like talk to the EP. We do know that our comments are read and probably have a similar weight as other things on the whole.[51]

Exemptions and adaptations

Although it is generally considered a better approach to try to influence EU decision-making early on before acts are adopted,[52] the EFTA states do have an opportunity to negotiate exemptions or adaptations before acts are incorporated into the EEA Agreement. As noted in the previous sections, measuring the decision-shaping impact of the EFTA states during the EU policy-making process is quite difficult, as there are many other states and interest groups involved in the process. Therefore, this last uploading stage is arguably where the impact of the EFTA states is most easily identifiable.

Legislation does not automatically become part of the EEA Agreement once it has been passed by the EU. Rather, acts that are likely to be EEA-relevant are examined by experts within the EFTA states. They are then reviewed and discussed by experts and officials in EFTA working groups and subcommittees,[53] which are often attended by representatives of the Commission. The EFTA Standing Committee, comprising EFTA Ambassadors to the EU and representatives from the Ministries of Foreign Affairs, then shapes a joint position of the EFTA countries. Finally, the EFTA Ambassadors meet with representatives of the European External Action Service (EEAS)[54] in the EEA Joint Committee approximately eight times per year to decide whether EU Acts are relevant to the EEA countries and, if so, how they should be incorporated into the EEA Agreement. Representatives of EU member states may also attend these meetings, but seldom do (Thorhallsson and Ellertsdottir 2004: 99). Figure 2.1 shows a diagram of EEA decision-making procedures through which EU acts are incorporated into the EEA Agreement.

During this process, the EFTA states can try to influence the EU side and request exemptions or adaptations. According to Article 102 of the EEA Agreement, the Annexes to the Agreement must be as similar as possible to the original European legislation, which means that there is considerable pressure on the contracting parties to submit fully to all EEA-relevant legal acts (Bjorgvinsson 2006: 59). Nevertheless, certain exemptions and adaptations have sometimes been made for the EFTA states. For example, Iceland

EEA decision-making

Figure 2.1 EEA decision making

has been granted exemptions in relation to security at local airports, animal health, energy use, safety regulations in fishing vessels and daylight savings (Forsaetisraduneytid 2007: 32). One EFTA official observed that the EU side could often appear quite tough and to have limited patience with the EFTA states wanting special arrangements. However, in practice they had not been unreasonable.[55] Indeed, analysis conducted by Frommelt and Gstohl (2011: 45), based on data from the EFTA Surveillance Authority and the EFTA Secretariat, shows that as of June 2011, 1,119 legal acts in the EEA contained country-specific derogations.[56]

Out of the three EEA EFTA states, Liechtenstein has by far the highest number of derogations (1,056), followed by Iceland (349) and then Norway (55). Frommelt and Gstohl (2011: 45) argue that Liechtenstein's particularly high number of derogations can be traced to its close relations with Switzerland, its small size and a lack of regulatory need, i.e. Liechtenstein has no inland waterways rendering the implementation of the corresponding EU *acquis* superfluous. They also note that derogations are relatively frequent within technical policy fields such as trade of goods and transport, whereas legislation related to the free movement of services or persons rarely contains country-specific derogations.

In general the EFTA states have found it difficult to negotiate adaptations if similar requests have been made by EU member states and refused (Forsaetisraduneytid 2007: 32). Therefore, it is necessary to demonstrate convincingly why conditions in Iceland or the other EFTA states are different from those in the EU member states.[57] This requires a lot of preparatory work and it is not certain that an agreement will be reached (Forsaetisraduneytid 2007: 33). As noted by one official:

> It is not generally something which is agreed at one meeting, but can take years. Often it is necessary to invite representatives from the Commission to Iceland to show them first hand why circumstances there are different than in other countries. For example, after they had been to Iceland they realized that their security requirements would be ridiculous for the tiny rural airports in Iceland. It is generally better to do this only in cases where we really have a problem.[58]

A Commission representative noted that they looked at requests on a case-by-case basis. The general rule was not to grant adaptations but, if the reasoning was founded or the circumstances were special, this would be taken into consideration, for example legislation on railways. As Iceland does not have any railways, something could be agreed. However, if the EFTA side asked for derogations because they thought something was inconvenient or, even worse, to protect their markets, then the answer would be a resounding 'No'.[59]

A study of the Joint EEA Parliamentary Committee found that, as the EU had become larger and more heterogeneous, the EFTA states were finding it more difficult to gain understanding for particular sensitivities, and that the EU had become less flexible and less willing to accommodate special concerns of the EFTA states through adaptations, exceptions and transition periods as it was disinclined to create precedents (Juliusdottir and Wallis 2007: 6). Officials at the EEA Coordination Unit in Liechtenstein did not agree that the EU side had become less understanding over the years. Rather, they felt it depended more on the individual dealing with the matter as well as the reasoning of the EFTA states.[60]

One way of avoiding the incorporation of undesirable legislation into the EEA Agreement is by arguing that it is not EEA-relevant, i.e. that it falls outside the scope of the EEA Agreement. The EEA Agreement has a strong focus on the internal market and covers the majority of the old pillar I legislation, albeit with certain exceptions. The EU has, however, evolved over the years. Legislation has become more comprehensive and often spans diverse areas. As such, the question of EEA-relevance has become more and more prominent, as will be seen in the case studies. In these cases, the EFTA states have often argued that acts are non-relevant while the EU has been in favour of incorporating them into the EEA Agreement.[61] However, the situation can be reversed, and in some instances the EFTA states are eager to adopt EU *acquis*.

In cases where a piece of legislation is controversial and there is no question of EEA-relevance and no adaptations or exemptions can be agreed, the EEA Agreement gives the EFTA states the right to refuse the incorporation of acts into the EEA Agreement at this point in the process. However, an outright refusal to implement EEA-relevant legislation would have grave consequences for the continuation of the EEA Agreement as it could be interpreted as a suspension of part of the Agreement.[62] This undoubtedly gives the EU considerable leverage over the EFTA states when it comes to incorporating legislation into the EEA Agreement,[63] as will be discussed further in the next chapter of this book which focuses on the downloading side of the Europeanization process.

Conclusions

This chapter has sought to shed light on Iceland's uploading potential, looking first at Iceland's administrative capacity and then at its opportunities to influence EU policy at each stage of the decision-making procedure within the EEA framework. Over time government administrations in EU member states generally develop more effective structures and strategies for dealing with EU requirements (S. Berglund *et al.* 2006: 713; Thorhallsson 2004b). This chapter has shown that this is also true of Iceland, although a non-member. Nevertheless, Iceland faces many hurdles when it comes to uploading.

The Icelandic administration has made several changes to enable it to play a more active role in the EU's decision-making process. The Foreign Service has been expanded substantially and Iceland now has embassies in many EU states. The Ministry of Foreign Affairs has a department dealing particularly with EEA matters and government ministries have EU experts and generally employ a counsellor at the Icelandic Mission to the EU. Furthermore, the government has augmented its resources through extensive collaboration with Icelandic interest groups active at the European level. Nonetheless, Iceland's small size and lack of resources has meant that it has not been able to participate as actively in the EU policy process as it would have liked, particularly in the wake of the financial crisis.

The EEA framework also places considerable restrictions on the access of the EFTA states to the EU decision-making process and there is evidence to suggest that the role of the EFTA states has been further diminished by recent developments in the EU. The EEA Agreement was drafted pre-Maastricht, with the institutional and decision-making structure of that era in mind. The Commission is the EFTA states' main point of access as they are allowed to participate in its expert groups and comitology committees. However, over the years the Council and particularly the EP have gained power in the legislative process at the expense of the Commission. Participation in the Commission's policy-formulation process has therefore arguably become less important (Gudmundsen 2008). As one official explained:

> The EEA Agreement was designed during a time when all the power was with the Commission, and the EEA gives a lot of access to the Commission. However, a few years later the Council and the EP started having more of a say and changing the Commission proposals. Everything has changed since the EEA Agreement was negotiated. The

Commission used to be the centre of power and Delors was at the top and controlled everything.[64]

Another official also criticized the situation:

> In my view it is quite remarkable that we can live with a situation like that. Our representatives adopt laws after they have been made and sometimes they don't even know what is coming. It is perplexing that the political elites have been able to accept this situation for such a long time.[65]

It is, however, clear that Iceland and the other EFTA states have developed various strategies to compensate for these changes. Evidence suggests that Iceland engages in coalition-building with EU member states to some extent, particularly the Nordic countries, and has also increasingly begun to focus its attentions on the EP as well as making use of ties with its EFTA partners. In some areas, such as the Maritime Strategy, where the EFTA states have demonstrable expertise, the EU has even actively sought contributions from them. Finally, the EEA framework allows, as a last resort, the possibility of negotiating exemptions or adaptations when decisions are being incorporated into the EEA Agreement. There are quite a few examples of success at this stage of the process and in fact this is where the impact of the EFTA states is the most measurable and concrete as it is not diluted by contributions from other actors.

In sum, Iceland is clearly at a disadvantage in uploading policy preferences in comparison to the EU member states. The Icelandic administration is and will always be considerably smaller than those of most EU member states, which, in addition to the limitations of the EEA Agreement, places some constraints on Iceland's ability to present its case at the EU level (Thorhallsson and Ellertsdottir 2004: 91). But Iceland does not have unrealistic ideas as to its status. As one official noted: 'We'll never be a great power in Europe. But that is ok because 90 per cent of the time the things we are adopting are absolutely fine.'[66] Although uploading success is far from guaranteed, an interesting conclusion of this chapter is that Iceland does not always appear to sit idle while policies that affect its interests are being decided on at the EU level. The case study chapters will go further towards exploring whether it has fulfilled its gloomy destiny of becoming an inactive policy-taker or whether it has developed some identifiable uploading capacity as a result of EEA membership.

Iceland's ability to have an impact on the legislation it adopts is important in its own right but also because of the repercussions it has for the downloading side of Europeanization. In the first place, having an impact on EU policy decreases incongruence between the EU and national levels and thus the material costs of EU policy adoption. Secondly, the perception of having a say in the decision-making process increases the legitimacy of EU legislation, making the adoption of EU rules more palatable to national actors. The next chapter looks at downloading in the institutional context of the EEA Agreement. How does adaptation pressure stemming from the EU manifest itself through the EEA Agreement, and which domestic intervening variables facilitate or hinder downloading?

3 Downloading in the EEA

In this chapter, the focus turns from uploading preferences to the EU level to the process of EU rule adoption, or downloading, in Iceland through the EEA Agreement. As noted in the previous chapter, it is important to bear in mind in this context that in most cases EU legislation corresponds relatively well with pre-existing domestic arrangements in Iceland and does not necessarily require much change to the national legal framework. State actors may also often feel that EU policy poses an effective solution to domestic needs and challenges.[1] Therefore, Iceland willingly adopts the majority of the EU legislation which it is required to take on board through the EEA Agreement.[2] Yet, as in all states adopting EU rules, situations do arise where EU requirements effectively clash with domestic policies or preferences, and this may be a more likely scenario in Iceland for various reasons.

First, as outlined in the previous chapter, Iceland's uploading capacity is somewhat restricted due to its small size and limited access to EU decision-making. This has been further exacerbated by the fact that the Commission's role in EU decision-making has deteriorated, as it is the main point of access of the EFTA states. Iceland has developed strategies and capacities which have counterbalanced these developments to some extent. Nonetheless the chances of success in uploading are arguably relatively slim in comparison to other states. Furthermore, Iceland's isolated location and sparse population could mean that many of the EU's policies, designed with more densely populated states on the mainland in mind, might not be ideally suited to Icelandic conditions. Finally, before Iceland joined the EEA, Icelandic policy in a number of areas had not followed the same trajectory as the EU countries. High levels of policy incongruence were, for example, noticeable in areas such as competition, finance, telecommunications and consumer affairs (Thorhallsson 2002).

Overall, it is therefore relatively likely that EU policy requirements will differ significantly from existing traditions or preferences in Iceland. As explained in Chapter 1, the institutionalist literature assumes that domestic structures and institutions will exert pressure on state actors to resist change imposed by the EU if there is a high degree of mismatch between EU policy requirements and existing structures and practices. Nevertheless, the effective application of divergent EU policies is necessary for change within the political system or 'Europeanization' to occur. The question of why and to what extent Iceland would adapt to costly changes required by EU policies is thus crucial to the Europeanization debate.

It is generally agreed that there are two external factors which may serve to counter the domestic tendency to maintain the status quo: either through mechanisms which put pressure on states to comply by tilting their cost/benefit calculations in favour of change or through a process of socialization whereby states internalize EU norms. These are based on the logics of consequentialism and appropriateness, respectively. For the EU member states, the former mainly involves the Commission issuing infringement proceedings which can result in the Court imposing financial penalties. The latter assumes that a willingness to adopt EU policy can be promoted through high levels of social interaction at the EU level, which makes states want to become 'good' members of the society (Borzel and Risse 2003: 67–68; Checkel 2001: 561–62; Schimmelfennig and Sedelmeier 2005b: 6 and 9).

The existing Europeanization literature has found that these mechanisms, whether they are geared at cost/benefit calculations or persuasion, are often not enough to ensure domestic compliance or downloading in the member states. Rather, EU member states are frequently reluctant to adopt EU policies if there is a high degree of mismatch between the national and EU levels. Domestic intervening variables such as mobilization in society, administrative capacity, a particular culture that facilitates or hinders compliance and the existence of veto points within the political system play a large role in determining whether or not an EU policy is downloaded effectively (Borzel *et al.* 2008; G. Falkner *et al.* 2005; Grabbe 2002; Haverland 2003; Knill 2001; Risse *et al.* 2001).

On the other hand, in studies of candidate countries during the eastern enlargement the carrot of membership and the threat of exclusion from the accession process were almost always found to be enough to ensure (at least formal) adoption of EU policies, no matter how high the adaptation costs (Grabbe 2001: 1015; Jachtenfuchs and Kohler-Koch 2004: 110; Schimmelfennig and Sedelmeier 2004: 672; Vachudova 2005). It can therefore be argued that the type and strength of mechanisms at the EU's disposal to induce domestic change vary depending on the implementing state's relations with the EU.

The aim of this chapter is to gauge how likely Iceland is to download the EU's policies effectively, even when they impose high adaptation costs and require considerable changes to pre-existing policies and administrative and political structures. EU policy initiatives are thus considered to be the independent variables, while domestic responses to these initiatives are seen as the dependent variable. In Iceland's case, the EEA Agreement is the key intervening variable which determines the framework through which EU policy is adopted in Iceland. There may, however, be other intervening variables present within the domestic sphere.

As noted, certain domestic factors such as administrative capacity, culture, civil society and veto points have been identified as prominent factors in hindering or promoting compliance in existing member states. An attempt is made to estimate to what extent these factors are present within the Icelandic political system, i.e. are internal conditions generally favourable to EU rule adoption? The chapter then moves on to examine the mechanisms to ensure downloading that have been built into the EEA Agreement, drawing comparisons between them and the EU's means of promoting rule adoption in member states and candidate countries. In other words, which external pressures are there on Iceland to adopt EU policy and how conducive is this environment to effective downloading? What are the consequences of non-adaptation in the EEA? Also, are there opportunities for socialization which might mean that rule adoption is generally regarded as appropriate? This will provide the essential backdrop for the following chapters in which the processes of both uploading and downloading will be examined in depth in four specific cases.

Domestic intervening variables

In order to explain variation in downloading across the EU member states, previous studies have posited various explanations as to which domestic conditions are likely to promote or hinder rule adoption. These approaches place differing degrees of emphasis on the importance of factors such as material interests, pressures from civil society, structural limitations and social norms in guiding actors' behaviour. Previous empirical studies have found evidence to support each of these explanations (Borzel *et al.* 2008; G. Falkner *et al.* 2005; Grabbe 2002; Haverland 2003; Knill 2001; Mbaye 2001; Risse *et al.* 2001; Tallberg 2002). Although it is difficult to measure precisely each factor's influence, they are all thought to play a role in a state's willingness and ability to adopt EU policy requirements and hence for Europeanization to occur. Based on the assumption that these factors can work in tandem to induce political action, this section looks at the different domestic variables which are thought to affect EU rule adoption and evaluates them against the Icelandic context. No consensus has yet been reached on a key variable or on the relative importance of each of these factors (Sedelmeier 2008a: 3), but they all help paint a general picture of the domestic conditions in which EU policy is adopted in Iceland and how favourable these conditions are to the downloading of EU requirements.

Administrative capacity

Institutionally oriented management approaches have noted that actors have to be capable of abiding by EU law, i.e. administrative departments must have the time, resources and expertise necessary to adopt EU rules (S. Berglund *et al.* 2006: 692 and 713). A certain level of organizational and administrative capacity within states is therefore necessary to facilitate downloading, and adaptation may not occur if the institutional preconditions that enable states to adopt the EU's requirements are absent (Borzel *et al.* 2008: 9–10). The need for inter-ministerial coordination and administrative inefficiency were, for example, found to be strongly associated with delays in transposing EU social directives in Germany, Greece, the Netherlands, Spain and the United Kingdom (Haverland and Romeijn 2007: 757). Furthermore, a study by Featherstone and Papadimitriou (2008) found that, in Greece, the state administration is weak in implementing and upholding EU commitments (Featherstone and Papadimitriou 2008: 9 and 34). In general, countries with the most efficient government administrations such as the UK and the Nordic countries have the best transposition records even though they are generally considered some of the most Eurosceptic countries in the EU (S. Berglund *et al.* 2006: 713). With respect to administrative capacity, it is important to note that, even if a state controls sufficient resources, its administration may still have difficulties in effectively putting them to use. Therefore, it is necessary to distinguish between resource endowment and the actual ability of a state to mobilize and channel its resources (Borzel *et al.* 2008: 9–10 and 56; Haverland and Romeijn 2007: 757).

The distinction between resource endowment and organizational efficiency is important when analyzing Iceland's overall administrative capacity. Iceland has an extremely small administration. However, much like the other Nordic states (S. Berglund *et al.* 2006: 713; Borzel *et al.* 2008: 3), Iceland is also generally thought to have a fairly well-functioning administration. The World Bank's 'Governance Matters' report includes an indicator of government effectiveness which has been used to operationalize administrative capacity (S. Berglund *et al.* 2006: 704). It takes into consideration aspects such as the quality of the bureaucracy, the competence of the civil service, the independence of the civil service from political pressures and the credibility of the government's commitment to policies. According to this report, Iceland's percentile score ranged from 89.6–100 per cent during the period 1996–2008 in terms of government effectiveness (World Bank 2009). In most years, its scores were above 96 per cent, with the exception of the years 1996 and 2008.[3]

These rankings are best viewed in comparison with other states. During the period in question, the OECD regional average ranged from 86.9 to 91.1 per cent, which is considerably lower than Iceland's rankings. Iceland on average ranked higher than most of the large EU member states. For example, the UK ranked between 93.8 and 97.6 per cent, Germany 90.5–94.8 per cent, France 85.8–91.5 per cent and Italy 67.3–82.5 per cent. It ranked similarly to the small EU and EFTA states, Luxembourg (92.4–99.1 per cent) and Liechtenstein (90.5–96.2 per cent), and, in general, its rankings were also comparable to the other Nordic countries: Denmark (95.3–100 per cent), Sweden (95.7–98.6 per cent), and Norway (95.3–98.1 per cent) (World Bank 2009).

In sum, Iceland is among the highest ranking countries in terms of government effectiveness, which would seem to indicate that its administrative capacity would be sufficient to implement EU requirements. Furthermore, Iceland has been improving its capacity to deal with EU legislation over the past 15 years. Officials are now generally more aware of what is in the pipeline, what the aim of the legislation is and how it should be implemented.[4] One official noted that, when adapting the Icelandic legal framework to EU acts, working groups were set up with the relevant experts from within the government administration and various interest groups, which helped to set more comprehensive and higher-quality legislation than was applicable to Icelandic conditions.[5]

In addition to government effectiveness it is also important to bear in mind Iceland's resource endowment when evaluating its overall administrative capacity. Iceland has an extremely small administration which has made it difficult to cope with EU requirements, especially during the first years of EEA membership (Laergreid et al. 2004: 363–65). Although studies have shown that the Icelandic administration is slowly becoming more accustomed to dealing with EEA requirements (Thorhallsson 2004b), it is probably fair to say that Iceland may be less able to deal effectively with the transposition and implementation of EU legislation than many larger states due to its limited amount of resources. As one official noted: 'It often takes time. Sometimes we are late, which has to do with how few we are, but it happens in the end.'[6]

Another official explained that there was a lot of pressure on the ministries and it was often challenging for a small administration to implement EU requirements on time.[7] The REACH Regulation was mentioned as an example, as it was very extensive and required a lot of financial and human resources to put into practice. Delays therefore occurred due to lack of capacity rather than a lack of will.[8] Some of the environmental legislation has also been challenging as it requires a lot of data-gathering and reporting which has been difficult as Iceland lacks the necessary internal structures for this work.[9]

Iceland has also had significant capacity problems in translating EU regulations, which has led to severe delays in adopting them at the domestic level (EFTA Surveillance Authority 2008b).[10] One official explained that the regulations which need to be translated were often extremely long and technical and so translating them could be difficult and time-consuming for an understaffed and overworked translation service.[11] Another official admitted that translation had been a bottleneck but that improvements were underway.[12] All of this seems to indicate that lack of administrative capacity might sometimes cause non-adaptation in Iceland.

Cultures of compliance

Studies have found that in some countries a particular 'culture' can exist which is thought to facilitate downloading. Sociological institutionalism emphasizes norm-guided behaviour. It is argued that one social norm can be respect for formal legal rules. The intensity of this norm may, however, vary between countries. If there is a strong tradition for law-abidance in a member state, political and administrative actors will be more likely to consider it their duty to abide by the law, including the obligation to adopt European directives correctly and on time (S. Berglund *et al.* 2006: 701).

The Nordic countries are generally thought to have a strong tradition for law-abidance, and political and administrative actors in these countries are likely to consider it their duty to abide by the law, including the application of European directives (S. Berglund *et al.* 2006: 701). Falkner *et al.* (2005) have, for example, observed that the Nordic countries belong to the 'world of law observance', where the compliance goal typically supersedes other domestic concerns and breaking EU law is not considered socially acceptable, even if there is a high degree of conflict between the EU and pre-existing national policy (Falkner and Treib 2008: 296–97). Sverdrup (2004) has also noted that, historically, the Nordic states have been more 'consensus-oriented' than other European countries. They constitute a distinct family of legal traditions and principles where the courts have played a relatively limited role. When resolving conflicts the Nordics frequently use 'sounding-out techniques' while avoiding voting and legal confrontations. At the same time relatively high levels of trust in the legal system and support for the rule of law can be found in the Nordic countries (Sverdrup 2004: 27–28).

Although no particular study has yet been conducted on Iceland's compliance culture, Iceland is culturally most closely related to the other Nordic countries. Interview evidence also seems to suggest that Iceland likes to be 'good' and that Icelanders perceive themselves as belonging to a law-abiding culture. The phrase 'more Catholic than the pope' came up more often than once in interviews with officials. As one official put it: 'We have certain obligations under the EEA Agreement and so we try our best to live up to them.'[13] Another noted: 'I think people are generally very scrupulous and try their hardest to do well. Having a high standing on scoreboards is seen as important.'[14] A third official said he often had the feeling that Icelanders were 'more Catholic than the pope' when it came to implementation and usually tried to transpose legislation conscientiously even though they could not see the purpose of it.[15]

One Eurosceptic former Minister of Social Affairs even seemed slightly annoyed by the 'over-eagerness' of the Icelandic administration to implement EU requirements:

> There is a tendency among Icelandic officials to do everything literally and extensively and be more Catholic than the pope. The pressure to implement was mainly from the domestic sphere. I think sometimes we adopt legislation too extensively. People are just so eager to do a good job. If we don't like something we just shouldn't do it. We could get away with it just like the Italians. It is only natural that this legislation should be more like guidelines and people can decide whether or not to adopt it.[16]

Other officials also compared the Nordic culture of compliance with other supposedly less conscientious states:

I believe we have a culture of avoiding conflicts and we are law-abiding. Our national identities are law-oriented ... . One can compare this with other parts of Europe, where it often seems that the culture is rather one of non-compliance.[17]

We Icelanders are pretty conscientious about implementing the rules and are much better than the southern Europeans. I've been to conferences and spoken to colleagues and I know in a lot of places these rules are just not applied.[18]

Thus, based on the findings that the Nordic countries exhibit a particularly strong tendency towards complying fully with EU requirements as well as the quotations from various interviews which suggest that Icelandic officials generally want to do their best, it might be expected that a relatively salient 'culture of compliance' exists in Iceland.

Civil society and veto points

Other authors have argued that downloading can occur in cases of policy mismatch if there is sufficient mobilization in domestic civil society to put pressure on authorities to 'bear the costs' of implementing incongruent policies (Borzel 2000: 141). For example, mobilization by environmental groups, political parties, trade unions and local municipalities has sometimes led authorities to implement incongruent EU policies, thus initiating domestic change (Haverland 2003: 210–12). On the other hand, implementation failure can be expected when there are no domestic advocates that compel public authorities to adopt EU rules (Borzel 2000: 141).

Mobilization of civil society hinges on the existence of influential domestic actors who support the EU legislation and thus will depend on both the particular policy and the overall policy area in question. It is also important to bear in mind that in some cases civil society actors might mobilize in opposition to a particular EU requirement, decreasing the chances that it will be effectively applied (Radaelli 2003: 46), so domestic mobilization can both work to hinder or promote domestic adaptation.

Haverland (2003) has found that interest group opposition is particularly effective in countries that provide institutional veto points such as a second chamber of parliament or strong regional government. For example, in implementing the Packaging Directive (94/62/EC), the German government was faced with strong resistance by the German Bundesrat, which represents the German states (Lander), and was controlled by opposition parties with ties to interest groups opposing the Directive. In the end Germany implemented the Directive late and inappropriately (Haverland 2003: 212–14).

Iceland does not have strong regional government bodies or a second legislative chamber and thus arguably has few veto points. It does, however, have active interest groups both on the management and labour sides of industry as well as various other groups, such as the Association of Local Authorities, the Farmers Association and the Federation of Icelandic Fishing Vessel Owners. Many of these groups follow the EU legislative procedure closely, as EU policies in various areas impact on them. As noted in the previous chapter, many of them have been active at the European level and participated in European umbrella organizations. Due to the smallness of Icelandic society, these groups have close and often personal ties with the government. Apart from associations related to agriculture and fisheries, most organizations in Iceland are generally fairly positive towards European integration. However, according to Ministry of Foreign Affairs officials, it is likely that interest groups in Iceland, as in other states, mobilize in favour of or opposition to EU requirements depending on the issue at stake.[19]

An official at the Confederation of Employers noted that they often attempted to ensure that EU regulations were not too oppressive when implemented at the national level. In other cases, pressure was put on the government to adopt EU legislation correctly and on time, for example with respect to the REACH Regulation. It was important for Icelandic companies that these rules be adopted on time so that they would have the same opportunities regarding registration of chemicals as companies in Europe. Therefore, according to the official, the Confederation successfully pressured the government to adopt the regulation as quickly as possible.[20]

Lack of interest groups in a particular area can also mean that legislation does not receive much attention and may therefore perhaps not be implemented properly. For example, Rognvaldardottir (2006) explored how each of the 22 directives related to the New Approach for the marketing of products was implemented in Iceland.[21] Her findings were that compliance was lacking with respect to nearly all of the directives (Rognvaldardottir 2006: 3). One of the most likely explanations proposed in the study is that production in the fields that fall under the New Approach is limited in Iceland, and participation of Icelandic companies in European standardization is very nearly non-existent in the areas which fall under the New Approach. Therefore, unlike in other states, there was little pressure from interested parties on domestic authorities to correctly implement these directives (Rognvaldardottir 2006: 91–92). This corresponds to findings that domestic mobilization in society is an important factor in determining whether EU rules are adopted at the national level.

In sum, it might be said that domestic factors in Iceland are relatively conducive to adaptation to EU policy requirements. Iceland appears to have a fairly strong 'culture of compliance' and there are many interest groups which are likely to exert pressure on the government to adopt EU legislation. There is also a lack of veto points which would make it more difficult for opponents to stall the implementation process. Nonetheless, Iceland's lack of access to decision-making institutions is likely to increase adaptation costs which might in turn make domestic actors less inclined to comply fully with EU policy. Furthermore, although Iceland has a reasonably efficient administration, its small size might potentially pose problems in dealing with EU requests.

Therefore, some outside pressure will most likely be necessary in order to counter the possible negative impact of domestic factors and induce compliance in Iceland. The next section gives an overview of the types of compliance mechanisms in the EEA Agreement, with the aim of evaluating their effectiveness.

External pressures

As noted, EU policy requirements are the independent variable in this study and they are filtered through the EEA framework. This section traces the process by which EU legislation becomes part of Iceland's legal structure through the EEA Agreement, paying particular attention to the tools for ensuring domestic adaptation at each stage of the process. First, a few general words about the potential impact of socialization as well as the asymmetry of power between Iceland and the EU.

Opportunities for socialization

With respect to the potential impact of socialization, Iceland is allowed to participate in the preparatory work of the Commission when new legislation is being drawn up, as discussed in the previous chapter. Furthermore, Iceland works in close collaboration with EU officials through the EFTA structure in working groups, subcommittees and the EEA Joint Committee. This is greater access than candidate countries enjoy. Iceland also has closer ties with European states (especially the other Nordic states) than with any other states and has been generally keen to strengthen cooperation with the EU and be as extensively involved in European integration as possible, short of membership (Eiriksson 2004: 17 and 54–55). It is therefore likely that Iceland experiences some degree of socialization, which is important as studies have found that a willingness to adopt EU policy can be promoted through high levels of social interaction at the EU level (Borzel and Risse 2003: 67–68; Checkel 2001: 561–62; Schimmelfennig and Sedelmeier 2005b: 6 and 9). Through this interaction with the EU institutions, Iceland could potentially acquire new interests through social learning which entails argumentation, deliberation and persuasion and may, as a result, act in ways that cannot easily be explained by material incentives (Eilstrup-Sangiovanni 2006: 396).

Despite some degree of socialization, unlike the EU member states, Iceland does not participate directly in EU decision-making, which might pose a similar legitimacy problem as encountered in the candidate countries, giving EU legislation a hint of foreign imposition. This can, for example, be illustrated by a comment made by Halldor Asgrimsson, former Icelandic Minister of Foreign Affairs: 'It is difficult for us to take over results in sensitive sectors when we have been excluded from the preparations' (EFTA Secretariat 2002: 7–8). In addition to the potential lack of legitimacy of EU legislation, Iceland is far less exposed to the EU's rules, norms, practices and structures than the member states and is thus perhaps less likely to be socially persuaded to comply with EU policy. The logic of appropriateness might therefore be less relevant in the Icelandic case. The motivations for rule adoption will be explored in greater detail in the case studies. Meanwhile, this chapter will focus mainly on the more the rationalist cost-benefit based incentives for compliance through the framework of the EEA Agreement.

Asymmetry of power

It is important to bear in mind that, although Iceland applied for EU membership after having been hit particularly hard by the financial crisis, it has not traditionally aspired to become a member of the Union, and opinion on the topic remains divided. Therefore, the EU has not been able to use the carrot of membership to induce compliance in Iceland, which has in the past proved so effective in the candidate countries. Nevertheless, the EEA Agreement grants access to the internal market upon which Iceland is highly dependent. The vast majority of Iceland's trade is with the EU and Iceland is therefore reliant on the EU economically. In 2005, 75 per cent of all exports from Iceland went to the EU while 62 per cent of all imports came from member states of the Union (National Statistical Institute of Iceland as cited in Forsaetisraduneytid 2007: 14). It can be said that losing access to the EU's internal market is generally not considered a viable option by the Icelandic government or by Icelandic businesses and interest groups. As the material interests invested in participation in the internal market increase, so to do the costs of exclusion.

The EU on the other hand probably does not attach equal significance to the EEA Agreement. When the Agreement was negotiated in the early 1990s between the then seven EFTA states[22] and the then 12 member states of the European Community, EFTA included the EC's largest trading partners (Einarsson 2003: 89; Wallis 2002: 7). Today, however, only the three smallest EFTA states remain party to the EEA Agreement, while, with the eastern enlargements of 2004 and 2007, the EU has grown to include 27 states.[23] Therefore, when considering the extent of the EU's leverage over Iceland, it is necessary to note that the power relationship between the EFTA states and the EU is extremely asymmetrical.

Both EU and EFTA sides are aware of this asymmetry. When asked whether the EU was losing interest in the EEA, one Icelandic official replied that, considering recent enlargement of the EU and the reduction in size of EFTA, it was normal that the EEA was not as high a priority for the EU as it once was.[24] Another noted: 'Although the EEA is supposed to be an equal two-pillar system between the EFTA side and the EU side, it is clear which side is stronger.'[25] When asked the same question, a Commission official simply shrugged his shoulders and replied: 'When the EEA was negotiated it was 12 EU states versus seven EFTA states. Now it is 27 versus three.'[26]

This is not to say that the EU has no advantage in maintaining the EEA Agreement. The Agreement has, in many ways, been a convenient way for it to structure its relations with its nearest neighbours and has even been suggested as a framework for other neighbouring states. However, it cannot be denied that the EEA currently encompasses only a small and ever-decreasing portion of the EU's overall engagements with third countries. The dependence of Iceland on the EEA alongside the EU's relative indifference potentially gives the EU considerable leverage over Iceland through the threat of exclusion from the internal market. Whether or not the EU is able to channel this leverage effectively will depend on the institutional set-up of the EEA and the credibility of the threat. This relates to the second research question posed in this study, which asks whether the tools provided for in the EEA Agreement are generally sufficient to ensure compliance with EU requirements.

The threat of suspension

The EFTA states are required to adjust their legal systems to EEA-relevant legislation. However, the EEA Agreement has various clauses to allow them to participate in EU cooperation without giving up their sovereignty, at least not in the *de jure* sense. For example, as noted in the previous chapter, legislation does not automatically become part of the EEA Agreement once it has been passed by the EU. Rather, an agreement has to be reached between the EEAS (formerly the Commission) and the EFTA states in the EEA Joint Committee as to its incorporation into the EEA Agreement. All decisions of the Joint Committee are taken by unanimity between the EFTA and EU sides (EFTA Secretariat 2008b) and, if approved, the acts are listed in the relevant Annexes to the EEA Agreement.

Although decisions in the Joint Committee require the approval of both the EFTA and EU sides, it will be argued here that in practice the EFTAns have little alternative but to abide by the EU's wishes during this stage of the adoption process. As discussed in the previous chapter, this provides one last forum for the EFTA states to impact the content of the legislation that they are required to adopt, and certain exemptions and adaptations have sometimes been made for the EFTA states (Bjorgvinsson 2006: 61–62), although it is up to the EU whether or not to grant these exemptions.

If the EFTA states find a piece of EEA-relevant legislation unacceptable, they have the right to refuse its incorporation into the Agreement. However, Article 102 of the EEA Agreement states that:

> If ... the EEA Joint Committee has not taken a decision on an amendment of an Annex to this Agreement, the affected part thereof, as determined in accordance with paragraph 2, is regarded as provisionally suspended, subject to a decision to the contrary by the EEA Joint Committee.

Although Article 102 only calls for a suspension of the relevant parts of the Agreement, internal market issues are all interlinked and so this would be difficult in practice. Accordingly, there is fear that the entire Agreement could be called into question by the EU if Article 102 were put into force (Forsaetisraduneytid 2007: 34; Thorhallsson and Ellertsdottir 2004: 99). This clause thus undoubtedly gives the EU considerable leverage over the EFTA states as the threat of suspension of the Agreement, in part or in whole, makes it difficult, if not impossible, for the EFTA states to say 'No'. As one official put it:

> Our democratic deficit is much stronger in the EEA than in the EU even though we have formally retained our sovereignty. In 15 years we have never used the possibility of saying 'No' and you wonder whether it is a reality or a fiction, i.e. it has no real value.[27]

Another noted: 'It's not like we really have the right to say "No". It's not very balanced. They do what they want and we have to accept it.'[28]

The EFTA states must speak with one voice when deciding on the incorporation of acts into the Agreement. This was a strong precondition on the EU side during negotiations of the Agreement.[29] However, the EFTA states also feel that it strengthens their position vis-à-vis the EU and so is in their interest.[30] Normally, forming a common position is not problematic, but certain issues are more politically sensitive in some states than others, which can lead to difficulty in arriving at an agreement.[31]

Any decision to suspend the Agreement will impact all of the EFTA-3 and so if they do not all agree, the reluctant state/s is/are likely to be under some degree of pressure from their EFTA partners to give way. The EFTA states are generally quite considerate of each other's opinions.[32] Nonetheless, if they have interests in a particular area they might become impatient if another state is causing delays. For example, an Icelandic official remembers having felt quite strong pressure from Norway regarding the adoption of the Directive on the Energy Efficiency of Buildings.[33]

Despite considerable pressure to incorporate legislation into the Agreement, there have been many cases where acts have been subject to significant delays and in some instances they have not been incorporated until several years after they were adopted by the EU. Examples include the Emissions Trading Scheme (2003/87/EC), the Water Directive (2000/60/EC) and the GMO Directive (2001/18/EC) (Juliusdottir and Wallis 2007: 11). Liechtenstein's opposition towards the Second Money Laundering Directive (2001/97/EC) also generated substantial problems (Frommelt and Gstohl 2011: 33). At the time of writing, the Third Postal Services Directive (2008/06/EC) was among the largest stumbling blocks due to opposition from Norway. Indeed, the Norwegian government indicated that it would veto its incorporation into the EEA Agreement, which would mark a historic development in the EEA. EU officials have responded by acknowledging Norway's position and proposing further dialogue (N. Berglund 2011). However, despite informal negotiations and clarifications regarding the content of the Directive, the Norwegian Minister of Foreign Affairs reaffirmed Norway's opposition at a meeting of the EEA Council on 15 November 2011 (*Nationen Politikk* 2011). Thus, at the time of writing, it was still unclear whether a veto would be successfully wielded by an EFTA state and what the consequences of such an action would be.

Perhaps the EU's relative tolerance regarding delays can in part be explained by the fact that the EU also has an interest in maintaining the good functioning of the EEA Agreement. Indeed, Article 102 also states that 'the EEA Joint Committee shall, in particular, make every effort to find a mutually acceptable solution where a serious problem arises in any area' and 'shall examine all further possibilities to maintain the good functioning of this Agreement'. Nonetheless, acts have so far always been incorporated into the Agreement in the end if the EU has wanted them there.

The EFTA states have not, however, transferred binding legislative powers to the EEA Joint Committee. Therefore, although legislation has been incorporated into the EEA Agreement, one or more EFTA state may have socalled constitutional requirements according to which their respective national parliaments must ratify the act before it can take effect in the EEA. Once the Joint Committee has incorporated such an act into the EEA Agreement, the EFTA states must adopt it at the national level and notify the other parties to the Agreement once constitutional requirements have been fulfilled (EFTA Secretariat 2007; Forsaetisraduneytid 2007: 30–31). The EFTA states have different criteria to decide whether or not constitutional requirements apply and so it is not always the same acts which trigger this procedure in all states. It is estimated that approximately 10–15 per cent of acts incorporated into the EEA Agreement generate constitutional requirements in at least one of the EFTA states (Nordgaard 2011).

The national parliaments of the EFTA states have never rejected the adoption of an act which has been incorporated into the EEA Agreement. This is not surprising as a notification refusing to transpose EEA-relevant legislation at the national level would have the same effect as refusing to incorporate it into the EEA Agreement, i.e. the suspension of part of the Agreement.[34] Therefore, much like refusing to adopt an act into the EEA Agreement, explicit refusal to transpose legislation into national law is generally not a viable option for the EFTA states and again seems to highlight the strength of the EU's leverage during the downloading process. However, in theory the EFTA states have six months to fulfil their constitutional requirements and it often happens that this procedure takes longer. In fact, according to Frommelt and Gstohl (2011: 26), the average time between the adoption of a Joint Committee Decision (JCD) with constitutional requirements and its entry into force was almost one year (331 days) during the period 1995–2010.

In sum, the EEA Agreement, which gives Iceland its much-needed access to the internal market, can relatively easily be revised through the suspension clause in EFTA Article 102. Because of this threat of exclusion, Iceland, as well as the other EFTA parties to the EEA Agreement, are under strong pressure to agree to incorporate acts into the EEA Agreement and transpose legislation at the national level. They are unlikely to refuse such action, no matter how inconvenient it is for them; indeed they never have, although the EEA Agreement has been in force for almost two decades. They are, therefore, in some ways in a similar position to candidate countries that are also faced with the threat of exclusion from the accession process if they should refuse to adopt a piece of EU legislation. However, the structure of the EEA Agreement also seems to give the EFTA states an opportunity to delay both the incorporation of acts into the EEA Agreement and the fulfilment of constitutional requirements. The EEAS has recently voiced concern over this trend. As a result, measures have been discussed to improve the processing of *acquis* in the EEA Agreement (EFTA Secretariat 2011).

It is not enough to incorporate acts into the Agreement and officially transpose them into national legislation; EU policies must also be effectively put into practice. Yet, importantly, the threat of exclusion seems only to be applicable if an EFTA state overtly refuses to adopt a piece of legislation. Adoption may be delayed or legislation might be incorrectly transposed or poorly implemented without the threat of exclusion applying to the same degree. There are some mechanisms in place for ensuring correct transposition as well as full implementation but, arguably, as will be seen in the following sections, the EU's leverage weakens at this stage of the adaptation process.

EFTA infringement procedures

The Commission is in charge of monitoring compliance with the *acquis* in the EU member states. However, as the EFTA states do not have representatives in the Commission, it was not thought fitting during negotiations of the EEA Agreement that the Commission should be in charge of monitoring compliance within the EFTA states (Einarsson 2003: 93). Therefore, a two-pillar system was set up whereby the EU member states are supervised by the European Commission and the Court of Justice of the European Union (CJEU)[35] and the EFTA states by the EFTA Surveillance Authority (ESA) and the EFTA Court. The EFTA institutions are made up mainly of officials from the EFTA states, so in a way the EU loses control over the monitoring process. This is very different from the EU's relations with other third countries such as candidate countries, where the Commission monitors their progress at all stages of the process. This system may be a remnant of the fact that, when the EEA Agreement was negotiated, the EFTA side was a much larger block, involving the EU's closest partners. Indeed, it can be considered unlikely that such a system would have been negotiated between the current

70 *Downloading in the EEA*

EU and EFTA sides (Mellvang-Berg 2011). Figure 3.1 shows the two-pillar structure of the EEA.

According to the two-pillar system, ESA has powers corresponding to those of the Commission to ensure that European legal acts are properly transposed and implemented. If ESA believes that an EFTA state has failed to comply with EEA legislation, it can issue infringement proceedings which are in most respects similar to those issued by the Commission in cases of member state non-compliance, i.e. beginning with a letter of formal notice, followed by a reasoned opinion and finally a case before the EFTA Court. Before infringement proceedings are initiated, ESA generally attempts to sort out the situation in informal discussions with representatives of the respective state; in practice the majority of problems identified by ESA are solved as a result of these exchanges and most cases are therefore resolved before they are brought before the EFTA Court (EFTA Surveillance Authority 2008a).

The EFTA Court consists of three judges, one from each of the EFTA states, and is competent to deal with infringement actions brought by ESA against any of the EFTA states (EFTA Secretariat 2008d).[36] It does not, however, have the same authority as the CJEU as it does not have the power to issue binding decisions, only recommendations and advisory opinions (Bjorgvinsson 2006: 162). The Court can, therefore, neither formally annul a national provision which is incompatible with EEA law, nor force a national administration to respond to a request of an individual, nor order the state to pay damages to an individual adversely affected by an infringement by the

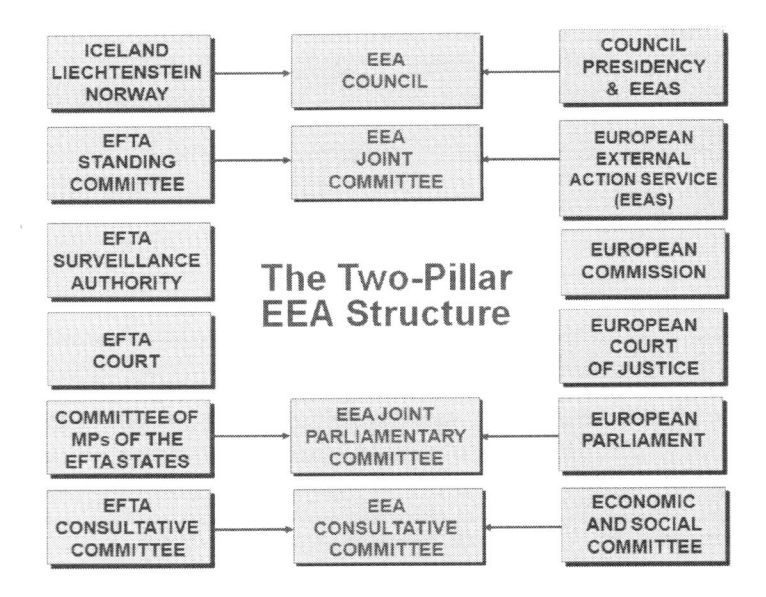

Figure 3.1 Two-pillar structure of the EEA

state of EEA law (EFTA Surveillance Authority 2008a). Nevertheless, according to Article 33 of the Agreement between the EFTA states on the establishment of a Surveillance Authority and a Court of Justice, it is the duty of an EFTA state to 'take whatever measures are necessary to comply with the judgment, and in particular to resolve the dispute, which gave rise to the procedure'.

In addition to infringement procedures initiated by ESA, the EFTA Court also has the jurisdiction to give advisory opinions on the interpretation of the EEA Agreement, i.e. court's or tribunals in the EFTA states may request such an opinion from the EFTA Court. This is much like the preliminary reference procedure in the EU. However, unlike in the EU, there is no obligation on courts in the EFTA states to request advisory opinions from the EFTA Court, and the Norwegian Supreme Court has not done so since 2002, although this practice is used more frequently by courts in Iceland and Liechtenstein (Baudenbacher 2012). Such a two-pillar system undoubtedly begs the following question: How effective is surveillance and enforcement in a system whereby non-member states monitor and sanction themselves? This question will be explored in the following section.

How effective are these mechanisms?

At first glance it might seem that the fact that the EFTA states are in charge of monitoring and sanctioning themselves and that the relevant institutions do not have binding authority over the EFTA states would significantly limit the external pressure to comply with EU requirements. However, as will be argued here, it appears in practice that the EEA monitoring and sanctioning mechanisms are not weaker than those used within the EU, although this is difficult to measure.

ESA maintains an Internal Market Scoreboard which is published in parallel to the Commission's report on transposition rates and infringement proceedings. In terms of transposition rates over the past ten years, the EFTA average has generally been comparable to the EU average. However, these figures only take into account directives that have been incorporated into the EEA Agreement and so they do not take into consideration delays in incorporating acts into the Agreement. The Scoreboard also shows the number of infringement proceedings against the EFTA states for non-conformity or incorrect application of legislation, which is usually quite low in comparison with the EU member states (EFTA Surveillance Authority 2008b). This could suggest either that the EFTA states are more correctly transposing and more fully implementing EU legislation than the EU member states or that ESA is for some reason hesitant to issue infringement proceedings. It could also mean that infringements are less likely to be discovered in the EEA EFTA states.

Because the quality of transposition and implementation are extremely difficult to monitor, the Commission largely relies on aggrieved parties such as individuals, firms or interest groups to bring complaints against member states that do not properly apply and enforce EU law (Sedelmeier 2008a: 14).

Citizens of the EFTA states may submit complaints to ESA if they believe that their rights under the EEA Agreement are being infringed (EFTA Surveillance Authority 2005). Nevertheless, a much higher share of cases is opened as a result of complaints by the Commission than ESA, and among the EFTA states the vast majority of complaints come from Norway (usually around 90 per cent) (EFTA Surveillance Authority 2008b). There might be no reason to raise complaints if application and enforcement are correct. However, another explanation could be that non-state actors are not as aware of their rights (Sedelmeier 2008a: 15–21) or choose not to complain to European-level surveillance institutions. Then again, Iceland and Liechtenstein are very small countries, so personal ties are strong and it is therefore perhaps easier to settle disputes internally. It is, however, interesting to note that ESA has received an increasing number of complaints from Iceland in the wake of the financial crisis (Mellvang-Berg 2011).

Interview evidence suggests that the fact that the institutions are run by the EFTAns themselves has not made them any more lax. Within the member states, ESA is often accused of being 'more Catholic than the pope' (Sejersted and Sverdrup 2012). Indeed, even the name 'EFTA Surveillance Authority' has quite an imposing ring to it. As one official noted:

> ESA goes over things really well and there are Icelandic lawyers that work there too. They make sure everything is adopted correctly and if we don't respond to any warnings there is a process that is started. Letter of formal notice, etc. So we have to do a good job.[37]

An official at the Ministry of Social Affairs said that they clearly felt the presence of ESA in their work:

> They make sure we adopt the legislation. We have to send it to them and they go over it and if they don't like it they contact us and tell us to make improvements. There are lots of examples of this. For instance, regarding the Working Time Directive, we had to change our legislation.[38]

An official at the Environmental Agency explained that they met with ESA twice a year where they went over everything that had been adopted in that period, so she felt that the surveillance was quite strict.[39] The Counsellor for Environment at the Icelandic Mission also said he often met up with his ESA counterparts to go over the status of various acts and that they regularly visited Iceland, noting that once legislation was in the Agreement there was no point in struggling against ESA.[40] An expert at the Ministry of Business said that once legislation had been incorporated into the EEA Agreement Iceland had to apply it just like the member states of the EU: 'I can't imagine ESA is any more lenient than the Commission in its monitoring. There is clearly pressure on us for implementation.'[41] Officials in Liechtenstein agreed with their Icelandic counterparts: 'ESA is surveying us. We just don't have a choice. We have to apply because sooner or later ESA will know about it and open a case.'[42]

Despite fairly strict monitoring, it is clear that instances of non-compliance do come up, particularly in terms of delays. For example, the transposition of a directive on ceilings on atmospheric pollutants was problematic in Norway, but this was not noticed until a few years later and it was only caught because the Norwegian industries notified surveillance bodies.[43] In Iceland, a framework directive on risk assessment was severely delayed.[44] As one official explained: 'In general we have done well, although of course there are certain gaps in the implementation where we could do better. Waste matters are our Achilles heel.'[45] Another described the overall situation as follows:

> I mean there are often delays mainly due to lack of capacity, but I think once something is transposed it is implemented properly in the end. But it takes time. Yes there is pressure. ESA makes sure we are transposing things correctly.[46]

There are also signs that ESA is not unreasonable if there is just cause for non-implementation. For example, an official at the Ministry of Industry noted that ESA had shown considerable understanding in relation to the implementation of the Gas Directive, as Iceland does not use gas as a power or heating source. The Directive was incorporated into the EEA Agreement and so Iceland should have transposed it like any other state, but did not do so. ESA was aware of the situation but turned a blind eye. The same official also mentioned a Directive on oil searching. It was adopted into the EEA Agreement but not transposed in Iceland as they did not foresee that any oil exploration would be taking place in Iceland. Ten years later, it was decided that this might be a possibility, so they transposed the Directive and notified ESA. Therefore, in general the strategy of the government has been to convince ESA that some things would be a waste of the Parliament's time and hope that ESA will understand, which is often the case as long as there is a reasonable explanation.[47]

ESA also appears to be relatively hesitant to bring cases to the EFTA Court. According to an EFTA Court official, the reason for the low caseload at the EFTA Court can partly be explained by the fact that ESA officials are afraid of offending their national administrations/governments by bringing them to Court. ESA officials are hired on a temporary basis and are often hoping to go back to work for their national administrations once their terms at ESA have expired and therefore they might go easy on the EFTA states in terms of litigation.[48] Another reason for the low caseload could be that matters are generally resolved before they reach this stage. In recent years there has, however, been an increase in the caseload of the EFTA Court, quite a few of which deal with the legal impact of the financial crisis in Iceland (Baudenbacher 2012).

When matters have been brought before the Court, the fact that it does not have the same power as the CJEU to issue binding decisions or fines does not seem to have had much impact on its behaviour or on the compliance of the EFTA states with its decisions. If an EFTA state does not comply with the Court's judgement, ESA may again bring the matter before the EFTA Court (EFTA Surveillance Authority 2008a). Failing to comply with the Court's decisions is, however, extremely rare. Indeed, according to the ESA information officer, this has only happened on one occasion where infringement proceedings were re-issued against Norway for non-compliance with a judgment of the EFTA Court on survivor's pension (Mellvang-Berg 2011).

The EFTA Court has not been hesitant to issue controversial decisions that have had far-reaching effects. The President of the EFTA Court notes that some of these rulings have set precedents for the CJEU, although it is not bound to take EFTA rulings into account (Baudenbacher 2012). It can also be argued that some of the EFTA Court's advisory opinions[49] have made strides towards establishing a form of 'quasi-direct effect' of EEA legislation as it has ruled that the EFTA states should be liable to provide compensation for loss and damage caused to individuals or economic operators by incorrect legal transposition of directives incorporated into the EEA Agreement (EFTA Court 1998).[50] Although not formally bound by the EFTA Court's decision, courts in the EFTA states have confirmed the Court's opinion that EFTA governments are liable for any damages due to incorrect transposition of EEA legislation.

There are various reasons why monitoring and surveillance within the EEA may indeed function relatively well despite apparent weaknesses. First, having institutions controlled by the EFTA states themselves may serve to increase the legitimacy of the Agreement and may thus in fact serve as a strength rather than a weakness when it comes to compliance. As one official argued:

> The fact that we have our own separate institutions that monitor and decide issues related to the implementation gives us the impression or feeling that we are actually in charge of these matters ourselves. This is, in my view, an important reason why the Agreement is politically acceptable in the EFTA states. Even though we are not there when decisions are taken at least we have our own people and institutions to look after it. I believe this explains why we have been willing for many years to accept everything that is coming in. If you look at other neighbouring states, they do not have their own institutions and it makes it more difficult for these states to go all the way.[51]

Second, there are three EFTA states and so it is not the case that each state monitors itself, as the monitoring institutions have representatives from each of the EFTA states and are meant to be independent from any government. Furthermore, although the ESA College and the EFTA Court are composed of one representative from each EFTA state, there are actually many non-EFTA nationals working for ESA. There might, however, be a problem if Iceland or any of the other EFTA states joined the EU and there were only two EFTA states left. As noted by one official:

> It is important to note that we are not monitoring ourselves. There are independent institutions with appropriate decision-making structures. You have a Court with three judges which means that you never have a situation where there is a deadlock. That partly explains why there are discussions about what would happen if Iceland were to join the EU. If there were only two EFTA states, the Agreement would not work for practical reasons without any institutional adjustments. This is basic but important and should not be underestimated.[52]

Third, there is close cooperation between the European Commission and ESA. They exchange information and consult each other on general surveillance policy questions and on individual cases (EFTA Secretariat 2008c; EFTA Surveillance Authority 2008c). In some ways it is likely that ESA may act like the little brother in this cooperation and want to be seen by the Commission as doing a good job. For example, ESA often asks for the Commission's views on matters of interpretation, and Commission officials often accompany their ESA counterparts on monitoring trips to the EFTA member states. In the area of transport they have been to each of the EFTA states to ensure how various security rules have been implemented. So the Commission still maintains a link to the monitoring of the EFTA states.[53] As noted by an ESA official: 'If the Commission and ESA are dancing partners, it is no question who is in the lead.'[54]

Finally, although the EFTA states are officially in charge of collectively monitoring themselves, there may still be a lingering fear of exclusion from the internal market. Particularly given the close cooperation between ESA and the Commission, there may be concern among the EFTA states regarding the potential consequences if the EU got the impression that the EEA Agreement was not functioning well. This might spark a debate over the viability of the EEA Agreement. As an ESA official noted:

> The EFTA Court may not have the same official capacity to take binding decisions as the ECJ, but the political pressure on the EFTA states to comply is very great as overt non-compliance with an EFTA Court decision would quickly be discovered by the EU and could put the EEA Agreement at risk. It would potentially be relatively easy to deliberately undermine the EEA Agreement, but the whole thing is based on trust.[55]

An extensive Norwegian review of the functioning of the EEA Agreement recognized the importance of both ESA and the EFTA Court for the functioning of the EEA Agreement. The authors of the report noted that this was a difficult balancing act as both institutions had to constantly keep in mind what they thought the Commission or the European Court would do (Sejersted and Sverdrup 2012). The report concluded that both institutions had generally been successful in treading this line. In relation to questions as to whether the EFTA institutions were 'more Catholic than the pope' or stricter than their EU counterparts, the report found that this was not the case with respect to ESA. However, the EFTA Court had perhaps in some cases been more stringent than the EU Court of Justice (Dypvik 2012). If this is indeed the case, the authors of the report argue that the Court must be careful, as overstepping its role could undermine the functioning of the EEA Agreement (Sejersted and Sverdrup 2012).

Conclusions

Having examined both domestic intervening variables and the external pressures that Iceland faces while downloading EU policies, it seems that conditions are in many ways favourable to EU rule adoption. In terms of the domestic sphere, Iceland appears to have a fairly efficient administration that should generally be capable of implementing EU policies. It also seems to have a relatively strong 'culture of compliance' or willingness to abide by rules. Finally, there is potential for mobilization in society in favour of EU requirements and a lack of veto points which would serve to facilitate opposition. The main domestic obstacle Iceland might face is lack of resources and capacity to put EU requirements into practice due primarily to the small size of its administration.

The EEA framework also appears to be relatively conducive to domestic adaptation. The EEA is considered to have far-reaching economic benefits and so the threat of exclusion from the internal market through the discontinuation of the EEA Agreement potentially gives the EU considerable leverage over Iceland. It does seem that Iceland feels pressure to adopt legislation into the EEA Agreement and transpose it at the national level, as it has never refused to do so. Nonetheless, there is considerable scope for delays during this process. Furthermore, the threat of exclusion has its limitations, as it only applies to the incorporation of EU legislation into the EEA Agreement and approval by national parliaments, but not to ground-level application, where EFTA infringement procedures apply.

The mechanisms for monitoring compliance in the EFTA states and the procedures to deal with non-compliance are similar to those used by the EU in its member states. The EFTA Surveillance Authority has more or less equivalent powers to the Commission to issue infringement proceedings. However, the EFTA Court has less formal power than the CJEU, as it cannot issue binding decisions or fines. Furthermore, the fact that the EFTA states formally monitor themselves means that the infringement mechanisms appear to be rather weak. Nonetheless, they seem to function relatively well for various reasons. Namely, having their own institutions may serve to increase the legitimacy of the Agreement. Each EFTA state is also subject to control, not only by its own officials but also by officials from its EFTA partners. The EFTA institutions remain in close contact with the EU throughout the monitoring process and the EFTA states are in all likelihood still aware of the asymmetry of power and the potential threat of exclusion if the EU should perceive that the EEA Agreement was not functioning well.

EU member states have formally submitted to a supranational treaty by which they pool their sovereignty and are required to adopt EU legislation. This is not the case for the EFTA states. EU acts do not have direct effect in the EFTA states and the EEA Agreement contains various clauses to formally protect them against loss of sovereignty. Nonetheless, there is arguably not much difference between EU membership and the EEA in practice in those areas covered by the EEA Agreement. In fact, due to the asymmetry of power between the EU and EFTA, the EFTA states may even to some extent feel stronger pressure to adapt to EU requirements.

Along with Chapter 2, this chapter provides a point of departure for the follow-up case studies, which look in detail at the processes of uploading and downloading in Iceland, focusing on legislation in the areas of energy, the free movement of persons, the environment and food law. These subsequent chapters will attempt to gauge the motives and attitudes behind the actions of the Icelandic government, as well as identifying the structural and behavioural changes that have occurred within the Icelandic political system as a result of the Europeanization process.

4 Market competition in the electricity sector

The liberalization of the electricity sector is a key example of policy mismatch between the EU and Iceland. At the end of the twentieth century marketization and liberalization were common themes in sectors that had traditionally been under public control such as banking, telecoms and energy.[1] At that time, creating an internal market in electricity came to be regarded by the EU as an important component of the internal market. The so-called 'First Electricity Directive' (96/92/EC) was adopted in 1996 with a view to establishing an internal market in the electricity sector. In light of the experience gained from this Directive, further steps were considered necessary by the Lisbon Council of 2000, and in 2003 the 'Second Electricity Directive' (2003/54/EC) was adopted, repealing the First Directive. In 2009 a 'Third Electricity Directive' (2009/72/EC) was approved, further revising EU policy in this area.

The EEA-relevance of these directives is clear as energy is considered a product to be traded on the internal market.[2] However, the incorporation of the First Electricity Directive into the EEA Agreement met with considerable resistance on Iceland's part. The key aims of the Directive were to liberalize trade in electricity between member states and promote competition in production and sales of electricity. As the Icelandic electricity market is both very small and completely isolated from the rest of Europe, there was concern that the proposed measures would be inconvenient and unsuitable for Iceland (Idnadarraduneytid 2007a: 7).

This chapter focuses on the First Electricity Directive, its incorporation into the EEA Agreement and adoption at the national level in Iceland. The Second Directive also comes into play as, by the time the First Directive was being transposed in Iceland, the Second Directive was on the verge of being approved by the EU and so its aims and objectives were also taken into consideration during the transposition and implementation phase. At the time of writing, the Third Directive (2009/72) had not yet been incorporated into the EEA Agreement and so will not form part of this discussion. First, the origins and the main objectives of the EU's electricity package are discussed. In line with the Europeanization framework outlined in previous chapters, the level of mismatch is then determined, i.e., the extent to which pre-existing conditions in Iceland clashed with the EU's requirements. Third, the focus turns to the first research question posed in this volume, which asks whether non-member states potentially have any uploading capacity. To shed light on this question, Iceland's attempts to gain an exemption from various aspects of the First Directive are explored. The second research question of this study relates to downloading. The chapter therefore goes on to identify the degree to which the Directive has been implemented or the changes which have taken place within the Icelandic electricity sector as a result of EU requirements.

Origins and objectives of the Electricity Directive

The EU liberalization agenda for the electricity sector originated in a Council resolution from 1986 followed by a Commission White Paper in 1988 (Padgett 2003: 231–33). In 1990 two fairly minor steps were taken towards liberalization with the adoption of Council Directive 90/547/EEC, which aims to facilitate and increase transmission between high-voltage systems in the member states, and Council Directive 90/377/EEC concerning transparency of gas and electricity prices charged to industrial end-users (Idnadarraduneytid 2000: 88). The process gained momentum in the early 1990s under new Energy Commissioner, António Cardoso e Cunha, who was strongly committed to liberalization (Padgett 2003: 231–33). The liberalization of the European electricity sector was also driven to a large extent by the United Kingdom (Padgett 2003: 228). The UK model included non-discriminatory access for all market participants (i.e. producers and sellers of electricity) to transmission and distribution systems. This necessitated the operational independence of the network operators from generation and supply, either through full legal separation or through management unbundling. Some form of independent regulatory authority was also required to guarantee the transparency and fairness of the access regime (Padgett 2003: 230).

These principles contrasted sharply with the state monopoly character of the sector that was prevalent at the time in most other member states. Perhaps not surprisingly, the Commission's original proposals, which included the core principles of the UK model, met with considerable opposition and in 1992 the first draft was rejected by all member states in the Council, bar the UK (Padgett 2003: 231–33). The French, in particular, wanted to preserve the Electricité de France (EDF)[3] model and to keep its advantages in regard to its technological expertise and its nuclear industry (Bauby and Varone 2007: 1049–50). However, the French position soon became more and more isolated within the EU (Bauby and Varone 2007: 1049–50). European governments had a wider interest in economic liberalization in the pursuit of competitiveness. In Sweden, the Netherlands and Germany domestic liberalization initiatives began to undermine resistance to the UK model. Finland and Sweden had already undertaken independent liberalizations. Furthermore, countries outside Europe such as the USA, New Zealand, Australia and a few Latin American states had also begun the process of liberalization in the early 1990s (Padgett 2003: 230).

A compromise was reached in 1996, whereby the French Minister of Industry was pressured into altering his position (Bauby and Varone 2007: 1050–51). The Electricity Directive did, however, deviate from the UK model in a number of ways, as various prescriptions had been significantly watered down. It set out the main principles of a liberal governance regime while allowing fairly broad scope for national discretion in its transposition and practical implementation (Bauby and Varone 2007: 1050; Padgett 2003: 234). In the Directive, a distinction is made between the different aspects of the electricity sector, i.e. generation, transmission and distribution. Electricity generation (or production) is the process of creating electricity from other forms of energy or the first process in delivering electricity to consumers. Transmission involves the bulk transport of electrical power through a high-voltage system, which usually connects power plants to multiple substations near populated areas. Electricity distribution is the final stage in the delivery of electricity to end-users carrying electricity on medium- or low-voltage systems from the transmission system to consumers.

In order to stimulate competition, the Directive distinguishes between the competitive and regulated parts of the market. Generation and supply are subject to market competition, while transmission and distribution are subject to regulation or private licence as they are in a position of 'natural monopoly' (Asgeirsdottir 2008: 42). This mandates an 'unbundling' or minimum level of separation of any 'vertically integrated undertakings', i.e. companies performing two or more of the functions of generation, transmission and distribution of electricity (EFTA Surveillance Authority 2006: 5). Member states are obliged to designate transmission and distribution system operators (respectively, TSOs and DSOs) to be responsible for operating and ensuring maintenance and development of the transmission and distribution systems in a given area. TSOs and DSOs must be independent from each other, at least in management and financial terms, as well as from generation activities (EFTA Surveillance Authority 2006: 5; Idnadarraduneytid 2007a: 3–4). As transmission and distribution are subject to private licence, customers cannot choose their system operators. Unlike transmission and distribution, generation is subject to market competition. As such, the Directive calls for the removal of legal monopolies in generation and enables customers to choose their electricity suppliers. In order for competition to work properly, transmission and distribution system operators must grant access to their networks to all suppliers under non-discriminatory conditions (Nordic Competition Authorities 2007: 75).

After the First Directive had been in place for some years, further steps were considered necessary in order for the market to function more effectively. The Second Electricity Directive, adopted in 2003, required additional separation between the competition and private licence aspects of the sector in order to guarantee suppliers access to the transmission and distribution networks. According to the Directive, distribution and transmission systems should be operated through legally separate entities, and independent management structures must be put in place between distribution and transmission system operators and any generation/supply companies. Although legal separation did not require ownership unbundling or a change of ownership of assets, these requirements went further than the accounting and management unbundling which was required by the First Directive and in essence meant that transmission and distribution operators could not participate in the competition aspects of the market. The Directive did, however, permit the postponement of legal unbundling of distribution companies until 1 July 2007 and allowed member states to exempt companies from legal unbundling if they served fewer than 100,000 connected customers (Nordic Competition Authorities 2007: 75-76).

Mismatch between the EU and national levels

The EU's energy agenda is frequently at odds with existing policies or conditions in Iceland. For example, the EU's energy policy is generally geared at reducing pollution and encouraging increased use of renewable energy sources.[4] Iceland has abundant renewable resources and almost all of its electricity and heating needs are fulfilled with relatively clean hydropower or geothermal energy. Therefore, EU requirements to increase the proportion of renewable energy do not fit well for Iceland. Furthermore, much of the EU's energy policy is focused on gas, which is not used in Iceland due to the abundance of other sources. In some cases special conditions in Iceland have met with understanding at the European level.[5] As noted in the previous chapter, Iceland has a silent agreement with ESA not to transpose any of the Gas Directives. Exemptions have also been granted regarding rules on the energy efficiency of buildings. Despite these allowances, special treatment is never guaranteed.

The Electricity Directive is no exception from the general mismatch between the EU's energy agenda and Icelandic conditions. One of the key issues to cause conflict between the EU legislation and Icelandic conditions is that the EU's objective behind establishing common rules for the electricity market is to stimulate cross-border trade between the member states.[6] The Icelandic market is geographically isolated, with no interconnections with other countries. The scope of the Icelandic market is therefore restricted to the national level and trade with other countries is currently impossible. The Directive is not solely confined to facilitating trade across borders. It also aims to generally encourage competition in the generation and supply of electricity. In absolute terms, the electricity system in Iceland is very small in size despite the presence of a few large energy-intensive (mainly aluminium) manufacturers. Therefore, there is limited scope for competition as there are very few large potential buyers and likewise few suppliers of electricity (EFTA Surveillance Authority 2006: 28-29).

Before the adoption of the Directive, none of the electricity companies in Iceland had any clear separation between generation, transmission and distribution aspects.[7] Although the exact costs likely to be involved in the

82 *Market competition in the electricity sector*

implementation of the Directive were not calculated precisely, it was obvious that it would involve extensive and costly changes in terms of the organization of the electricity sector.[8] It is true that many countries in Europe also had monopoly systems prior to the adoption of the Directive. However, in Iceland the benefits of the required changes were less clear due to the isolation and limited size of the market.

Prior to the adoption of the Electricity Directive, the Icelandic market was closed for competition and almost all electricity was generated by a publicly owned company called Landsvirkjun (Nordic Competition Authorities 2007: 14). Landsvirkjun had a *de facto* monopoly position on investment in generation, although some DSOs such as Orkuveita Reykjavikur (OR), Hitaveita Sudurnesja (HS) and RARIK (Iceland State Electricity) had obtained limited and conditional concessions to generate electricity (Nordic Competition Authorities 2007: 14). According to the pre-existing legislation they were allowed to produce small amounts of electricity for their own markets. If they wanted to make large agreements with heavy industry, they had to negotiate with Landsvirkjun which then consulted with the relevant buyer, so negotiations were not direct but had to be mediated through Landsvirkjun.[9] There was clearly no free market competition in the generation and sales of electricity as prescribed by the Directive. In addition to controlling the vast majority of production, Landsvirkjun was also in charge of about 70 per cent of the country's transmission system (EFTA Surveillance Authority 2006: 28–29), without any separation between the two.[10] Again, mismatch between the Directive and national conditions is striking, as the Directive states that there should be competition in generation and supply, while the transmission system should be in the hands of a privately licensed single operator. RARIK, which was in charge of distributing electricity to rural areas that were not covered by local DSOs, had also laid an extensive system of transmission lines between different regions of the country or about 24 per cent of the transmission system (RARIK 2009). As Landsvirkjun and RARIK together controlled most of the transmission system, there was no independent transmission system operator who was not engaged in other relevant activities such as distribution and generation.

In sum, the Icelandic electricity sector was very small with relatively few large potential buyers and one company with a monopoly position in generation. None of the companies operating in the sector had any clear separation between the competition and private licence aspects.[11] Due to the high level of market concentration, vertical integration in the market and cross ownership, the unbundling and third party access requirements imposed by the Directive would entail significant changes for Iceland (EFTA Surveillance Authority 2006: 34). It was clear from the beginning that this Directive would have a great impact on Landsvirkjun as well as the small producers and distributors with respect to organization, pricing, surveillance, etc.[12] Perhaps unsurprisingly, there was considerable animosity towards the new Directive among the main stakeholders, as well as various politicians and civil servants who all voiced doubts as to whether it was suitable to adopt legislation about competition in the electricity sector in a small isolated market.[13] There was, nonetheless, some limited support for marketization as some of the large DSOs, mainly OR and HS, were interested in developing their production capacities further. This was, however, tinted with apprehension regarding potential costs of the changes and doubts as to their ability to compete effectively with Landsvirkjun.[14]

The EU did foresee that the Directive might cause additional complications for small isolated systems and accepted that provisions should in some cases be made for recourse to transitional regimes or derogations for the operation of such systems.[15] During the decision-making phase at the EU level as well as the incorporation of the Directive into the EEA Agreement, Iceland attempted to ensure that it would be able to claim special treatment based on such a clause and gain exemptions from the Directive or certain aspects of it. The following section explores Iceland's efforts to upload these preferences to the EU level.

Attempts to gain an exemption as a small isolated system

The original Commission proposal for the Electricity Directive came forward in January 1992, before the EEA Agreement came into effect. Therefore, the Icelandic government first got wind of the proposal at an EFTA working group meeting after it had been passed to the Council and the Parliament.[16] Iceland is highly dependent on these working groups and its EFTA partners, particularly Norway, for information on EU legislation which is in the pipeline and as a venue for making its views known.[17]

The Directive was frequently discussed at EFTA working group meetings,[18] which Commission officials often attended (Idnadarraduneytid 2007a: 5). It was mainly through this channel and EFTA comments that Iceland tried to make its voice heard and increase awareness of its unique position, rather than lobbying the Council, the EP or other countries with similar interests.[19] During the first years of the EEA, Iceland had not yet developed relations with the other institutions or sophisticated lobbying tactics and its attention was very much focused on the Commission and the other EFTA states.[20] Iceland felt that it was a good strategy to continue to lobby the Commission even once the proposal had been passed to the Council and the EP.[21] This is probably because it had direct access to the Commission and the Commission also has the ability to influence legislation even after it has been sent to the decision-making institutions through its role as mediator and conciliator in the decision-making process (Nugent 2003: 187–88). Another reason for the rather primitive lobbying strategy in this case may be that there are relatively few interest groups in this sector and none that belong to the private sector.[22]

An internal report by the Ministry of Industry (Idnadarraduneytid 2007a: 5) notes that, at an EFTA working group meeting on 27 November 1995, the Icelandic representative voiced strong doubts that the Directive would function for small isolated systems and stated that Iceland would ask for an exemption at least until the Icelandic electricity system was connected with the mainland. This view did not meet with much sympathy and the Commission did not feel that small isolated systems should be treated differently from other systems. The Commission representative said that, according to a Commission survey, other small isolated systems within the EU would not be asking for exemptions and he could not see any reason why the Directive would cause problems for Iceland.

Iceland was not the only country to have reservations about the Directive. Greece and Spain had also started voicing doubts within the Council about the suitability of the Directive for some of their islands.[23] In an EFTA working group meeting two months later, on 26 January 1996, the Icelandic government had become aware of proposals within the Council to include a clause in the Directive on potential exemptions for small isolated systems. The proposed exemptions did not, however, include all chapters of the Directive. Furthermore, it appeared that Iceland would not fall under the scope of the definition because its consumption of electricity was too high due mainly to the large amount of electricity supplied to heavy industry.[24]

At that time, the Icelandic government was not used to dealing with comprehensive EU directives and did not have the manpower to analyse in depth what repercussions it would have for Iceland.[25] Therefore, at first the government did not have a clear view of its aims with respect to the Directive other than to assert reservations about its suitability.[26] However, it seems that, from that point, Iceland's attention became focused mainly on pressing for the extension of the scope of the clause on small isolated systems to incorporate more parts of the Directive, and on a definition which would include Iceland. At the January 1996 working group meeting, the Icelandic representative said that he found it strange that small isolated systems would not be exempted from Chapter III of the Directive, which deals with generation, because the provisions of that chapter would make the organization and running of such systems unnecessarily complicated. The Icelandic representative further criticized the definition of small isolated systems for being too narrow and restrictive. Finally, the Icelandic representative pointed out that, according to the proposal, Luxembourg would be allowed to apply for an exemption even though it did not fall under the definition of a small isolated system. The Commission representative responded that the definition of small isolated systems was based on Greek and Spanish islands such as Rhodes and the Canaries and that Luxembourg would also be allowed to apply for an exemption because it had many of the same problems as these islands even though it was not isolated. However, there was no reason why the third chapter of the Directive on generation would entail any specific problems for small isolated systems (Idnadarraduneytid 2007a: 5).

Although there was a golden opportunity for developing strategic partnerships with countries with similar interests such as Greece and Spain, during its campaign Iceland focused primarily on gathering support from its EFTA partners. Although Norway was very much in favour of the Directive, it was also quite understanding of Iceland's position, and the chairman of the energy working group frequently highlighted Iceland's unique situation.[27] In EFTA comments from 1 February 1996, the EFTA side stated their concerns regarding the Directive. It was emphasized that the Icelandic electricity system was small and disconnected from other systems. Additionally, it was noted that electricity in Iceland was produced from clean, renewable sources which should receive special consideration. The letter urged that the chapters of the Directive dealing with generation, transmission and organization of access to the system should take such unique conditions into account (Idnadarraduneytid 2007a: 5).

At another EFTA working group meeting at the end of March 1996, the Icelandic representative asked the Commission to update the group on the status of the debate within the Council on small isolated systems. The Commission delegate again emphasized that, according to the Commission's view, derogations for such systems were not necessary. Nevertheless, the Council seemed set to allow derogations. Finally at a meeting on 28 May 1996, the chairman of the working group reiterated the unique position in small isolated systems (Idnadarraduneytid 2007a: 5–6).

The Directive was adopted by the Council and Parliament on 19 December 1996. It permitted the Commission to grant certain exemptions for small isolated systems. However, it did not include Chapter III on generation as part of the exemption clause and it defined small isolated systems as 'any system with consumption of less than 2,500 GWh (gigawatt hours) in the year 1996, where less than 5 per cent of annual consumption is obtained through interconnection with other systems'.[28] Even though Luxembourg did not fall under this definition in terms of interconnection with other systems, the Directive stated that Luxembourg would also be allowed to apply for exemptions. As Iceland has an abundance of energy sources and supplies a relatively large amount of electricity to heavy industry, it did not meet these requirements, as its total electricity usage was 5,100 GWh in 1996. Iceland, therefore, fell outside the definition of a small isolated system in terms of size, although it was sufficiently isolated (Idnadarraduneytid 2007a: 2–3).

After the Directive had been adopted by the EU and it was clear that the definition of small isolated systems would not apply to Iceland, the government's attentions turned towards obtaining an adaptation period and/or exemption for Iceland during the process of incorporating the Directive into the EEA Agreement. The Commission made it clear that it thought the Directive should be considered EEA-relevant and come into force in the entire EEA. Although Norway supported Iceland's reservations as to the suitability of the Directive for Iceland, it also agreed with the Commission's view that the Directive should be considered EEA-relevant (Idnadarraduneytid 2007a: 7). Norway had already made most of the changes required by the Directive and so it would not have much impact there.[29] The Icelanders therefore realized that it would be difficult to argue against the EEA-relevance of the Directive, especially as it was clearly an internal market issue.[30]

86 *Market competition in the electricity sector*

After having discussed the Directive with Icelandic stakeholders, the Ministry of Industry agreed that the Directive could be incorporated into the EEA Agreement and Iceland did not ask to be exempted from the Directive as a whole. Nevertheless, it argued that it would be necessary to have more time to implement the Directive and asked for a two-year adaptation period. Furthermore, it wanted a guarantee from the Commission that Iceland would also be allowed to apply for the exemptions reserved for small isolated systems if the new system turned out to be very problematic (Idnadarraduneytid 2007a: 7), even though technically the Icelandic system did not fall under the definition given in the Directive.

The Electricity Directive was incorporated into the EEA Agreement on 26 November 1999 and came into force in the EEA on 1 July 2000 (JCD no. 168/99). As requested, the Icelandic government received a two-year adaptation period for the implementation of the Directive. Iceland and Liechtenstein[31] were also added to the Directive's exemption clause, so that even though the definition of small isolated systems did not cover Iceland, it would still be allowed to apply for an exemption if it could demonstrate significant problems with the adoption of the Directive (Idnadarraduneytid 2007a: 7–8). Therefore, it seems that, although Iceland was not able to have any impact on the policy while it was being formulated and decided on by the EU, it was able to achieve an adaptation period and permission to apply for an exemption to most aspects of the Directive prior to its incorporation into the EEA Agreement.

This case has been hailed as a success by Icelandic government officials.[32] Nevertheless, the Commission made it clear that no exemptions would be granted regarding Chapter III on electricity generation for Iceland or any other state. Furthermore, it was of course not self-evident that any exemptions would be granted to Iceland as it would first need to demonstrate convincingly substantial problems in the adoption process (Idnadarraduneytid 2007a: 7–8). In any case, the end result was that Iceland made no attempt to apply for an exemption. The next section focuses on the adoption of the Electricity Directive at the national level and asks why Iceland adopted the Directive without attempting to gain any exemptions, what impact the Directive has had on the Icelandic electricity sector and to what extent the transposition and implementation of the Directive has met the EU's requirements and objectives.

Transposition without exemption

Despite having lobbied for and won the right to apply for exemptions from certain aspects of the Directive, a decision was made not to make use of this option. There are various reasons for this. First, there was considerable uncertainty as to whether such a request would be granted. In fact, it can be deemed fairly unlikely that Iceland would have received any exemptions. The exemption clause requires that the relevant state must show substantial difficulties in transposing the proposal before any exemptions are granted. Exemption clauses are generally interpreted rather narrowly and the Commission had already underlined that the Directive was not restricted to dealing with cross-border trade, but also aimed at standardizing rules between countries. Furthermore, by the time the Directive was incorporated into the EEA Agreement all the EU states had already transposed the Directive without any exemptions (Idnadarraduneytid 2000: 105), making it more implausible for Iceland to argue for special consideration.[33] However, interestingly, when the island states Malta and Cyprus later joined the EU both countries received derogations from certain provisions of the Electricity Directive as they were thought to have limited scope for the development of competition for electricity (European Commission 2005b).[34] An official at the Icelandic Ministry of Industry noted that, with the accession of these countries, the Commission's views appeared to become more lenient towards small isolated systems.[35]

Another reason why no exemptions were sought might be that there was in fact growing support for the Directive both within the Icelandic administration and government. It has been suggested that the Permanent Secretary at the Ministry of Industry at the time played an important role in pushing the Directive through. According to a representative of Landsvirkjun: 'He was extremely pro-EU and did not like asking for exemptions from Brussels.'[36] The CEO of HS agreed that this man had been instrumental in the adaptation process, noting that he had very liberal economic views and had wanted to have a market economy and competition in the electricity sector. He was therefore adamant that Iceland should accept the Directive without any special treatment.[37]

One official could not, however, single-handedly have arranged for the adoption of such a comprehensive piece of legislation. The centre-right government also appears to have been increasingly in favour of the Directive, although it wanted to ensure that no damage was done to any of the publicly owned companies in the process.[38] The Minister of Industry at the time was of the opinion that transposition of the Directive would not be a problem (Idnadarraduneytid 2007a: 8). She met with various stakeholders and encouraged them to see the new legislation as an opportunity rather than a threat (*Morgunbladid* 2003). Members of her party also advocated the Directive in the national media, emphasizing the importance and necessity of liberalizing the electricity market (Hreinsson 2003).

The reasons for this government support most likely vary. First, the aims of the Directive were in line with the general government policy of liberalization and marketization. Icelandic officials may also have been persuaded to some extent of the benefits of the Directive during meetings with the Commission. In all likelihood there was a will to be seen as a 'good' state and live up to the obligations of the EEA Agreement. In fact, a senior official at Landsvirkjun suggests that the government was being 'more Catholic than the pope' in this case, as it did not want to get a 'black mark' from the EU.[39] Some of the

88 *Market competition in the electricity sector*

larger non-heavy industry electricity buyers in the market such as SA, the Confederation of Icelandic Employers, and the fishing industry were also pressing for the adoption of the Directive, as they wanted the freedom to choose their own suppliers on an open market. Therefore, opting out of any aspects of the Directive would have been politically difficult.[40] Finally, there had been some talk over the years of building an electricity cable to Scotland to be able to sell Icelandic electricity on the mainland. In that case, it was argued that implementing the Directive was a necessary prerequisite.[41]

The decision not to ask for an exemption was not taken without consideration being given to the main stakeholders.[42] Nevertheless, an official from one of the largest DSOs noted that there was considerable political pressure on them not to ask for an exemption as the government was in favour of adopting the Directive.[43] For whatever reason, opposition among stakeholders appeared to die down to some extent during the consultation process which took place in advance of adopting the new legislation. The government asked the main interested parties to begin reviewing and forming an opinion of the Directive while it was still being discussed at the European level. Meetings were also arranged with Commission officials to answer any questions about the Directive's aims and obligations. At the end of the consultation process, Samorka, the federation of Icelandic energy and utilities, noted on behalf of the main electricity companies that it was clear that the Directive would impose substantial changes to the Icelandic electricity sector which would certainly be controversial. It did not, however, oppose the adoption of the Directive outright or promote the use of the exemption clause but urged that the electricity companies be closely consulted during the formulation of the legislation required to implement the Directive.[44] Orkustofnun (the National Energy Authority) also came to the conclusion that the adoption of the Directive would be feasible (Idnadarraduneytid 2007a: 6).

In agreeing to adopt the Directive, some of the stakeholders may have seen opportunities in opening the market.[45] There was considerable dissatisfaction with the pre-existing system, as one company had a monopoly over generating electricity and also owned most of the transmission grid. There was a view that the market had to be opened up somehow.[46] The companies also appeared to have taken Iceland's obligations under the EEA Agreement into consideration. When asked why the electricity companies agreed to the new legislation, an official from Samorka noted the following: 'When we decided to participate in European cooperation we agreed to undertake certain obligations to fulfil the requirements of the internal market and must adjust our legal system to these requirements'.[47]

Despite increasing support within the Icelandic administration and government and even among stakeholders, the Directive was still highly controversial and politically flammable, and finding a compromise regarding transposition proved to be a difficult and time-consuming process.[48] The first legislative proposal was submitted to Althingi in 2000–01 but was sent back to the Energy Committee for revision. A second attempt was made the following year, but there was still substantial controversy mainly surrounding the transmission aspects of the new system (Asgeirsdottir 2008: 73). The Electricity Act (no. 65/2003) was finally adopted by the Icelandic Parliament in the spring of 2003, nearly a year after Iceland's two-year adaptation period had expired. Notwithstanding the delay, the act transposed the First Electricity Directive 96/92/EC, without any exemptions, paving the way for the opening of the Icelandic market for competition (Nordic Competition Authorities 2007: 14).

By the time the Icelandic Electricity Act was adopted, the EU was on the verge of agreeing on the Second Electricity Directive (2003/54/EC) so the Icelandic Act also took into consideration many of the changes required by the new Directive. On 2 December 2005 Directive 2003/54/EC was incorporated into the EEA Agreement. The Joint Committee Decision confirmed that Iceland would be considered a small isolated system and so it would be allowed to apply for the relevant derogations. However, the Ministry of Industry did not feel that the electricity legislation had caused severe problems and so it did not foresee that Iceland would apply for any of these derogations (Idnadarraduneytid 2007a: 12–13). Although the original Act from 2003 took into consideration some of the aims of the Second Directive, it was further amended twice in 2004 and again in 2008 in order to more fully transpose the new requirements (Asgeirsdottir 2008: 73).[49]

With Electricity Act no. 65/2003 considerable changes were made to the Icelandic electricity sector and the environment in which electrical companies operate (Idnadarraduneytid 2007b: 19). Asgeirsdottir (2008) has compared the EU Electricity Directive to Icelandic legislation, concluding that the Icelandic Electricity Act is to a large extent based on the EU Directive, but also appears to have strong national flavours (Asgeirsdottir 2008: 90). According to Article 1 of the Electricity Act, its purpose is to:

> Promote an economic electricity system and thereby strengthen the Icelandic industries as well as regional development in Iceland. To this end: 1) A competitive environment shall be ensured for the generation and trade of electricity, with such restrictions as may prove necessary for the security of supply and other public interests. 2) Effectiveness and efficiency in the transmission and distribution of electricity shall be promoted. 3) The security of the electricity supply system and consumer protection shall be ensured. 4) The use of renewable energy sources and observance of other environmental criteria shall be promoted.

As can be seen, the overall purpose of the Icelandic legislation appears to coincide fairly well with the EU requirements. In line with the Directive, the legislation distinguishes between the competitive side of the sector, i.e. generation and sales, and the private licence side, or transmission and distribution, with the aim of achieving competition in the generation and sale of electricity (Skarphedinsson 2007: 8). In other words, the legislation ensures

90 *Market competition in the electricity sector*

that customers are free to choose their electricity suppliers, third-party access to transmission and distribution systems is guaranteed, the sector is placed under surveillance from an independent supervisory authority which has the power to make decisions on the pricing and maximum income of transmission and distribution, and there is separation between generation, transmission and distribution activities (Asgeirsdottir 2008: 91–92).

Originally, companies that engaged in both generation and distribution were only required to place an administrative separation between the two activities. However, more recent changes to the national legislation based on the Second Electricity Directive also require a company separation for DSOs covering more than 10,000 inhabitants.[50] This is far stricter than the requirements of the EU Directive, which allows member states to decide not to apply a legal separation to integrated electricity undertakings serving less than 100,000 customers.[51] In fact, most DSOs in Iceland cover less than 100,000 customers and so legal separation would not have been necessary in the vast majority of cases. The Icelandic authorities did consider using this possibility (Idnadarraduneytid 2007a: 12). However, in the end they made their decision not because it was required by the Directive but because they though it was right in terms of competition to separate between the competition side and the private licence side. Although the Minister did say that it was natural that the very smallest companies should get an exemption, as separation would not be economical.[52]

One of the main changes that was made to the legislation in the spring of 2004 (89/2004), which had been a particular bone of contention during the transposition phase, was the creation of a separate company called Landsnet to serve as the transmission system operator in Iceland. Although its owners were still allowed to participate in generation, sales and distribution, the board of Landsnet was required to be independent from these activities. The 2004 legislation also specified more clearly maximum revenues for private licence companies, i.e. Landsnet and the distribution system operators. Another change in 2004 (149/2004) meant that the full opening of the electricity market was pushed forward by one year, and so all eligible customers were free to purchase electricity from the supplier of their choice from 1 January 2006 instead of January 2007. Overall, the Icelandic Electricity Act appears to meet the requirements of the EU Directive and in some cases even goes further than is required in terms of separation between distribution and generation activities and it was put into practice earlier than required. But to what extent has the landscape of the electricity sector really changed with the new laws?

Over-implementation?

It is clear that significant changes have taken place within the Icelandic Electricity sector since the Electricity Act came into effect. Landsvirkjun no longer has a monopoly on the production of electricity. A new company has been set up as the country's Transmission System Operator and companies previously engaged in both generation and distribution activities have been split up. However, the extent to which the overall aims of the Electricity Directive have been achieved can be considered questionable.

The opening of the Icelandic electricity market proceeded in stages, with larger buyers being allowed to choose their supplier from 2003 and full market opening in 2006. Nonetheless very few customers have used the opportunity to switch supplier (Nordic Competition Authorities 2007: 15). A low switching rate does not necessarily mean ineffective competition, since it might imply that competition is strong and customers have little to gain from changing supplier (Nordic Competition Authorities 2007: 77–78). Although there is little price disparity between suppliers and the price of electricity is generally fairly low in Iceland, there are reasons to believe that market competition is not functioning ideally (EFTA Surveillance Authority 2006: 29–30).[53] One of the most prominent features of the Icelandic electricity sector is the dominant position of one company, Landsvirkjun, in the generation of electricity. Iceland is different to other countries in that there are far fewer producers and sellers of electricity, and the share of Landsvirkjun in overall generation is extremely large (Skarphedinsson 2007: 18). The Electricity Act has not led to the entry of any new participants into the market and Landsvirkjun is still by far the dominant producer and wholesale supplier of electricity in Iceland, even if its share has decreased somewhat since the new legislation came into effect.[54]

Although other companies besides Landsvirkjun, primarily HS and OR, generate a limited amount of electricity which is also sold on the open market, in effect all retailers have to buy electricity in wholesale from Landsvirkjun (Nordic Competition Authorities 2007: 75). As an official from the National Energy Authority observed:

> Landsvirkjun still controls most of the generation and wholesale of electricity and everyone else has to buy from them, even though others are increasing their generation capacities. While everyone buys from the same company at the same price there won't be much competition in sales, so it is an interesting question to explore why Iceland is doing all this when there is hardly any competition in sales and can't really ever be.[55]

A representative of Samorka agreed:

> We are meant to have a competitive environment, but one company produces such a vast majority of the electricity. This obviously retards competition. If we could buy and sell across borders, then it might work.[56]

On a similar note, the Head of Corporate Communications at OR complained that in Iceland Landsvirkjun generated most of the electricity and so all the companies had to buy electricity from them. The competition therefore came from generating cheaper electricity than Landsvirkjun and 'subsidizing' the electricity bought in wholesale from Landsvirkjun. 'The price we are selling at and those companies that produce their own electricity, is lower than Landsvirkjun's wholesale price so the competition is who can "subsidize" Landsvirkjun the most. So it is a very strange market.'[57]

A particular grievance among Landsvirkjun's competitors is that Landsvirkjun is state-owned and so the state is liable as a guarantor for all Landsvirkjun's obligations.[58] This, they argue, serves to further bolster the company's dominant position on the market. As noted by the CEO of HS:

> One thing I don't think is compatible with competition policy is that Landsvirkjun has a 100-per-cent state guarantee on everything it does and we have to try to compete with them. All these changes have been used to empower the state in the energy market. They do what the EU legislation asks but also promote their own agenda.[59]

Furthermore, although there has been a legal separation between companies engaged in generation, transmission and distribution, there is still a high degree of cross-ownership between companies engaged in the different aspects of the electricity sector. For example, the transmission system is now in the hands of a new company, Landsnet, which began operations in January 2005, but the owners of Landsnet are Landsvirkjun (64.7 per cent); RARIK, one of the largest DSOs owned by the state (22.5 per cent); Orkubu Vestfjarda, a small local producer and distributor which is also owned by the state, (6 per cent); and OR (6.8 per cent) (Skarphedinsson 2007: 11). The board of Landsnet is meant to be independent from producers and distributors of electricity. However, as each of its owners is engaged in other activities, i.e. generation and/or distribution, this could distort competition. Furthermore, all Landsnet's owners except OR are owned by the Icelandic state.

Companies previously engaged in both generation and distribution have also been split into legally separate entities. However, there is also still a high degree of cross-ownership in these sectors. When the Electricity Act first took effect, seven companies were granted licences to be distribution system operators in their designated areas: HS, OR, RARIK, Nordurorka, Orkubu Vestfjarda, Orkuveita Husavikur, and Rafveita Reydarfjardar (Skarphedinsson 2007: 8). Each of these companies also had some production capacities, particularly HS, OR and RARIK. Now most of these have been split into separate companies either dealing with generation and sales or distribution. Nevertheless, there have been fairly limited changes in terms of ownership.[60]

The EFTA Surveillance Authority has received complaints from generators that a supply company affiliated to a particular DSO obtained better quality and more timely information than its competitors. There have also been complaints from generators that supply affiliates of DSOs had knowledge that final customers intended to switch and were able to take steps to prevent this from occurring (EFTA Surveillance Authority 2006: 32). For reasons such as this, according to the Icelandic Competition Authority it would be best to separate ownership of production and distribution (Skarphedinsson 2007: 18). But this might prove difficult in such a small sector in which all companies are publicly owned. As noted by a senior official at Landsvirkjun:

> We are all like elephants in a porcelain shop. They are trying to set up different teams that are supposed to be competing with each other, but in reality everyone is on the same team as we are all public companies and there are also so few of us that the price is not really based on competition.[61]

As an OR official noted:

> Lack of a connection to other markets means that the competition here is lame. Iceland is in a completely different position from those that have connected systems and now they are trying to set up a spot market for electricity here. Again, people are trying to imitate the European market in this small market where there is one company dominant in generation. I don't really know what people foresee. Some dreams about competition. I thought the debate on the real need for adoption of the Directive was very relevant.[62]

Finally, it is important to bear in mind that the sales portion of the total electricity price is very small, so there is really fairly limited scope for substantial differences in prices. The main costs are for the private licence aspects, i.e. transmission and distribution, for which there is a fixed price under observation from OS. The sales part is just a very few per cent and so it is not really able to create a lot of upheaval on the market.[63] Despite increasing costs, electricity in Iceland is still cheaper than in most other countries.[64]

The fact that market liberalization has not proved to be glitch-free in Iceland is not surprising based on the experience of other larger states that have connections with other markets. Many of the more controversial obligations have caused problems for everyone, not just small isolated systems.[65] In France, adoption of the Directive faced substantial challenges because of historical attachment to public service obligations, the strong position of the incumbent operator (EDF) and the high degree of public satisfaction with the existing service (Bauby and Varone 2007: 1050). Despite the European aim to break down national monopolies and introduce competition with foreign operators, control over the French market remains in the hands of French groups (Bauby and Varone 2007: 1049).

An examination of regulatory reforms in the Spanish and Portuguese electricity sectors also shows that adherence to the rules of EU regimes has not curtailed uncompetitive behaviour by governments and market incumbents and they have been able to adhere to EU rules while also finding ways to continue to be engaged in mercantilist policies (Jordana *et al.* 2006: 460). A

Commission report indicated that, although many of the necessary measures to implement competition had been taken, markets remained concentrated in many parts of the EU and only those regions with an adequate number of players, i.e. the UK and Nordic markets, had been able to deliver a competitive market (European Commission 2005b). There had also been limited business between countries and limited reinvestment in transmission systems. Furthermore, the rules on legal separation have not had the desired effect, and there is evidence of discrimination in favour of companies in the same conglomeration (Utanrikisraduneytid 2007: 19–20). In sum, it is questionable how well market competition can function in the electricity sector, particularly in a small isolated system such as Iceland. This does not, however, appear to have been due to any hesitation or neglect on behalf of the Icelandic government in implementing the Directive's requirements, but rather due to the nature of the sector.

Conclusions

This chapter has explored the Europeanization of the Icelandic electricity sector, i.e. Iceland's response to the EU's Electricity Directive in terms of uploading and downloading as well the mismatch between the EU's Electricity Directive and Icelandic conditions. With respect to mismatch, the Electricity Directive was designed with much larger electricity systems in mind and was furthermore geared towards enabling cross-border trade within Europe, which does not apply to Iceland as it is an isolated system. In order to achieve a competitive market in the electricity sector, the Directive required a separation between generation and sales of electricity, which would be subject to market competition, and network activities (i.e. transmission and distribution) which would require a private licence. There are very few electricity companies in Iceland and prior to the adoption of the Electricity Directive none of them had any administrative or legal separation between generation, transmission and distribution activities. Thus it was clear that implementation of the Directive would involve extensive and costly changes in terms of the organization of the electricity sector. The benefits of these changes were, however, less obvious as there is limited scope for competition in a small isolated market with few potential large-scale buyers and one dominant supplier.

Prior to the incorporation of the Directive into the EEA Agreement, Iceland was able to secure the right to apply for exemptions from certain aspects of the Directive, based on its small size and isolated location which can be deemed a partial uploading success. This possibility has not, however, been used by the Icelandic government. Rather, the Icelandic Electricity Act conscientiously fulfils the aims of the Directive and in some cases even goes further than EU requirements in demanding the company separation of DSOs covering more than 10,000 inhabitants rather than 100,000 as stipulated by the Directive. The implementation has also been dutifully carried out with full market opening being put into effect earlier than required and the establishment of Landsnet as the country's transmission system operator, as well as a separation between the generation/sales and distribution activities of all but the very smallest vertically integrated companies. It can therefore be argued that in this case downloading EU requirements has led to a 'transformation' of the Icelandic electricity sector.

It is, however, important to bear in mind that in many ways these changes appear to have come about because of domestic preferences rather than as a result of external pressure to suspend the EEA Agreement or issue infringement proceedings. When the Directive was incorporated into the Agreement there was in fact growing support for its aims within the Icelandic centre-right government, as they corresponded with its policy of liberalization and marketization. It is not certain whether these changes would have been implemented as enthusiastically by a left-leaning government. There was also some degree of pressure from within society as many of the larger non-heavy industry electricity buyers in the market wanted the freedom to choose their suppliers. Therefore, domestic actors saw some potential benefits in adopting a market system, despite a relatively high degree of mismatch between the national level and EU requirements.

In spite of these changes, competition in the Icelandic electricity sector does not appear to be flourishing, but this probably has more to do with the smallness and isolation of the Icelandic electricity sector than any reluctance to implement the Directive on behalf of the government. In this case it is important to note that, although it was EU requirements that initiated the changes within the Icelandic electricity sector, domestic support also seems to have been essential in bringing them about. In the following chapters, EU policies which have received a less enthusiastic domestic response will be examined in order to ascertain whether they are downloaded to the same extent.

5 European citizenship and free movement of persons

One of the key questions posed in this study relates to the extent to which the EU can ensure that its policies are downloaded in a non-member state, such as Iceland. In other words, which incentives and/or sanctions apply with respect to EU policy adoption? As noted in Chapter 3, the EEA Agreement contains various clauses which allow the EFTA states to participate in EU cooperation without formally giving up their sovereignty. The right to refuse EU legislation was, for example, seen as an important protection against the loss of sovereignty by the EFTA states.[1] Nevertheless, it is questionable whether they can actually 'veto' the incorporation of a piece of legislation into the EEA Agreement, as Article 102 of the EEA Agreement threatens a partial suspension of the Agreement if the EFTAns refuse. As argued in Chapter 3, this provides a relatively strong incentive for the EFTA states to agree to the adoption of EU rules because of their dependence on access to the internal market. This clause, therefore, gives the EU considerable leverage over the EFTA states and makes it difficult, if not impossible, for them to use their right of refusal. This chapter examines how Article 102 works in practice.

Most pieces of legislation are adopted without dispute and so Article 102 has seldom been put to the test. However, one issue that has increasingly begun to spark conflict is the question of EEA-relevance. The EEA Agreement was drafted in the early 1990s and has a strong focus on the internal market and the four freedoms. Thus, it covers the majority of the old pillar I, albeit with certain exemptions. The EU has, however, evolved since then. New concepts, such as EU citizenship, have been introduced and expanded upon. Directives have become more comprehensive, often spanning diverse areas, which can pose problems in defining EEA-relevance.[2] In many cases some elements of EU legislation may be applicable to the EEA while others are not.[3] This can make the task of determining EEA-relevance a difficult one. In some cases the EU has been more eager to incorporate acts into the EEA Agreement, while the EFTA states have not been as enthusiastic.[4] But can the EFTAns prevent the EEA from expanding into new areas which were not perhaps envisioned in the original Agreement? Or is there an element of 'mission creep' in the EEA framework?

The case of the 'Citizenship Directive' or the 'Free Movement Directive' (2004/38/EC) as the EFTA states refer to it, is a prime example of this type of conflict. The EEA Agreement is based on the pre-Maastricht conception of free movement of persons as workers or economic entities within the internal market, rather than a right to be enjoyed by Union citizens as outlined in the Directive. Accordingly, Iceland and Liechtenstein argued that the Directive overstepped the legal boundaries of the EEA and that various aspects of it, mainly those dealing with immigration law, should not be considered EEA-relevant. Norway was rather indifferent towards the Directive and did not oppose the Commission's interpretation that it should be incorporated into the Agreement. A long period of dispute and deadlock ensued in which the EFTA states were running the risk of the relevant Annex of the EEA Agreement being suspended (Juliusdottir and Wallis 2007: 11). In the end, Iceland and Liechtenstein backed down and the Directive was taken into the Agreement, paving the way for full downloading at the national level.

This chapter begins by looking at the origins, content and aims of the Directive, particularly the expanding concept of Union citizenship and the changing interpretation of free movement as a key right to be enjoyed by EU citizens. In line with the Europeanization framework, the chapter goes on to explore mismatch between the European and national levels and the reasons behind Iceland's resistance to the Directive. Although there were doubts early on regarding the EEA-relevance of the Directive, Iceland did not take much action to upload its preferences until the Directive had been adopted by the EU.[5] Therefore, a large portion of the chapter focuses on the discussions between EFTA and the EU that led to the incorporation of the Directive into the EEA Agreement, which is both the last chance for the EFTA states to upload their preferences as well as the first step in the downloading process. The debate is examined with a view to understanding how Article 102 works in practice, the dynamics between the EFTA states and the EU, and the real scope for the EFTA states to say 'No'.

It is not enough, however, for legislation to be incorporated into the EEA Agreement. It must also be transposed and implemented at the national level for domestic change to occur. Incorrect transposition and implementation failure incur relatively mild sanctions in comparison to the threat of discontinuation of parts of the EEA Agreement and exclusion from the internal market through Article 102. Therefore, this chapter also examines how well Iceland has followed through with the adoption of the Directive at the national level. Finally, some concluding remarks are made on what this case can tell us about the EU's overall ability to ensure that its policies are downloaded in Iceland.

Free movement as an integral part of EU citizenship

Citizenship generally refers to a status of individuals which is tied to a political unit, usually a state (E. D. H. Olsen 2008: 43–44). In other words, it refers to a legal and political position which confers various civil, political and social rights to individuals. In its modern form, the concept dates back to the emergence of the nation-state as the dominant mode of political organization. Only in recent years has it been extended to the supranational level, particularly within the framework of the European Union.

Some would argue that European citizenship has existed since the early days of European integration (E. D. H. Olsen 2008: 40). Indeed, the establishment of the European Economic Community in 1957 did grant certain rights to the nationals of its member states, primarily the right of free movement within the Community. This right was, however, based on economic considerations necessary to achieving a common market and was linked to an individual's capacity as a factor of production rather than a citizen (European Commission 2006). The right of free movement was attached to the status of individuals as workers or market participants, rather than democratic citizens, and was meant to facilitate what the Treaty referred to as 'movement of labour' (E. D. H. Olsen 2008: 45–48 and 54).

In the 1960s and 1970s a broader conception slowly began to evolve in which individuals mattered at the European level not only as workers but also as citizens who should enjoy certain fundamental rights (E. D. H. Olsen 2008: 50–51). The concept of EU citizenship was not, however, formally introduced until the Treaty of Maastricht.[6] Although it was initially perceived as mainly symbolic or decorative, this was undoubtedly a significant event as it was the first time that a concrete form of citizenship beyond the nation-state emerged (Kostakopoulou 2007: 623–26). European citizenship is reserved for every person that has the nationality of an EU member state with the view to strengthening the protection of their rights and interests. As a result, citizenship is said to entail a fundamental right to move and reside freely within the European Union, without reference to an economic activity (European Commission 2006).[7] It also includes political rights such as the right to vote and stand in local government and European Parliament elections in the country of residence, the right to certain diplomatic and consular protection from the authorities of any member state and the right of petition to the European Parliament and appeal to the European Ombudsman.[8]

The concept of European citizenship has since evolved further and become widespread in the EU's legal texts and policies. For example, the Treaty of Amsterdam included various advances with regard to human rights and non-discrimination and a commitment to raising the quality of, and free access to, education. In addition to rights explicitly mentioned in the Treaties, there is a series of fundamental rights and obligations which stem from various sources such as the case law of the European Court of Justice, the Council of Europe's Convention on Human Rights and the constitutional traditions of the member states. The European Commission can also put forward proposals to strengthen or expand the rights associated with EU citizenship. In relation to democracy and citizens' participation, the Lisbon Treaty provides various new initiatives designed to give a richer meaning to European citizenship

(Editorial Comments 2008). In sum, European citizenship entails a fairly large bundle of expanding rights and freedoms.

Despite the constant expansion of rights included in European citizenship, the original right of free movement is considered to be one of the most visible advantages of Union citizenship (E. D. H. Olsen 2008: 41–42; Vitorino 2004). It provides the focal point through which other elements of European citizenship, such as social rights and the right of residence, gain substance. As such, it forms the core of Union citizenship (E. D. H. Olsen 2008: 53). The rights resulting from EU citizenship are in most cases triggered by transborder movement involving, for example, discrimination on grounds of nationality (Editorial Comments 2008).

It is true that nationals of the EU member states have enjoyed the possibility of moving freely (albeit with some limitations) within the territory of the member states since the beginning of the European integration process. However, the introduction of Union citizenship has challenged the economic paradigm that once formed the basis for free movement provisions (Spaventa 2008: 13–14). European citizenship is still associated with internal mobility of labour and the creation of an internal market, but the right of free movement and residence has also become tied to the political status of a citizen of the Union (Kostakopoulou 2007: 634–35). Migrant workers have thus been transformed into Union citizens with broad rights of equal treatment in the member state of their residence (Kostakopoulou 2007: 646). This is in stark contrast to the original right of free movement, which was conditional on a person's economic function within the host state.

Even if it is still subject to certain limitations and conditions, the right of free movement has been extended considerably through Treaty revisions, legislation and case law. Article 21(1) TFEU (ex-Article 18(1) TEC), which came into effect with the Treaty of Maastricht, grants EU citizens the right to move around the Community and to reside in any of the member states. The reach of this Article is much greater than that of previous economic free movement provisions as it confirms that it is no longer necessary to establish a connection between an economic activity and right to move (Spaventa 2008: 22–23). The European Court of Justice has recognized the direct applicability of this Article (European Commission 2006). The Amsterdam Treaty of 1999 strengthened the right of free movement linked to European Union citizenship by integrating the Schengen Convention[9] into the Treaty, while the Treaty of Nice (2003) introduced QMV into the EU decision-making process in the field of free movement and residence (European Commission 2006).[10]

The so called Citizenship Directive (2004/38/EC) represents an important step in the definition of a strong concept of citizenship of the Union (Vitorino 2004). In many ways it embodies the change in understanding towards free movement being considered a fundamental right of EU citizens, rather than being based on their economic activities. The Directive gives legal effect to residence rights and spells out the conditions and limitations referred to in Article 18(1) (Borgmann-Prebil 2008: 335–36). Thus, its main objective is to guarantee Union citizens and their family members the right of entry and residence in any of the member states and establishes the only acceptable reasons for restricting the free movement of citizens by member state authorities.

The Directive merges together various pre-existing pieces of secondary legislation and European case law into one comprehensive legal act (Europa 2009).[11] Therefore, many of the rights contained in the Directive had already been established. Most notably, in the early 1990s, three directives were adopted which guarantee rights of residence to categories of persons other than workers: retired persons, students, and economically inactive people (European Commission 2006).[12] Thus, in the pre-Maastricht era, formal rights of free movement and residence were also conferred on the economically independent, retired persons, students etc. on the condition that they had sufficient resources to avoid becoming a burden on the host state and were covered by health insurance (Kostakopoulou 2007: 634–35). Consequently, perhaps the most important contribution of the Directive was to reconceptualize free movement into a right of Union citizens. Moreover, it made some important tangible changes to the pre-existing legal environment and extended free movement rights.

The right of citizens to reside in the territory of another member state is still subject to certain limitations. However, the new measures included in the Directive aim to make it easier for Union citizens to exercise their right to move and reside freely within member states by cutting back the administrative formalities necessary when moving between member states. Residence permits are, for example, abolished for Union citizens, although host member states may still require EU citizens to register with the competent authorities if they deem this to be necessary (Europa 2009; Vitorino 2004). The Directive also adds substance to Union citizenship by establishing permanent right of residence for Union citizens and their families (Kostakopoulou 2007: 645). It distinguishes between categories of residence rights, introducing a gradual approach to equal treatment rights for migrant citizens in a host state (Borgmann-Prebil 2008: 343–45). European citizens have the right to enter, reside and remain in the territory of any other member state for a period of up to three months simply by presenting a valid passport or national identity card (European Commission 2006).

In order to guarantee member states protection against an excessive burden on their public funds, EU citizens must either exercise an economic activity or possess sufficient resources in order to take up residence in another member state (Vitorino 2004). Therefore, after the first three months of stay, the right of residence is conditional upon possession of sufficient economic resources and comprehensive health insurance (Spaventa 2008: 26). However, after five years, the right of residence becomes permanent, which means there are no longer any preconditions or restrictions concerning access to public funds such as unemployment benefits or a state pension, although in some cases these are lifted earlier. This clearly enlarges the social content of citizenship (Kostakopoulou 2007: 641).

The Directive further extends the rights of family members who are not Union citizens to reside in the member states. Family members, irrespective of their nationality, have the right to accompany and establish themselves with a European citizen who is residing in the territory of another member state (European Commission 2006).[13] In addition, the death of the Union citizen, his or her departure from the host member state, divorce, annulment of marriage or termination of partnership does not affect the right of family members to continue residing in the member state in question, subject to certain conditions. After a five-year period of uninterrupted legal residence, family members who are not nationals of a member state also acquire permanent residence and benefit from equal treatment with host country nationals in the areas covered by the Treaty (Europa 2009). The definition of 'family members' also covers registered partners for the first time, if the legislation of the host member state treats registered partnerships as equivalent to marriage (European Commission 2006). Finally, the Directive limits the scope for refusing entry or terminating the right of residence of Union citizens and their family members (Europa 2009). Citizens and their family members may thus only be expelled on serious grounds of public policy and security. Citizens who have resided a minimum of ten years in a host state and minors may only be expelled based on imperative grounds of public security (Borgmann-Prebil 2008: 343–45).

EEA-relevance as a convenient excuse for non-adoption?

One of the main complications of the EEA frameworks is that EU policy-making has progressed a great deal, while the EEA Agreement has remained static.[14] The purpose of the EEA Agreement was to grant the EFTA states access to the internal market. Free movement of persons was considered one of the four freedoms upon which the internal market is based. However, it has now been reconceptualized within the EU as a right to be enjoyed by its citizens. Although changes had been taking place with respect to the relationship between free movement and European citizenship throughout the 1990s and early 2000s, the Citizenship Directive was the first legislative revision in the area of free movement of persons since before 1993. Therefore, the rules on free movement that were adopted by the EFTA states when the EEA Agreement first came into effect had never been changed and the Citizenship Directive was the first occasion that this new conceptualization was put to the test in the context of the EEA.[15]

An important aspect of citizenship is exclusivity. In other words, those who have citizenship and those who do not are treated differently. Although they are bound by the EU's rules, nationals of the EEA states do not have European citizenship. They do not, for example, enjoy any of the other rights of Union citizens such as voting in EP elections or petitioning the Ombudsman.

Adopting legislation into the EEA Agreement which is based on the concept of citizenship therefore provokes certain questions. A key demonstration of this is that officials from the EFTA states never refer to the Citizenship Directive by that name, even though that is what it is often called within the EU and by academics. Instead, they consistently refer to it as the 'Free Movement Directive'.

Icelandic officials first became aware of the Directive around 2002 when the proposal was still being formulated by the Commission. The EFTA Secretariat notified relevant officials that it was in the pipeline and an Icelandic representative from the Directorate of Labour attended some of the Commission's expert group meetings. At that early stage, the view had already emerged that the Directive should not be considered EEA-relevant.[16] A representative of the Ministry of Justice elaborated on the Icelandic government's position:

> The Commission is working towards the idea of turning European Citizenship into a meaningful concept. The legislation from 2004 builds on the idea of European citizenship. In other words, as a European citizen you have certain rights, not because of the internal market. In the future it is likely that the Commission will try to push forward a legal framework which makes it just as easy to move from Copenhagen to Lisbon as from Copenhagen to Roskilde. As the EU moves closer to being a confederation with political rights that are related to citizenship rights, it becomes more difficult to connect rules that are built on these views with rules that are built on the EEA Agreement and the four freedoms. We wanted a legally correct outcome and we did not feel that the EEA Agreement contained any commitment or obligation to adopt this type of legislation.[17]

A representative of the Icelandic Mission to the EU further explained that Union citizens had certain rights that were based on the Treaties as well as case law. The idea was that they should have the same rights in other member states as they did at home. The Directive combined free movement of persons with a specific purpose that served the internal market and the right of citizens to make themselves at home anywhere in the EU. If the Directive were incorporated into the EEA Agreement, it would mean that EU citizens and their family members could move to Iceland permanently without the Icelandic authorities having any say in the matter. They would not have to be there for any internal market purpose, they just had that right. But that wasn't part of the EEA Agreement.[18] It is true that, based on pre-Maastricht legislation, citizens of EU member states, such as students and pensioners, already had the right to move to Iceland even if they were not engaged in any economic activity. However, a key change brought about by the Directive was the right of their family members to move and reside freely with them, even if they were not citizens of EU or EFTA states.

On the basis that the concept of citizenship is not part of the EEA Agreement, Icelandic officials queried whether certain specific clauses of the Directive should be considered EEA-relevant. Directive 2004/38/EC contains aspects of both social policy and immigration policy. The part of the Directive that falls under social policy has to do with work permits and such. This portion of the legislation was not controversial as it had a basis in the EEA Agreement. Furthermore, it did not require any changes to existing legislation. The immigration side was far more contentious.[19] The main doubts had to do with whether the right to reside permanently after five years and the rights of third-country nationals who are family members of EEA nationals to reside in the EEA states should be part of the EEA Agreement.[20] As one official put it: 'Should the Nigerian wife of a Polish worker who comes to Iceland and divorces her husband be allowed to settle here on the basis of the EEA Agreement?'[21]

The officials interviewed consistently argued that the Icelandic Authorities opposed the incorporation of the Directive on the basis of the legal principle of EEA-relevance, not because they disagreed with the content of the Directive. The previous legislation upon which the Directive is based was already part of the EEA Agreement. Furthermore, they maintained that the Icelandic legal framework in this area was already fairly lenient, so the real tangible impact of the Directive was limited. In some ways, the Icelandic legislation even gave more rights than the Directive required.[22] For example, the Icelandic legislation previously stated that EEA citizens could obtain a permanent residence permit after three years, while the Directive allowed for permanent residence after five years.[23] Representatives of the Foreign Ministry agreed that it was not the requirements of the legislation that were problematic. It was the principle regarding the scope of the EEA Agreement because the Directive would give third-country nationals an independent right of residence even though immigration law is not part of the EEA Agreement. There were concerns that incorporating such legislation into the EEA Agreement would set a precedent.[24]

The Counsellor for Justice and Home Affairs at the Icelandic Mission to the EU explained that the dispute was of a legal nature regarding the scope of the EEA Agreement. It was not about opposition to the content of the Directive. The EEA Agreement only applies to the free movement of persons between member states with a certain purpose such as employment and the provision of services or to people like students or pensioners. These are clearly defined groups that have a right to move and reside for a specific reason. Immigration is not part of the EEA and so the EFTA states should be able to control their own immigration laws. Icelandic law should decide who is allowed to reside permanently in Iceland, as this is not part of being able to move freely within the context of the internal market. Adopting the Directive would mean admitting that the EU can decide how immigration affairs are handled in Iceland.[25]

Despite assertions that the dispute was primarily a matter of principle, it is clear that the Directive would have entailed some legislative changes that the Icelandic government would perhaps have preferred to avoid. One of the biggest changes was that EEA nationals would no longer need a residence permit to stay in Iceland. Another change had to do with deportation and the right to return. These rules needed to be made more lenient as EEA nationals could no longer be deported for life. The Directive meant that the maximum period would have to be 20 years. Perhaps the most controversial change had to do with the extensive rights of third-country nationals who are family members of EEA nationals. For example, if people divorce or separate or if the partner dies or goes back to his/her home country then the third-country spouse still has a right to remain in Iceland. Icelandic authorities did not want to adopt this because they believed this system could easily be abused with marriages of convenience.[26] Finally, one of the changes that the Directive entailed is that foreigners residing in Iceland could no longer be required to learn Icelandic, which was a concern for Icelandic authorities.[27]

In some ways the argument against EEA-relevance may, therefore, have been an excuse to attempt to avoid downloading policies that the Icelandic government did not particularly want. It would not be the first time that lack of EEA-relevance has been used in an attempt to avoid or at least postpone the adoption of a particular act. One example is Norwegian opposition to the Services Directive (2006/123/EC). Norway had an internal political issue with that Directive, as they were afraid it would lead to social dumping. Therefore, they tried to argue that it was not EEA-relevant, even though their reasoning was fairly weak as services is one of the four freedoms.[28] This may be because arguing against EEA-relevance is seen as a more viable strategy than just saying 'we don't like something'.[29] As noted by one official:

> The EEA Agreement is not pick and choose and doesn't leave much room to say I think this is a stupid rule and I just don't like it. We know that it doesn't matter if we don't like the rule. The debate can, however, be about whether a particular rule should be EEA-relevant or not.[30]

In sum, it appears that the reasons behind Iceland's objections were mixed. They mainly had to do with the question of EEA-relevance, as they did not want to set a precedent for the expansion of the EEA into new areas. However, opposition to certain substantive elements of the Directive may also have played a role. These feelings were expressed by Foreign Ministry officials:

> What we mainly look at is whether legal acts are EEA-relevant and whether they fall under the scope of the EEA Agreement. We want to make sure we don't extend the scope of the Agreement unnecessarily. Of course it also depends on the legislation. We have to protect our interests. But the main principle is whether or not a certain act is legally EEA-relevant.[31]

Can the EFTA states say 'No'?

There is no independent arbitrator who decides whether or not legislative acts should be considered EEA-relevant. Instead, questions of EEA-relevance must be agreed upon in negotiations between the EU and EFTA sides. Unlike Iceland, the Commission considered the Directive to be essential to the functioning of the EEA Agreement and the internal market.[32] The EU pointed out that the EEA already went much further than allowing the free movement of workers by allowing students and pensioners to reside freely inside the EEA even though they were not contributing economically.[33] Accordingly, the Commission was in favour of a total incorporation of the Directive into the EEA Agreement and had marked it as EEA-relevant from the very beginning.[34]

As explained in Chapter 3, the EFTA states are required to speak with a united voice when deciding whether to incorporate acts into the Agreement. This can be challenging if they do not all agree. It soon became clear that Iceland, Liechtenstein and Norway were not all on the same wavelength with respect to the EEA-relevance of this Directive.[35] The Directive was much more politically flammable and controversial in Iceland and Liechtenstein than in Norway.[36] Norway shared some of its EFTA partners' concerns, but adopted a much more positive stance towards the Directive. Although Liechtenstein generally agreed with Iceland's view, it had additional concerns. Prior to the adoption of the Directive, Liechtenstein had a special arrangement for the free movement of persons provisions stating that only a certain number of persons per year could obtain a residence permit. There were quite substantial restrictions regarding the free movement of persons due to the country's small size, and it was afraid that the new Directive would challenge these special arrangements. On this basis, and also as a matter of principle, Liechtenstein argued that the Directive should not be considered EEA-relevant.[37]

The Norwegian view was that the practical effects of the new legislation were miniscule.[38] They had already adopted most of the rules required by the Directive and so they could not see the problem. Unlike Iceland and Liechtenstein, they did not think it mattered that the new rules would be based on the EEA Agreement and not national legislation.[39] As outlined by officials in Liechtenstein:

> Norway was always of the opinion that they could live with the Directive. With regard to their national legislation they were already in conformity, so they thought it wouldn't be difficult to implement it. For us and for Iceland it was more a question of principle not to mix immigration issues with free movement of persons issues and we wanted to be very clear on that point.[40]

It was very difficult for the EFTA states to agree on a common position regarding this Directive. This problem has arisen more frequently in recent years because the EU has changed its method of developing new policies. As noted, instead of adopting narrowly defined legal acts, it now develops broad-based policies which include a number of different measures, some of which go beyond the EEA and the internal market as it was conceptualized at the time when the EEA Agreement was signed.[41] In some cases, Norway has been more interested than its EFTA partners in taking on policies even though they are not totally within the strict formalistic borders of the EEA. Iceland and Liechtenstein have taken a more formal, legal approach and have been rather hesitant to incorporate new measures as a matter of principle because it sets a precedent. They argue that once you start broadening the scope of the EEA you do not know where you will end up and that this is not what the national parliaments of the EFTA states agreed to when they adopted the EEA Agreement.[42]

Any decision to suspend the EEA Agreement will impact all of the EFTA states, and so it would seem likely that the reluctant state(s) would be under some degree of pressure from its EFTA partner(s) to agree to the EU's demands. However, in this case representatives from both Iceland and Liechtenstein generally agreed that it was the EU side that posed an obstacle, rather than Norway. Although Norway had separate views, they did not put pressure on the others to change their opinion, rather the process was very civilized and polite.[43] It is also important to bear in mind that no vital interests in Norway depended on the adoption of this Directive, which may have meant they were fairly relaxed about delays. As noted by one official:

> Even though the interests of the EFTA states don't always coincide, they respect the fact that there can be problems in any of the other states because it happens to us all. Its not like we are always the ones with the problem. Sometimes the Norwegians need our support. So everyone usually agrees when it comes to delaying the adoption of a piece of legislation. It is not in the interest of any of the EFTA states to always try to be on top. Though of course we can't deny that the Norwegians are very big in this context and they know it. But Iceland and Liechtenstein have been able to have their way too, in some cases. The obstacle is usually not any of the other EFTA partners. It is always the EU side that needs to be convinced. The three EFTA states work very well together and they realize that it is in their interest to support each other. So they speak with one voice opposite the EU even though the EU always knows which state has the problem.[44]

Another official explained:

> If you have special interests you obviously try to promote these interests within EFTA. In some cases this may be important for us. But generally the tougher negotiators are from the EU side, not from the other EFTA states. We seek to avoid open conflict, which means we would rather

postpone things than address them head on. We are only three countries but sometimes we spend quite some time arriving at a common position. I think this partly has to do with the political culture. Also, we don't have the same decision-making procedures as the EU. They have QMV which means you can be out-voted. In EFTA there is no QMV, we operate by consensus.[45]

In the end, the citizenship/free movement issue was discussed at all levels within the EFTA framework for over three years. The EU repeatedly asked whether the EFTAns were making any progress and in return they would ask questions about how this and that would work in the context of the EEA.[46] The EFTAns attempted to get exemptions from various aspects of the Directive, mainly to do with the independent right of third-country nationals to settle in EEA states.[47] However, it was the EU's view from the beginning that the Directive should be wholly incorporated into the EEA Agreement. That opinion never changed and it was not flexible with respect to any adaptations.[48] As noted by a Commission official:

Sometimes our stance is that things should be EEA-relevant because we want them in. In these cases, we don't discuss the legal details. It is relevant because we say it is relevant. That was the case with respect to this Directive.[49]

As time wore on, the EU officials grew tired of the deadlock and invoked the dispute-settlement clause foreseen in Article 102 of the EEA Agreement,[50] which states that, if agreement on incorporating a piece of EU legislation into the EEA Agreement cannot be reached, the Joint Committee shall examine 'all further possibilities to maintain the good functioning of this Agreement', with the view to reaching an accord before a suspension of Agreement takes place within six months. The matter was not, however, solved until the end of October 2007, a year after the conciliation process had begun. A Commission official explained that in the end they had considered this Directive so important for the internal market that they had no choice but to start the conciliatory process referred to in Article 102. This process went on for almost a year, so in theory they should have introduced measures to suspend the relevant part of the Agreement.[51] According to an EFTA official, the conciliation process was fairly informal. The process was invoked at one of the Joint Committee Meetings and stopped again when the Directive was incorporated into the EEA Agreement. There was never anything written.[52] Another official noted that the Commission was generally reluctant to cause problems and gave the EFTA states considerable leeway with this Directive and were not very harsh.[53]

During the conciliation phase there were many meetings with EU officials. Finally the EU threatened to discontinue certain aspects of the EEA Agreement about free movement under the suspension clause in Article 102 if it was not adopted.[54] The EFTA side then had to make a decision whether to discontinue the cooperation. As noted by an Icelandic official: 'In the end what could we do? We agreed to adopt this Directive and continue EEA cooperation and that is that.'[55] Officials from Liechtenstein expressed a similar view, noting that the outcome was a result of political negotiations: 'We certainly wanted to go a step further with the adaptations, but the strength of the EU convinced us to take it over.'[56]

As an Icelandic Ministry of Justice official noted, Iceland and Liechtenstein were in a weaker position as there was no united EFTA position:

> When there is disagreement, you win some and you lose some. Especially when there is no agreement on the EFTA side and the EU has an uncompromising position. It is easier for them when there is disagreement among the EFTAns. They set a time limit for finding a solution and so we had to reach an agreement.[57]

Iceland and Liechtenstein did, however, insist on a special declaration accompanying the adoption of the Directive so it should not set a precedent for future legislation.[58] The Joint Committee Decision (no. 158/2007) incorporating the Directive into the EEA Agreement therefore includes a few disclaimers stating that the concept of 'Union Citizenship' is not included in the Agreement and neither is immigration policy and that the EEA Agreement does not provide a legal basis for political rights. Furthermore, the incorporation of the Directive into the Agreement will not form a basis for evaluating the EEA-relevance of future EU legislation or case law based on the concept of EU citizenship. The Decision also notes that the EEA Agreement does not apply to third-country nationals, with the exception of those who are family members of EEA nationals exercising their right to free movement, as these rights are corollary to the right of free movement of EEA nationals.

An EFTA official admitted that this was really only a technical change replacing the term 'EU nationals' with 'EU citizens'.[59] The Counsellor for Justice and Home Affairs at the Icelandic Mission to the EU also noted that the declaration was a bit strange as it said immigration policy was not part of the EEA Agreement but with that same decision immigration laws were being revised.[60] Liechtenstein, did however, manage to hold on to its restrictions on residence permits,[61] so the negotiations were not a complete disappointment for the EFTA side.

As noted, the suspension clause in Article 102 has never actually been put to the test. The Citizenship Directive is one of the few cases in which the conciliation process potentially leading to suspension has been activated. Based on this case, it seems that Article 102 provides a fairly strong incentive to conform to the EU's wishes. Nevertheless, EFTA representatives argue that the repercussions of Article 102 are vague and maintain that in this case it was never clear whether part of the EEA Agreement would have been suspended.[62] As explained by one official:

In reality we still don't know what the repercussions of a refusal would be. This is also being debated in Norway with respect to the Services Directive. No one really knows what would happen if an EFTA state refused to adopt a piece of legislation which the EU thinks is EEA-relevant. They say that a portion of the EEA Agreement would be suspended, but it is all very unclear. For example, would it only refer to free movement of services? Would it mean all legislation up until that point was still valid but nothing on top of that? It has never been tested, even though the Free Movement Directive was one of the closest calls. But during that process it was never made clear exactly which measures would be taken in the event of a no vote from the EFTA states. We always reach a solution even though this can take a long time. This one took many years. But, what right do the EFTA states actually have to say 'No'? Whether this is really possible and what implications it would have has never been tested, because people always look for a solution.[63]

Another official noted that the EFTA states had been very clever when they drafted the EEA Agreement, because they made it virtually impossible to apply Article 102. The Community at the time the EEA Agreement was negotiated wanted a much tougher automatic mechanism, whereby, if the EFTA states did not adopt the *acquis*, that area would be suspended automatically. But Article 102 has a conciliation procedure, whereby a certain period of time lapses and then discussions take place on which areas are actually affected. Another question is whether all parties to the Agreement have to agree to suspension. If so, the process could take an endless amount of time.[64]

EFTA officials also argue that the EU has an incentive to maintain good, structured, pragmatic and predictable relations with its neighbouring states, and the EEA gives it that. The EEA Agreement is arguably very easy for the EU to maintain as the EFTA states do most of the work themselves through the EFTA institutions. The negotiations and preparation of new acts and all the surrounding procedures are very rational and streamlined, and so it is very efficient from a civil service point of view. As expressed by one official:

It is a very convenient agreement for the EU. As long as we are not members of the EU they need to organize their relations with us. I do not think the EU is interested in maximizing a conflict because this would have consequences for the political opinion in the EFTA states, so in fact they are quite careful too. But it is a delicate balance. They have initiated the procedure, but without going further than just invoking it. There is some speculation about what could have happened. If we don't accept it and they would go all the way, there is no mechanism for us to appeal to a court arguing that they are in breach of the Agreement. In my view both sides have a clear interest in avoiding that this happens.[65]

110 *European citizenship and free movement of persons*

The same official noted that there might easily be a situation where Article 102 would be put to the test if things went on as they were with conflicts becoming more frequent. Perhaps it would be a good thing to find out what would happen, but of course it could also wreak havoc in the system. It also depended on the nature of the legislation in question. If it related to an important part of the *acquis*, it would be more dramatic. Sometimes this had been compared to dropping an atomic bomb.[66]

A Commission official agreed that it would be difficult to implement Article 102 and was relieved that they did not have to in this case. Nevertheless, he insisted that the relevant parts of the EEA Agreement would have been suspended: 'In my understanding a right of veto is a right to say no without consequences. In this sense the EEA EFTA states do not have a veto right.'[67] In sum, it is unclear what would have happened if the supsension clause of Article 102 had been invoked, and both sides have an interest in avoiding it.[68] Although neither party wants to test it out, the EFTAns, in particular, are afraid they would lose out in such a confrontation.[69]

On 7 December 2007, the Citizenship Directive was incorporated into the EEA Agreement and transposed at the national level in the EFTA states. Interestingly, Norway actually lagged behind Iceland and Liechtenstein in transposing the Directive, despite supporting its incorporation into the EEA Agreement.[70] The transposition phase went relatively smoothly in the Icelandic Parliament and the relevant changes were adopted in June 2008, within the six-month timeframe which the EFTA states have to transpose acts that have been incorporated into the EEA Agreement. ESA seems to have followed the process fairly closely and even commented on an aspect of the Icelandic proposal which the government then amended.[71] On the whole, the new legislation appears to meet all the requirements of the Directive.[72] The relevant changes have, for example, been made to the Act on Foreigners (no. 96/2002) regarding the right of third-country nationals who are family members of EEA citizens, residence permits, permanent residence rights and deportation requirements.

In this sense, Iceland seems to have downloaded the Directive more thoroughly than many of the EU member states. A report commissioned by the European Commission found that the overall transposition of Directive 2004/38/EC was far from satisfactory. Not one of the member states had transposed the Directive in an effective and correct manner. In most member states considerable parts and crucial aspects of the Directive were wrongly or not transposed (Milieu Ltd and Edinburgh Europa Institute 2008).

Conclusions

The concept of citizenship is one of the issues currently being extended to the supranational level within the framework of the EU. However, its impact is not limited to the European Union. European citizenship has been a particular bone of contention in negotiations between the EFTA states and the

EU regarding the extension of the EEA *acquis*, as citizenship is technically not meant to be part of the EEA Agreement. The adoption of the Directive on the right of citizens of the Union and their family members to move and reside freely within the territory of the member states almost caused a suspension of the certain parts of the Agreement, as Iceland and Liechtenstein were unwilling to adopt it. However, in the end the Directive was incorporated into the Agreement and has now taken effect in the EFTA states. This chapter has examined the deadlock between the EFTAns and the EU regarding the adoption of the Directive, with the end result highlighting the EU's leverage over the EFTA states and the strength of Article 102 as an incentive for incorporating EU acts into the EEA Agreement, which is an important first step in the downloading process for the EFTA states.

The EU has evolved considerably in the past years. Although the EEA Agreement was meant to remain static and focused on the internal market, it appears that in many ways it has been impacted by the EU's evolution. As expressed by one Icelandic official: 'Many things are now in the EEA Agreement that no one would have thought of when it was first signed. Sometimes we feel a little bit like we have got our glove caught in the shredder and we have to yank our hand back.'[73] Another official noted: 'They are always extending the EEA further and further. The EEA is often described as a tsunami. There was a gap that got bigger and bigger and now it is a flood.'[74]

Icelandic officials have expressed concern over this rapid development:

> The EEA Agreement includes certain areas and should not automatically be able to grow out of control. It should not be a unilateral decision of the EU to expand the Agreement. This is an agreement between two parties, but not something they decide and control.'[75]

Nevertheless, the EFTA states appear to be relatively helpless to control it. The right to veto was considered extremely important when the EEA Agreement was being ratified by the Icelandic Parliament.[76] Furthermore, because of concerns over sovereignty, legislation adopted by the EU does not automatically become part of the EEA Agreement, but must be agreed in the EEA Joint Committee. Many would, however, argue that this is all a mere formality. It is not the case that the EFTA states have any sort of real veto power as they do not have the right to refuse without considerable consequences. As they are very dependent on their access to the internal market, it is perhaps not surprising that they have never risked the consequences of suspending the Agreement. Norway has, however, recently indicated that it will refuse to incorporate the third Postal Services Directive into the Agreement, but at the time of writing the consequences of such an action are not yet known.

In some ways it could be argued that the EFTA states are condemned to download EU policies. However, it is important to bear in mind that the downloading process does not end with the incorporation of acts into the

EEA Agreement. As noted in Chapter 3, incorrect transposition and implementation failure incur relatively mild sanctions compared to the threat of suspension which applies to refusal to incorporate acts into the EEA Agreement. Nonetheless, it seems that Iceland has at least correctly transposed the Directive into its national legislative framework. Perhaps this is because the EFTA Surveillance Authority paid close attention to the national transposition process. Another reason could be that the measures required by the Directive were not highly controversial or politically flammable, although they were perhaps in some ways slightly inconvenient. This can therefore be interpreted as a case of accommodation to the EU's demands, and the Europeanization process appears to be having an impact on Iceland in an area that was not foreseen at the outset.

6 The Emissions Trading Scheme

In the past two decades the EU has increasingly sought to portray itself as a global environmental leader (Wettestad 2009: 313). Environmental issues make up a large portion of its agenda and their importance has been growing in recent years. As environmental policy was part of the old pillar I and was considered an important flanking policy to the internal market, it was included within the scope of the EEA Agreement. Iceland's participation in the EEA therefore means that it adopts nearly all the EU's environmental *acquis*. EEA-relevant legislation has, for example, been passed regarding pollution, waste disposal, and evaluation of environmental impact (Umhverfisraduneytid 2008).[1] In fact, this is considered one of the policy areas that has been most heavily impacted by the EU and it is estimated that as much as 70–80 per cent of Icelandic environmental legislation originates at the EU level.[2] One official described the change as 'a revolution in environmental affairs'.[3]

Because of the growing importance and substance of environmental policy within the EEA, the Icelandic foreign service's resources have increasingly been dedicated to lobbying in this field (Utanrikisraduneytid 2007: 13). One of the most extensive campaigns relates to the Emissions Trading Scheme, which is aimed at regulating greenhouse gas (GHG) emissions and establishes a system allowing trading of emission allowances within the Union. Companies are allocated emission permits which represent the right to emit a specific amount of GHGs. If they need to exceed that amount they must purchase excess allowances.

The ETS Directive (2003/87/EC) in its original form did not have much practical impact on Iceland, as most of the industries covered by the scheme were not present in Iceland. Nevertheless, adoption of the scheme into the EEA Agreement arguably infringed on Iceland's ability to conclude international agreements. An important aspect of sovereignty is being able to negotiate agreements with other sovereign states. As the EU member states have officially pooled their sovereignty in some areas, the EU frequently negotiates agreements with third countries on their behalf. These are not meant to be binding on the EFTA states. However, in some cases the EU transforms its international conventions into EU legislation, which it then deems to be EEA-relevant and expects the EFTA states to adopt. The ETS is one of these cases as it is meant to put the EU's obligations under the Kyoto Protocol into practice. Meanwhile, Iceland had negotiated a separate agreement under Kyoto allowing it to increase emissions, and so implementing the ETS system, as proposed by the EU, would potentially undermine its right to negotiate its own international agreements. In addition, this Directive has undergone several revisions since it was first adopted and further expansion is foreseen. The extension to include the aviation sector was an area of grave concern to the Icelandic government (Directive 2008/101/EC). Because of Iceland's isolated location, its aviation emissions are considerably greater than in countries on or closer to the mainland.

The EU ETS is problematic for Iceland in several other ways. In 2009 aluminium, which is a major industry in Iceland, was incorporated into the ETS (Directive 2009/29/EC). Furthermore, from 2013 the allocation of emissions allowances will be centralized at the EU level. Due to sovereignty issues and the fact that EU institutions are not meant to have direct control over the EFTA states, this system poses challenges with respect to the EEA framework. At the time of writing, the 2009 extension of the Directive had not yet been incorporated into the EEA Agreement, and so this chapter will focus primarily on the original Directive and its expansion to the aviation sector. In line with the Europeanization framework and the overall objectives of this book, this chapter will explore both Iceland's attempts to upload its preferences to the EU level and the downloading of the Directive at the national level.

The chapter begins by looking at the main objectives and requirements of the EU ETS, including changes potentially posing difficulties for Iceland. Thereafter, the debate between Iceland and the EU over the incorporation of the original Directive into the EEA Agreement is analyzed. As the initial framework Directive was incorporated into the Agreement, all subsequent revisions have also been considered EEA-relevant. Thus, although the original Directive did not substantially affect Icelandic interests, the expansion of the ETS to include aviation activities was set to have a considerable impact. The following section of the chapter therefore explores Iceland's attempts to have an input at the EU level so that the amending Directive incorporating aviation into the scheme would include special consideration for ultra-peripheral regions. Finally, the process of downloading the Directive at the national level is evaluated. Iceland opposed the initial incorporation of the Directive into the EEA Agreement and it could perhaps be argued that domestic adaptation was less than adequate, at least at the outset.

What is the EU ETS?

The EU considers the ETS to be a key policy in the fight against climate change. It is a 'cap and trade' system, in that it sets a limit to the overall level of emissions allowed and enables participants to buy and sell allowances within that limit.[4] In this way, member states allocate allowances to plants covered by the scheme in accordance with historical emissions, while also taking into consideration reduction commitments. Companies must then demonstrate that the extent of their emissions are covered by their allowances (Braun 2009: 470). Those that emit less than their total allocation can sell their excess allowances, while those that emit more must either take measures to reduce their emissions or buy extra allowances on the market (European Commission 2008). The EU ETS is the first large-scale international emissions trading system (Wettestad 2009: 311). At the end of 2008, it covered over 10,000 installations in the energy and industrial sectors which were responsible for almost half of the EU's CO_2 emissions and 40 per cent of its total GHG emissions (European Commission 2008).

The ETS is linked to the Kyoto Protocol, which commits industrialized countries to reduce their emissions of GHGs (UNFCCC 2010b).[5] Under the Kyoto Protocol, the EU agreed to reduce its targets jointly by 8 per cent below 1990 levels during the period 2008–12. The aim of the EU ETS was to provide a cost-effective way for EU member states to achieve their Kyoto commitments together (European Commission 2008). The Commission proposed the establishment of a European ETS in June 1998 in the wake of the adoption of the Kyoto Protocol. The proposal was followed by a Green Paper in 2000, a draft proposal in 2001 and finally a binding Framework Directive in 2003 (Braun 2009: 470). The so-called Linking Directive (2004/101/EC) created a formal tie between the EU ETS and the Flexible Mechanisms of the Kyoto Protocol, i.e. the Joint Implementation and Clean Development Mechanism. Companies undertaking emission-reduction projects outside the EU through these mechanisms would thus be able to convert their credits into EU ETS allowances (European Commission 2005a).

The EU ETS was formally put into practice on 1 January 2005. The first trading period ran from 2005–07, the second one from 2008–12 and the third one is due to begin in 2013. The first trading period was a pilot phase to prepare for the commitment period of the Kyoto Protocol which began in 2008. During the commitment period the EU and other industrialized countries are required to meet certain targets to limit GHG emissions. EU emissions were capped at around 6.5 per cent below 2005 levels in the 2008–12 period to ensure that it would meet its Kyoto obligations (European Commission 2008).

A key element in the ETS implementation process is deciding the upper limit for the emissions included in the ETS (Wettestad 2009: 311). The original ETS was fairly decentralized in the sense that member states were in charge of national allocations in line with their national emissions caps. They were required to formulate National Allocation Plans (NAPs) to determine the total quantity of CO_2 emissions they would grant to their companies and decide how many allowances each plant covered by the ETS would receive (European Commission 2005a; Wettestad 2009: 311). The Commission then acted as a watchdog, ensuring that NAPs were in line with Kyoto targets and adhered to the other criteria set out in the Directive, and could reject NAPs if the criteria were not observed (Wettestad 2009: 313–14). This decentralized system led member states to allocate too many allowances to protect their own interests, although the Commission was able to counteract over-allocation to some extent (Skjaerseth and Wettestad 2009: 115–16). For the third phase the cap-setting process will be centralized at the EU level, which means that there will no longer be NAPs. The Commission will set a single EU-wide cap and allocate allowances on the basis of harmonized rules. The total number of allowances will then decrease annually (Skjaerseth and Wettestad 2009: 117). As noted, EFTA participation in the scheme requires an acceptable solution for the allocation of allowances, which does not entail the EFTAns directly ceding power to the Commission.

In addition to becoming more centralized in nature, the ETS now covers a larger range of industries. One of the biggest changes was an amendment agreed in July 2008 (2008/101/EC) which brings the aviation sector into the system from 1 January 2012 (European Commission 2008). This change obliges airline operators to cap their fleet emissions during the year 2012 at 97 per cent of a predetermined benchmark based on 2004 emission levels. The quantity of allowances allocated decreases further in subsequent years.[6] Thus, although the emissions allowances are fairly generous to begin with, they decrease progressively over the years. The extension of the ETS has met with considerable resistance in the aviation sector, which has argued that the attention given to its emissions are not in proportion with the size of its contribution to global warming (Forster 2009). To demonstrate their performance, airlines must calculate fuel uptake, leftover fuel, fuel temperature, specific gravity and a range of other variables in accordance with an elaborate reporting and verification process which is long and costly (Taverna 2009).

The EU, on the other hand, considered the limitation of emissions from aviation to be an essential component of reaching its commitment to reduce GHG emissions to at least 20 per cent below 1990 levels by 2020.[7] As noted, the incorporation of the aviation sector into the ETS is set to have a proportionally greater impact on Iceland than most other European countries due to its isolated location and the absence of alternative transport links to the rest of Europe. Further expansion of the ETS to include maritime operations and aluminium and ferrosilicon production could also have a substantial impact on Iceland (Bragadottir 2008: 46–47) as it has a large fishing and cargo fleet, while aluminium smelting production is one of Iceland's largest industries. Therefore, there is a great deal of concern in Iceland over the development of the ETS.[8] The ETS is a fluid, constantly changing system. As it is now part of the EEA Agreement, future developments will potentially impact heavily on Iceland (Umhverfisraduneytid 2008). The following sections trace the incorporation of the original ETS into the EEA Agreement. Thereafter, Iceland's uploading attempts to gain an exemption for ultra-peripheral regions in the aviation sector are explored and finally the extent to which the ETS has been put into practice or downloaded at the national level is discussed.

Incorporation of the ETS into the EEA Agreement

When the proposal for the first ETS Directive came forward, it was not marked as EEA-relevant by the Commission, which, according to one EU official, was an oversight.[9] At that time, the EFTA states also discussed the scheme between themselves. Norway and Liechtenstein did not think it should be considered EEA-relevant and, as it had not been marked relevant by the Commission, the Icelandic government stopped worrying about it and did not attempt to have any impact on the proposal during the formulation stages, as they did not think it would be incorporated into the EEA Agreement.[10]

In the later stages of the legislative process the Commission changed its mind and argued that the ETS did in fact have high internal market relevance and should be incorporated into the EEA Agreement,[11] believing that companies would be able to flee to Iceland or the other EFTA states in order to escape the quota system.[12] Initially all of the EFTA states were sceptical and argued that the ETS would infringe on their international treaty obligations, i.e. Kyoto.[13] As officials from Liechtenstein noted: 'All three countries had doubts. There were legal reasons for this, but there was also the question of whether we wanted it in and whether we could avoid it by the EEA-relevance discussion.'[14]

During the course of the negotiations, Norway had a change of heart and became quite enthusiastic about incorporating the Directive into the EEA Agreement.[15] This was most likely because the Confederation of Industries in Norway realized that, by becoming part of the scheme they would not have to pay the carbon dioxide tax that they had been paying in Norway and they would then be in a similar competitive position to companies elsewhere in Europe. As a result, they lobbied the Norwegian government to incorporate the Directive into the EEA Agreement.[16] Furthermore, Icelandic officials believe that Norway generally wants to portray itself as an environmental leader and saw this as a step in that direction.[17] Although the EFTA states by and large have good relations with each other, the Emissions Trading matter caused some tension between Norway and Iceland after Norway's position had altered.[18] Liechtenstein had also looked more closely at the Directive and decided that it would not be heavily impacted by the ETS and so it would not oppose it. Liechtenstein's financial sector had also spotted opportunities in being part of the scheme, as they could purchase excess allowances while the market was new and sell them again when the emissions limit was further reduced and allowances became more scarce.[19]

In the end, Iceland was therefore the only EFTA state that had any reservations about making the Directive part of the EEA Agreement. This was primarily because of its pre-existing international agreements. As noted, the Directive was largely intended to help EU states meet their obligations under the Kyoto Protocol through a burden-sharing system which the Commission negotiated on behalf of the EU member states.[20] The EU agreed to an 8 per cent reduction as a whole compared to the 1990s' rates during the first commitment phase (2008–12). The member states share these obligations, but the reduction is not split equally between states. Thus, the EU member states spent a considerable amount of time deciding amongst themselves how to reach the EU's joint Kyoto targets, where some states would be allowed to increase their emissions and others would have to decrease them substantially.[21] In fact, prior to the Kyoto negotiations Iceland had asked to be part of the EU system, but was refused on the grounds that it was not part of the EEA Agreement.[22]

Iceland thus negotiated its own agreement at Kyoto, which allowed it to increase its emissions by 10 per cent.[23] The 2001 UN climate talks in Marrakech finalized most of the operational details of the Kyoto Protocol and set the stage for the ratification process. In Marrakech, Decision no. 14/CP.7 on the impact of single projects on emissions was agreed upon, which is also informally called the 'Icelandic clause' (Bragadottir 2008: 12–13).[24] The Decision recognizes Iceland's concerns that, for countries with very low emissions, a single project such as the construction of an aluminium smelter, can lead to a disproportionate percentage increase in emissions. It therefore allows states that meet certain criteria to exclude single projects from their total emissions during the first commitment period, provided they use renewable energy (UNFCCC 2010a). This was based on the small size and uniform nature of the Icelandic economy; it would not have been possible for Iceland to reduce its emissions as outlined by the Kyoto Protocol as the reduction obligations would have prevented Iceland from realizing projects that were already on the agenda.[25] Furthermore, the vast majority of Iceland's energy consumption is fuelled by renewable resources and therefore it was argued that, even though Icelandic industries were using more energy, they were still more environmentally friendly than plants elsewhere in the world that are run on oil and coal.[26]

With respect to the EU ETS Iceland, therefore, felt that it would in essence be losing its autonomy to negotiate international agreements on how it fulfils its obligations under Kyoto if it were required to adopt the EU scheme.[27] This was a rather complicated state of affairs, as one EFTA official explained:

> On one hand you have the ETS which impacts on the internal market, but on the other hand it is related to Kyoto obligations, which is an international agreement, so it is very complicated in relation to the EEA Agreement.[28]

Another official noted:

> The ETS is very technical and comprehensive. It is related to the Kyoto Protocol and the EEA EFTA states' participation in the system is linked to their obligations under the Kyoto Protocol. This makes it all quite complicated when it comes to incorporating the ETS into the EEA Agreement.[29]

EU officials were, however, adamant that the Directive should be incorporated into the EEA Agreement. Officials from Liechtenstein recalled that they were very clear on this matter:

> They said it was EEA-relevant because they wanted it in and did not want to discuss any of the legal details. This was probably a manifestation of the EU's vision of itself as a world environmental leader which meant that it did not want any blank spots within its field of influence. They also thought it might be too complicated to have two regimes within the EEA. For these reasons they were very strict on making sure that the EFTA states joined the scheme.[30]

The Commission admitted that the incorporation of the ETS Directive into the EEA Agreement had taken a great deal of haggling. One official noted that this was one of the hardest battles they had ever fought in the EEA and that they had been under a great deal of pressure to finalize the deal as the first phase of the ETS system was drawing to a close by the time the Directive was finally taken into the Agreement.[31] In the end, the EU side threatened to invoke Article 102, which ultimately foresees a suspension to the relevant part of the EEA Agreement, and so Iceland gave in.[32] On 26 October 2007 the Directive was incorporated into the EEA Agreement (JCD no. 146/2007) and as of 1 January 2008 the ETS has applied not only to the 27 EU member states, but also to the three EFTA members of the EEA (European Commission 2008).

The Directive was not, however, adopted without certain exemptions and clauses to appease Iceland. At that time, the ETS covered only specific types of operations such as combustion plants, oil refineries, coke ovens, iron and steel plants, and factories making cement, glass, lime, brick, ceramics, pulp and paper (European Commission 2005a). Because of this fairly limited coverage, only a very small portion of Iceland's greenhouse gas emissions actually fell under the scheme at the time of its incorporation into the EEA Agreement (Utanrikisraduneytid 2007: 15). Almost no companies in Iceland would therefore have been affected by the original ETS Directive.[33] Iceland was also able to negotiate an exemption for combustion installations with a rated thermal input exceeding 20 MW (megawatts) but which had reported emissions to the competent authority of less than 25,000 tonnes of carbon dioxide equivalent. The exemption was, however, only valid as long as the emissions from these installations were less than 25,000 tonnes per year and as long as ESA received proof that the installations followed the rules outlined in the Directive (Bragadottir 2008: 42). The result was that no Icelandic company fell under the scheme and so Iceland did not have to submit an NAP.[34] The incorporation of the original Directive, therefore, had a limited impact in Iceland. As one Icelandic official stated: 'We were able to solve the problem with the exemptions we achieved, so it was acceptable to us.'[35]

120   *The Emissions Trading Scheme*

The reason Iceland received an exemption was that such a small number of plants fell under the scope of the Directive: only ten fishmeal plants, of which just eight were functioning, as well as the back-up generators of one aluminium plant and one electricity company.[36] It would not have been cost-effective to set up a complicated system around such a small number of companies with relatively low emissions. Furthermore, various EU member states had already had problems with small operators such as these and new proposals had been made to exempt them from the scheme, so Iceland's exemption corresponded with plans that were already in motion at the EU level. Finally, the EU's main objective was to get Norway to join the system and it was prepared to grant exemptions to Iceland to ensure that the Directive was made part of the EEA Agreement.[37]

In addition to the exemptions, paragraph 10 of the Joint Committee Decision incorporating the ETS into the EEA Agreement states that:

> The different situation applicable in the EFTA states needs to be taken into account, particularly Iceland's commitments under Kyoto as Iceland has notified that it avails itself to the provisions of Decision 14/CP.7 of the Conference of the Parties to the Kyoto Protocol on the impact of single projects on emissions in the commitment period.

Paragraph 12 further clarifies that:

> The Decision does not affect the autonomy of the Contracting Parties with respect to international negotiations on climate change, in particular the UN Framework Convention on Climate Change and the Kyoto Protocol, other than in respect of the instruments incorporated by this Decision into the EEA Agreement. However, the EFTA states shall take due account of the obligations they have undertaken in the EEA Agreement.

Certain considerations were thus granted by the EU to Iceland in order to facilitate the incorporation of the ETS into the EEA Agreement, and Iceland's position with respect to Kyoto was also formally acknowledged in the Joint Committee Decision text. Nevertheless, the end result was that the ETS was incorporated into the EEA Agreement, which meant that all future developments of the ETS were likely to be considered EEA-relevant. As noted, the ETS is far from static in nature. Although Iceland gained an exemption from various aspects of the Directive, developments in this area move at a rapid pace. The expansion of the ETS to include aviation activities is one of these areas. These planned changes triggered an extensive uploading campaign during which Iceland attempted to impact the Aviation Directive, as will be explored in the following section.

Special recognition for ultra-peripheral regions?

The Commission proposal to revise the ETS scheme to include aviation caused a great deal of concern in Iceland (Umhverfisraduneytid 2008). Around the time that the proposal came forward, 80 large aeroplanes were registered in Iceland and it was estimated that their emissions were proportionally substantially higher than those of other European countries due to Iceland's location in the middle of the North Atlantic (Utanrikisraduneytid 2007). Officials at the Foreign Ministry noted that Iceland was in a completely different position from states on or closer to the mainland, as Iceland was much more isolated and there was no alternative but to fly in order to get anywhere.[38] Rising costs of air travel would therefore have a significant impact, not only on the Icelandic tourism industry, but also on the price of imported goods, upon which Iceland is highly dependent, and the price of exported goods would become less competitive.[39] The government thus made it a high priority for Iceland to participate in the shaping of this Directive (Umhverfisraduneytid 2008). However, the main attempts at uploading seem to have been made at the later stages of the decision-making process, after the proposal had been passed to the Parliament and the Council.

The Commission first outlined a strategy for including aviation in the ETS in September 2005.[40] In its Conclusions of 2 December 2005, the Council agreed that the inclusion of this sector in the ETS was the best way forward and asked the Commission to formulate a legislative proposal by the end of 2006. In its resolution of 4 July 2006, the European Parliament also recognized that aviation should be brought into the scheme, provided that its inclusion was appropriately designed. Icelandic experts did not participate in the formulation of this proposal,[41] despite the fact that the Icelandic government had become aware of the proposal quite early on. The Confederation of Icelandic Employers learned of the proposed changes through its ties with BUSINESSEUROPE and notified the government of its potential detrimental effects and urged it to lobby the EU. The government began to take action little by little, but its main campaign only began at the later stages of the decision-making process.[42] This rather late engagement may have been due to the fact that, when the proposal first came forward, the ETS had not yet been incorporated into the EEA Agreement and so it was still unclear whether Iceland would have to adopt these changes. Capacity issues may also have played a role. Whatever the reason for the late start, it may have decreased Iceland's chances of success as it is generally agreed that it is more difficult to impact legislation in the later stages of the decision-making process.

In mid-November 2007 the EP voted on the Commission's proposal and suggested changes to it. The EP proposed that all airlines should be required to have enough allowances for emissions required for all commercial flights within the EU and between the EU and third states from 2011. According to the proposal, the total quantity of allowances to be allocated to aircraft operators should be set at 90 per cent of the baseline emissions of the years 2004–06, and 25 per cent of the allowances should be auctioned. This would mean that all airlines that aimed to emit more than 75 per cent of the 90 per cent average from 2004–06 would have to buy allowances for excess emissions. Among the EP's proposed changes included a compromise between the environmental and the transport committees which stated that flights from 'ultra peripheral regions' should be given special consideration (Utanrikisraduneytid 2007).[43]

The EP did not specifically define the concept of ultra-peripheral regions, but the original proposal probably came from Portugal, with regions such as the Azores and Madeira in mind, and so was most likely intended for peripheral regions within member states, but not for entire states.[44] Nevertheless, Iceland believed that a clause such as this could apply to it and from that moment its lobbying efforts were aimed at making sure that a clause on ultra-peripheral regions which was applicable to Iceland would be part of the final Directive. The Icelandic Counsellor for Transport recalled that the EP had left a certain opening for Iceland after its first reading by noting that ultra-peripheral regions should get special consideration.[45]

The Icelandic government pursued a comprehensive campaign around this issue focused on all of the EU institutions as well as many of the member states. It prepared a memorandum endorsing the clause and outlining Iceland's unique position with respect to travel to and from the country. The Icelandic Mission to the EU arranged meetings to present Iceland's view within the Council, key member states and the Commission, and to the EP rapporteurs as well as its EFTA partners. The issue was also brought up at pre-council meetings of Nordic and Baltic transport and environment ministers, and Iceland sent information to, and arranged special meetings with, the permanent representations of potential allies such as Spain, Portugal, France, Germany and Finland (Utanrikisraduneytid 2007: 15).[46] As noted by one official:

> Our Ministers spoke to their counterparts in the EU member states, as is common practice when big important issues come up. The Minister for the Environment has been in touch with many colleagues in the EU, particularly those that might have similar interests, and we have sent letters to the Ministries of Environment, Transport and Foreign Affairs all over Europe to promote our cause.[47]

Iceland often focuses a large portion of its energy on lobbying its Nordic neighbours. In this case, however, the Nordic states were not very enthusiastic supporters of Iceland's cause and were reluctant to pursue the matter in the Council on Iceland's behalf. According to one official, this was most likely because Iceland's preferences did not correspond with their priorities. The Nordic states have seen themselves as environmental leaders so, although they understood Iceland's point of view, their support was lukewarm.[48]

In addition to the Nordic states, the Commission has traditionally been a primary target for the Icelandic government when pressing its case at the EU level. In this instance Icelandic government officials voiced their opinions about the proposed Aviation Directive at EFTA working group meetings attended by the Commission and also arranged for a Commission representative to go to Iceland and meet with stakeholders, authorities and the general public. According to Icelandic officials, cooperation with the Commission is generally good. If they ask them about something, they always get a response, and the Commission is often prepared to help if need be.[49] However, it is debatable how effective the strategy of lobbying the Commission is in the later stages of the decision-making process, when the matter is mainly in the hands of the Parliament and the Council.[50]

One of the most interesting aspects of this campaign is the extensive attention which Iceland paid to lobbying the Parliament and its environmental and transport committees, much more so than on any other previous occasion. Traditionally, Iceland has focused its attention mainly on the Commission and its Nordic allies, but it appears that the government is becoming more aware of the growing importance of the EP.[51] In this case, the Minister for Transport met with various MEPs and the Ambassador met with the rapporteurs of the environment and transport committees of the EP.[52] The Counsellor for Transport presented Iceland's view at working group meetings organized by the rapporteur of the environmental committee.[53] Icelandic MPs also tried to promote Iceland's position among MEPs in the Joint EEA Parliamentary Committee,[54] while the Confederation of Icelandic Employers' representative in the EEA consultative committee made Iceland's views know through that channel.[55]

According to Icelandic officials, the European Parliament was seriously considering the option that special consideration should be made for ultra-peripheral regions[56] and they were also very happy with the reception they received when lobbying the Parliament in comparison to the Council. One official noted that they had been able to take their comments to the EP at any stage of the process and that it had been very open to Iceland's views. The weakness was that Iceland did not have any access to the Council.[57] Another official also felt that in this case Iceland had been granted considerable access to EU institutions, particularly the Parliament. Government officials had met with many MEPs, which was a relatively new strategy but was considered a positive development. In general, he felt that the reception was good if Icelandic officials exerted themselves to arrange meetings. There was recognition that Iceland was part of the internal market and so there was interest in its views.[58]

Despite Iceland's efforts, a suitable clause for ultra-peripheral regions was not adopted at second reading. The Environmental Council met to discuss the proposal at the end of 2007. They agreed that aviation should be taken into the scheme, but proposed that the quota should be 100 per cent of the average of 2004–06 and that 10 per cent of the quota should be auctioned. The suggestion of the EP regarding ultra-peripheral regions was not adopted unchanged. The Council only wanted to exclude flights that were run as a public service or in regions where the yearly number of seats was under 30,000. This meant that only certain domestic flights in Iceland would be exempted, but not any of the international flights (Utanrikisraduneytid 2007).

At the Council meeting the environmental ministers of Malta and Cyprus argued that special consideration should be made for island states with few other alternatives but air travel. This proposal was rejected, although a clause was added which states that the Commission should write a report before 1 June 2015 which assesses the effects of the scheme on islands and peripheral regions within the EU (Utanrikisraduneytid 2007: 16). The Icelandic government continued to apply pressure for the inclusion of the clause on ultra-peripheral regions during the second reading phase. In this vein, it initiated work in cooperation with interest groups and stakeholders on analysing the impact of the proposed legislation for Iceland (Utanrikisraduneytid 2007: 16).

Iceland's efforts do not seem to have had much impact. Following a series of meetings between MEPs and the Slovenian Presidency of the Council, the two sides were able to agree on the details of how to include aviation in the EU Emissions Trading System (Zalewski 2008). A second reading in the European Parliament took place in July 2008 and the Directive was adopted on 19 November 2008. The key points agreed were that all flights starting and/or landing in the EU would be included in the ETS from 1 January 2012. Eighty-five per cent of emissions certificates would be allocated for free and 15 per cent would be auctioned. Based on airlines' average annual emissions in 2004–06, emissions would be cut by 3 per cent in 2012 and by 5 per cent from 2013 onwards. Some flights would be exempted from the scheme, including light aeroplanes, flights for humanitarian purposes under a UN mandate, emergency flights, police, customs and military flights, research flights and small airline companies producing low emissions (Duffin 2008).

The position adopted by the EP at second reading did not grant any exemptions to ultra-peripheral regions, although their potentially difficult position was mentioned. The final Directive (2008/101/EC) states that:

> By 1 December 2014 the Commission shall, on the basis of monitoring and experience of the application of this Directive, review the functioning of this Directive in relation to aviation activities in Annex I and may make proposals to the European Parliament and the Council pursuant to Article 251 of the Treaty as appropriate. The Commission shall give consideration in particular to: (f) the impact of the Community scheme on the structural dependency on aviation transport of islands, landlocked regions, outermost regions and peripheral regions of the Community.

Despite the lack of uploading success, there was a general view within the Icelandic administration that they had conducted a good campaign, although there was some frustration regarding Iceland's lack of access to EU decision-making institutions, particularly the Council. As noted by one official: 'Even though we didn't get any tangible results, the government went all out and did its best. We don't have direct access to the EU institutions, after all, so we can't always expect to win.'[59] Another explained: 'We have many potential ways to make our views known, but of course these are kind of lobbyist ways because we don't sit at the table where the actual decisions are made.'[60]

Once the Directive had been adopted by the EU, the question arose as to whether Iceland should attempt to gain any special considerations during its incorporation into the EEA Agreement. Prior to negotiations, most Icelandic officials appeared to be relatively pessimistic about being able to gain any special consideration for ultra-peripheral regions. One official noted that this would be difficult, as none of the EU states had received special consideration for their ultra-peripheral regions.[61] As the EU did not accept the views of Malta and Cyprus, it would be difficult for Iceland to receive special treatment.[62] They also appeared to have a relatively tough stance on aviation.[63] One official conceded that Iceland might just have to pay for its relatively high aviation emissions. After all, it was a global problem that was being tackled.[64] The line from the EU prior to negotiations was that they considered aviation to be an important part of the scheme, but that they would examine the matter with the EFTA states.[65]

It also appears that the Icelandic government had become less pessimistic regarding the potential detrimental effects of the Directive. One official explained that the Icelandic aviation sector had contracted in recent years and might shrink even more by 2012, so perhaps Iceland's emissions quota would be sufficient to cover all flights to and from the country. Furthermore, Icelandair had very recently renewed its fleet so they were fairly efficient in terms of emissions. In fact, it was one of the most environmentally friendly fleets in the world, which would put them in a strong position when the scheme was adopted. Therefore, the official noted that perhaps Iceland did not need any adaptations or special considerations for aviation and the government should save its energy for other issues.[66] Finally, a centre-left government came to power in the spring of 2009, which generally adopted a more environmentally friendly stance than its predecessor. At any rate, a decision was made by the Icelandic government not to apply for exemptions or adaptations for ultra-peripheral regions. The incorporation of the ETS Aviation Directive into the EEA Agreement did meet with some delays. However, this was due mainly to difficulties in finding a solution regarding the allocation of emissions allowances which adequately respected the two-pillar system of the EEA Agreement and the sovereignty of the EFTA states.[67]

The ETS Aviation Directive was incorporated into the EEA Agreement on 1 April 2011 (JCD no. 6/2011). With respect to the allocation of emissions allowances, the Decision states that the EEA Joint Committee shall decide on EEA-wide historical aviation emissions, the total number of allowances, the number of allowances to be auctioned, the number of allowances in special reserve and the number of free allowances, based on figures provided by ESA in cooperation with Eurocontrol (The European Organisation for the Safety of Air Navigation). The calculations of historical emissions for the EFTA states are made using the same methodology as for the EU-27 (European Commission 2012). The Commission then decides on the EEA-wide benchmark values which are used to allocate greenhouse gas emission allowances to aircraft operators free of charge. The Commission's benchmark decisions are incorporated into the EEA Agreement by the EEA Joint Committee and thereby extended to the EFTA states. Emissions from all domestic and international flights arriving at or departing from an EEA airport are thus covered by the EU Emissions Trading System as of 2012. The JCD incorporating the Directive into the EEA Agreement did not contain any special adaptations for ultra-peripheral regions. Icelandic airlines are therefore not exempted from the ETS system and all airlines in the EEA have to purchase allowances for their GHG emissions from 2012. This will potentially have a considerable impact on the Icelandic aviation sector.

Implementation at the national level – or lack thereof?

In this section, the focus reverts to the original ETS Directive which was incorporated into the EEA Agreement in 2007 and came into effect in the EEA in 2008. Although Iceland received some exemptions from the Directive, it did place certain obligations on Iceland. This section explores the extent to which these requirements have been downloaded. At the time of writing, the revision of the ETS to include aviation activities had not yet been put into practice, and so it is too early to evaluate the practical implementation of the ETS Aviation Directive. Nonetheless, some changes to the national legislation have already been made in order to transpose the Directive, which will be explored further in this section.

The ETS Directive places two sets of obligations on states. First, to distribute emissions allowances to the companies that fall under the scope of the Directive and second, to allow individuals and legal entities to trade allowances on the internal market (Bragadottir 2008). Companies may trade allowances with each other or buy and sell via a broker, bank or other intermediary. An electronic registry system keeps track of ownership of emission allowances as they change hands (European Commission 2005a).

The Icelandic exemption meant that Iceland would not need to distribute emissions allowances or form a National Allocation Plan as long as the conditions set out in the Joint Committee Decision were met. However, the question remains whether Iceland was exempted from assuring conditions for individuals and legal entities to conduct unobstructed trade in allowances on the internal market. Bragadottir (2008) argues that, despite the exemption received by Iceland from the first obligation, it does not appear that it should have been exempted from creating conditions for allowing trade in allowances. In order to ensure that trade in allowances can be conducted, it is necessary to establish a registration system which is tied to that of the EU member states and allow anyone who wishes to conduct trade to set up an account (Bragadottir 2008: 42–43).

According to Bragadottir, there was considerable misunderstanding in the Icelandic Parliament regarding Iceland's obligations to transpose the Directive. In discussions in Althingi regarding the incorporation of the Directive into the EEA Agreement it was stated that, as long as Icelandic emissions from the companies included in the scheme did not exceed 25,000 tonnes per year, the Directive would only take effect if any new installation exceeded this limit. Furthermore, if the scope of the Directive were expanded to include more sectors and gas types, the Directive would need to come into effect. The Minister of Foreign Affairs stated that, until that time, Iceland would not need to transpose the Directive (Bragadottir 2008: 44). An act on GHG emissions, which set up an allocation system for emissions allowances to industries emitting more than 30,000 tonnes of CO_2 per year, was adopted by the Icelandic Parliament in 2007 (No. 65/2007). This system was, however, unconnected with the EU ETS (Umhverfisstofnun 2010).

Bragadottir argues that, according to Article 12 of the Directive, which deals with transfer, surrender and cancellation of allowances, the interpretation of Icelandic politicians was incorrect (Bragadottir 2008: 44). Furthermore, a Commission Regulation (2216/2004/EC) especially outlining the implementation of a standardized and secured system of registries had been incorporated into the EEA Agreement in October 2007 at the same time as the Directive. Arguably, Iceland should therefore have introduced some changes at the national level despite having received an exemption from certain aspects of the Directive. It was clear that, if conditions in Iceland changed or if the scope of the Directive was expanded, amendments to Icelandic legislation would need to be made. However, in order to assure the interests of companies that might want to pursue any of the activities mentioned in the Directive, it should perhaps have been made clear from the start which rules applied in Iceland instead of waiting until something new happened to make the Directive applicable. Furthermore, arrangements should have been made in the Icelandic legal framework to allow trade in allowances on the internal market. It could thus be argued that Iceland was in breach of the EEA Agreement at the time (Bragadottir 2008: 44–45).

It was, however, clear that the Icelandic government was preparing to implement the EU's requirements with respect to aviation and the ETS as a whole. In December 2009, a Commission Decision (2009/339/EC) on the monitoring and reporting of aviation activities was incorporated into the EEA Agreement (JCD no. 148/2009), and the EFTA States commenced their monitoring and reporting in January 2010 (European Commission 2012). The Environment Agency had also arranged various meetings with stakeholders in the aviation sector to make them aware of their rights and obligations, should the ETS Aviation Directive be adopted (Umhverfisstofnun 2010). Furthermore, in July 2009, the Ministry for the Environment set up a committee with the purpose of preparing an action plan to ensure that Iceland reduced its GHG emissions by 19–32 per cent by the year 2020. According to the draft action plan issued in December 2009, the main recommendation of the committee was that Iceland should fully implement and align its legal framework with the EU ETS as this would provide industry with the necessary incentives to reduce their GHG emissions (Umhverfisraduneytid 2009).

According to the report the scheme did not at the time have much impact in Iceland and hence it had not been transposed into Icelandic legislation. However, it was foreseen that this would change in coming years. The report noted that, from 2012, aviation activities would be included in the scheme, and aluminium production from the year 2013. If these changes were incorporated into the EEA Agreement, over 40 per cent of Icelandic emissions would fall under the scheme. The report recommended that Iceland participate fully in the scheme, which would mean that Icelandic emissions reduction commitments would take into account the decisions of the EU regarding reductions for the period 2013–20. Heavy industry in Iceland was already obliged to apply for emissions permits in accordance with Icelandic law, but from 2013 this would most likely be part of the EU ETS through the EEA Agreement, which would involve a system change which the Icelandic government and Icelandic companies should prepare themselves for. According to the report, it appeared that the government had reconciled itself with these imminent changes and considered it natural for Icelandic heavy industry to submit to the same rules and requirements as other comparable companies throughout Europe (Umhverfisraduneytid 2009). Here again, it is important to note that a centre-left government with green credentials came to power at the beginning of 2009. It is unclear whether the previous right-leaning government that was in power during Iceland's uploading campaign would have accepted these pending changes as willingly.

With respect to Kyoto, the report observed that participating in the EU ETS raised various questions related to Iceland's status under the Kyoto Protocol, i.e. that participation in the ETS could clash with its international obligations. However, according to the report the Icelandic government was of the view that a dual system could be problematic for Icelandic industries and that the most simple and viable solution would be to participate fully in the EU ETS (Umhverfisraduneytid 2009). Therefore, in general it appeared that the new Icelandic government had adopted a rather positive stance towards the scheme.

Indeed, soon after the ETS Aviation Directive had been incorporated into the EEA Agreement, the Icelandic Parliament adopted an act (no. 64/2011) amending the legislation on greenhouse gas emissions and transposing both the original ETS Directive and the Directive extending the scheme to aviation activities. The new legislation pre-empted the expansion of the scheme, foreseeing that from 1 January 2013 all operators falling under the system would be required to hold emissions permits issued by the Environment Agency of Iceland as a prerequisite in order to qualify for the allocation of emissions allowances for the period 2013–20. A new chapter was also added specifically on emissions allowances in the aviation sector which would be put into practice on 1 January 2012. Furthermore, the legislation foresaw the establishment of a registration system to track the issue, holding, transfer and cancellation of allowances. It therefore seems that, despite an arguably slow start, Iceland will become a full participant in the EU ETS through the EEA Agreement.

Conclusions

This chapter explored Iceland's attempts to upload its preferences to the EU level with respect to the EU ETS as well as the downloading of the scheme at the national level. In line with the key questions posed in this study, an attempt has been made to gauge whether a non-member state such as Iceland can in fact leave its mark on the policies it is required to adopt and whether the tools provided for in the EEA Agreement are generally strong enough to ensure domestic adaptation to EU requirements.

Iceland opposed the initial incorporation of the ETS Directive into the EEA Agreement, arguing that the system infringed on its pre-existing international agreements under the Kyoto Protocol. However, its EFTA partners Norway and Liechtenstein favoured participation in the ETS, and the EU was also adamant that the scheme was highly relevant to the internal market and so should be included in the EEA Agreement. In the end the Commission threatened to make use of Article 102 which would potentially have involved a partial suspension of the EEA Agreement and so Iceland had little choice but to agree to the incorporation of the Directive, although the process was delayed and drawn out. Iceland was also able to secure certain special considerations, as it was able to negotiate an exemption for the very limited number of companies which would have fallen under the scheme at the time. Nonetheless, by incorporating the Directive into the EEA Agreement, Iceland was arguably surrendering its right to conclude its own international agreements to a certain extent. Much like the citizenship case in the previous chapter, this case also demonstrates the strength of Article 102 and the asymmetry of power inherent in the EEA Agreement.

Furthermore, as discussed in the previous sections, the Emissions Trading Scheme is not static, but is constantly being extended to include more and more industries. As the original Directive had become part of the EEA Agreement it was apparent that any expansions building on or amending the ETS would also be considered EEA-relevant. One academic has noted that the expansion of the ETS to include aviation was one of the harshest examples of the EEA impinging on Icelandic interests as, due to Iceland's isolated location, its aviation sector emits proportionately more GHG than those in other European countries.[68] The Icelandic government conducted an extensive lobbying campaign at the EU level focusing on each of the EU institutions in an attempt to ensure that a special clause for ultra-peripheral regions was included in the Aviation Directive. This campaign was unsuccessful and according to the Directive ultra-peripheral regions are subject to the same requirements as others. Despite lack of success, this case does show that Iceland's uploading strategies are becoming more sophisticated, particularly with the new and increased focus on the European Parliament. However, whether or not strategies are sophisticated is of limited importance if they do not deliver tangible end results, and it cannot be said from this case that Iceland is an effective decision-shaper in the EU policy process.

With respect to downloading the Directive at the national level, the Icelandic government arguably neglected its obligations to begin with. Although Iceland received certain exemptions from the original Directive, arrangements should have been made in the legal framework to allow trade in emissions allowances on the internal market. This was not done by the centre-right government which was in power when the Directive was incorporated into the EEA Agreement. Nonetheless, more recent reports commissioned by the new centre-left government indicated that Iceland began actively preparing for the implementation of the ETS once it had been expanded to include more industries which were relevant to Iceland such as aviation and aluminium smelting. In June 2011 an act was adopted by the Icelandic Parliament transposing the original Directive as well as the Directive extending the scheme to aviation activities. This change in policy could, however, to some extent be traced to internal political changes by which an environmentally friendly left-leaning government came to power in 2009, but not wholly from pressure emanating from the European level.

Thus far, it seems the Directive has had limited impact at the national level, but it is likely that its future impact will be substantial. In line with the Europeanization framework, the level of domestic adaptation can therefore be grouped as accommodation with a future potential for transformation. It is clear that the EEA framework was at least strong enough to ensure the incorporation of the ETS into the EEA Agreement, which provided a basis for significant change at the national level. When it came to putting the policy into practice at the national level, domestic adaptation was at first thwarted, but later facilitated by a change in government where the new leaders had more environmentally friendly views. In addition, domestic change had become more pressing due to the expansion of the scheme to new activities. This case, therefore, appears to highlight the importance of favourable domestic conditions in the downloading process, in addition to European level pressures.

7 The Food Law Package

Any mention of the so-called 'Food Law Package' carries with it a certain sense of foreboding among those who have overseen its progression through the EEA policy process. To date, it is among the most challenging legislative packages to have been incorporated into the EEA Agreement, involving substantial tension both between Iceland and the EU as well as between EFTA partners Iceland and Norway. It may even prove to be a sticking point in Iceland's accession negotiations with the EU. Unlike the other cases explored in this volume, which focus on single comprehensive pieces of framework legislation, this chapter looks at a bundle of acts grouped together under the common heading of 'Food Law'. This area underwent substantial reform in the early 2000s leading to the adoption of the General Food Law Regulation in 2002 (178/2002/EC), which lays down the general principles and requirements of food law, establishes the European Food Safety Authority (EFSA) and defines procedures in matters of food safety. This Regulation establishes an overarching legal instrument upon which subsequent acts are based. The entire package includes a number of amending acts, implementing acts and other related initiatives, namely the hygiene and control package[1] and rules on animal by-products.[2] In general, these measures aim to ensure a high level of food safety at all stages of the food chain.

Much of the EU's Food Law contains veterinary and phytosanitary (plant health) measures which are included in Annex I of the EEA Agreement. Chapter I of the Annex, which deals with veterinary issues, is particularly extensive, containing a range of acts from animal welfare to public health and control measures. Prior to the adoption of the Food Law Package into the EEA Agreement, Iceland had an exemption from most of this chapter, i.e. it only implemented measures relating to aquaculture and fisheries products. This general exemption was revoked with the incorporation of the package into the EEA Agreement, obliging Iceland to adopt most acts in this field. The review of Chapter I of Annex I for Iceland significantly expanded the scope of its adoption of EU policy, making all EU legislation concerning animal products applicable to Iceland.[3] However, this case is not one of quiet submission to new EU rules. Both the incorporation of the package into the EEA Agreement and the adoption at the national level were subject to

132 *The Food Law Package*

considerable delays, negotiations and special solutions. Indeed, although the Food Law Package was transposed at the national level, it appears that the contents of the national legislation deliberately included only those parts of the package which were deemed acceptable.

A key question posed by this study is whether domestic adaptation to EU requirements is inevitable in Iceland, given the asymmetry of power between the EU and the EFTA sides of the EEA Agreement and Iceland's dependence on its access to the internal market. Previous chapters have found that the potential threat of partial suspension of the Agreement has been sufficient to ensure the incorporation of EU legislation into the EEA Agreement, although Iceland has in some cases been able to gain certain adaptations. In these cases, incorporation of acts into the Agreement has generally led to the transposition and implementation of the acts at the national level, although domestic support (or at least lack of domestic opposition) has also played an important role in the downloading process. This case offers a different scenario, which merits attention. There was considerable opposition to the package among high-level members of the government, as well as influential interest groups in society, and the downloading phase was slow, problematic and incomplete.

In line with the Europeanization framework of this study, this chapter begins by examining the background leading up to the debate and the mismatch between the EU and the national levels. Why did Iceland have an exemption from Chapter I of Annex I, why did it resist adopting legislation in this area and why did the EU push for its adoption? The following section looks at Iceland's uploading attempts. Iceland did not make a concerted effort to influence the content of the legislation during the decision-making phase at the EU level. However, it did make a substantial attempt to secure various adaptations during the incorporation of the package into the EEA Agreement. Finally, the focus of the chapter turns to the downloading phase at the national level, paying particular attention to delays, the EU's threat to revert to an Article 102 procedure and the content of the implementing legislation. After almost a decade of debate, it is unlikely that this matter has been fully laid to rest. Concluding remarks will therefore also contain some reflection as to what the next steps in the process might be, particularly in light of Iceland's application for EU membership.

Mismatch between the EU and national levels

As the previous chapters have shown, the EU's policy domains have expanded over time and the content of the EEA Agreement has generally evolved correspondingly, often requiring the EFTA states to adopt legislation which they perhaps did not envisage when the Agreement first came into effect. Originally, the food and veterinary legislation adopted at the EU level did not apply to any of the EFTA states.[4] However, in 1997, there was a change of policy in Norway as it decided it would like to adjust its national legislation to EU requirements. A report from the Norwegian Ministry of Foreign Affairs cites various reasons for Norway's decision. The fact that the EFTA states were not party to the EU's veterinary legislation meant that trade with such products was difficult. Therefore, there was considerable pressure on the government from exporters to adopt the legislation. Furthermore, the former EFTA states, Sweden, Finland and Austria, had by that time joined the EU and Norway wanted to be able to trade more easily with its Nordic neighbours. The World Trade Organization (WTO), of which Norway was a member, had also begun adopting increasingly comprehensive legislation in this area which generally corresponded to the EU framework, making it more desirable for Norway to be part of that system (Det Kongelige Utenriksdepartment 1999). Finally, it is likely that Norway had become accustomed to the idea of adopting this legislation during its accession negotiations with the EU.[5] In response to Norway's request, the EU agreed to a revision of the contents of Chapter I, Annex I in 1998 (JCD no. 69/98). Accordingly, it was decided that all outstanding acts in the veterinary field which were of EEA relevance would be incorporated into Annex I of the EEA Agreement: a total of 644 new acts.[6]

Being a far more isolated market, Iceland did not share Norway's view on the desirability of expanding the EEA Agreement to all animal products. Nevertheless, Iceland was eager to be able to sell its fisheries products freely on the internal market.[7] Thus it was decided that the acts incorporated into Chapter I would only apply to Iceland if this were especially agreed upon. In practice this meant that Iceland only adopted acts related to aquaculture animals and products and fisheries products in order to ensure that it could export them to the EU. Annex I on veterinary and phytosanitary measures was not made applicable to Liechtenstein due to its participation in the Agreement between the EU and the Switzerland on trade in agricultural products. So, in practice, Annex I, Chapter I was mainly only applicable to Norway.

The adoption of the General Food Law Regulation and related acts in 2002–04 marked a considerable change in the EU's method of legislating in this policy area. With the package, the EU adopted a much more 'integrated approach', which aims to ensure a high level of food safety, animal health, animal welfare and plant health and is characterized by 'farm-to-fork' measures. In other words, the new legislation is now designed to cover all steps of the food chain, including feed production, primary production, food processing, storage, transport and retail sale (European Commission 2010a). This change in policy style is to a certain extent part of a more general trend which has been evident in other areas over recent years towards adopting more comprehensive 'horizontal' legislation which covers a wider range of areas. Another more specific reason for this change was increasing concern over BSE (commonly known as mad cow disease) and dioxin contamination in food products on the European market. Following a series of food crises in the late 1990s, the EU felt it was necessary to take measures in order to prevent such products from entering the market and regain the trust of consumers. Because food products could become contaminated at any stage of the food chain, it was deemed necessary to adopt comprehensive measures which cover the whole production process (Gunnarsdottir 2010). As a result, the Commission published a White Paper on Food Safety in 1999, followed by a proposal for a Regulation on Food Law in 2000. The Food Law Regulation, adopted in 2002, includes specific requirements for food business operators as well as rules on monitoring of safety, ensuring the traceability of food and feed and setting up response measures in case of food safety problems. It also sets up a special European Food Safety Authority as an independent source of scientific advice and communication on risks associated with the food chain (European Commission 2010a).

None of the new measures related to increased hygiene and safety were particularly controversial in Iceland. In fact, Iceland signed up to EEA EFTA comments which were sent to the EU institutions on 10 May 2001, generally praising and supporting the EU's initiatives to restore and maintain confidence in food safety. The comments did include some suggestions to clarify whether the labelling of food materials should be included on the package and proposed a slight change of wording of one of the Articles of Regulation (EC) no. 178/2002. However, their main aim was to ensure full EEA EFTA participation in EFSA.

The reason Iceland was eager to maintain its exemption from most aspects of Chapter I, Annex I thus had little to do with the content of the Food Law Package as such. Rather, Iceland's resistance was related to the fact that adopting the package would mean that it could no longer preserve its import ban on animal products from the EU. The main underlying motivation for the Food Law Package was after all to approximate food and feed safety requirements in order to prevent hindrances to the free movement of these products on the internal market. Although generally a full participant in most aspects of the EU's internal market, Iceland preferred to keep animal products outside the scope of its participation. Protectionism towards Icelandic producers who were afraid of competition from cheaper products imported from the EU is probably the main reason for this stance. There was also fear that, as Icelandic livestocks had been isolated for so long, they would be particularly susceptible to diseases brought in from the mainland.[8] In this context, it is important to bear in mind that the CAP is not part of the EEA and Article 8(3) limits the coverage of the Agreement with respect to agricultural products. Therefore, Icelandic farmers would still enjoy some level of protection. However, the EEA Agreement does contain certain provisions concerning trade in agricultural and fish products and, with the incorporation of the Food Law Package into the Agreement, Iceland would not be allowed to maintain a ban on imports.[9]

The EU, on the other hand, felt that its new comprehensive strategy spanning the entire food production cycle was incompatible with an 'à-la-carte' approach, as it would be impossible to separate measures pertaining to fish from those relevant to other animal products. Iceland would therefore either have to adopt the entire package as Norway had, or remain completely outside it, like Liechtenstein. The latter option would have had a devastating effect on Iceland's trade in fisheries and aquaculture products and so this was not considered an acceptable alternative. The disagreement between Iceland and the EU led to a prolonged deadlock regarding the incorporation of the package into the EEA Agreement and its adoption at the national level, as will be explored in the following sections.

Incorporation of the Food Law Package into the EEA Agreement

From the beginning it appears that the EU was reluctant to allow Iceland to be exempt from most acts in the veterinary field and had been applying pressure on Iceland to adhere to this legislation well before the adoption of the Food Law Package. In its view there was an imbalance between Iceland and the EU concerning the EEA Agreement in the veterinary sector, and Iceland should adopt acts for more products than fish.[10] The original decision of 1998 to incorporate veterinary acts into the Agreement contained a clause stating that the situation for Iceland should be reviewed in 2000. When the time came to discuss a potential revision of Iceland's exemption, Iceland informed its EFTA partners and the Commission that they had looked into the matter and concluded that they wanted to prolong their derogation. EU officials, on the other hand, argued that, in the spirit of the EEA Agreement, Iceland should begin taking over the veterinary *acquis* little by little. The fact that Iceland had to be considered a third country for certain food products but not for others was confusing and impractical. Therefore, it would greatly improve the situation if Iceland decided to extend the *acquis*.[11] Despite some grumbling of this nature, the EU did not insist on a review of Iceland's derogation at this point in time.[12]

The situation changed with the coming into effect of the new Food Law Regulation in 2002. At this point the EU became adamant that a review of Chapter I of Annex I for Iceland was necessary, whereby Iceland would adopt all legislation concerning products of animal origin. Soon after the adoption of the General Food Law Regulation, discussions began within the EEA framework as to its incorporation into the EEA Agreement, resulting in lengthy and difficult negotiations between the EU and the EFTA states which were ongoing for five years, from 2002 to 2007.[13] The EU side maintained that, due to its new horizontal mode of legislating, it would no longer be possible for Iceland to participate in certain areas of veterinary law and not others. Furthermore, they argued that the review clause for Iceland in the 1998 Joint Committee Decision to incorporate veterinary acts into the Agreement justified their stance. As one Icelandic official recalled:

> The Commission said that this was an all-inclusive package and if we didn't adopt it, we wouldn't be able to ensure the free movement of fisheries and

aquaculture products. As a result, the Icelandic government appointed a committee to examine the legislation and negotiate with the EU.[14]

Norway was eager to adopt the package into the Agreement and in the end became impatient with the delayed negotiations process between Iceland and the EU. At an internal meeting between the EFTA states in June 2007, Norway voiced its disappointment in having to repeatedly withdraw participation in EFSA from the budget as the fact that the Food Law Package was not part of the EEA Agreement meant that EFTA experts could not participate. Furthermore, Norway stated that they had never been happy with the proposal to finish negotiations between Iceland and the EU before incorporating the package into the EEA Agreement. It would have been a better solution for Norway to adopt the regulations into the Agreement from the beginning with an adaptation for Iceland, which would later be negotiated bilaterally.[15] Unlike the citizenship case, concrete interests were at stake both in Iceland and Norway. It therefore appears that Iceland was also under some pressure to adopt the package from its EFTA partner.

Various proposals and counter-offers from each side were made throughout the negotiations and in the end the most contentious issues had to be cleared at the highest levels within the Commission.[16] The negotiations resulted in five Joint Committee Decisions which were adopted on 26 October 2007 and reflected a degree of compromise between the EU and Iceland. First, it was decided that Iceland should adopt the acts referred to in Chapter I of Annex I, except for the provisions concerning live animals, other than fish and aquaculture animals and animal products such as ova, embryo and semen. Maintaining a ban on imports of live animals was a particularly important issue for Iceland due to the susceptibility of Icelandic livestocks to disease. One veterinarian argued that importing live animals from Europe could have a similar impact on Icelandic live stocks to that which was felt by native populations in the Americas when Europeans first set foot on the continent. Iceland was thus able to convince the EU that there was a valid scientific reason for hindering the import of live animals into the country.[17] However, EU officials have since hinted that negotiations regarding the application of legislation concerning live animals to Iceland should be reopened, while Iceland has maintained that it should retain third-country status in this respect.[18]

Furthermore, the EU agreed that Iceland could continue to feed fishmeal to ruminants.[19] At a meeting of the Joint Working Group on Veterinary Matters, the Commission claimed that the purpose of the ban on fishmeal was not that it considered it to pose a risk to ruminants, but rather that there was a risk of cross-contamination between fishmeal and animal products. However, fishmeal is the main source of protein for ruminants in Iceland and a very important industry. At the meeting the Icelandic delegation argued that there was no risk of cross-contamination in Iceland, since the processing plants for products of animal and fish origin were separate.[20] In the end Iceland's campaign for a derogation for fishmeal was successful. This debate did, however, have to be settled at the highest political level, requiring the intervention and approval of the relevant Commissioner.[21]

Thus Iceland maintained its ban on the import of live animals as well as its hard-fought right to be allowed to use fishmeal in animal feed. In addition, Iceland received a transitional period of 18 months from the entry into force of the package in order to comply fully with the provisions it was required to implement, despite concerns that this would create uncertainties, for example regarding Iceland's participation in EFSA.[22] It is likely that this transitional period was granted for practical reasons because, in addition to having to adopt the new Food Law Package, Iceland would also have to implement all relevant pre-existing *acquis* which had been incorporated into the EEA Agreement in this area, numbering hundreds of acts.

The end result can therefore be interpreted as a partial success for Iceland. Nevertheless, in effect the incorporation of the Food Law Package into the EEA Agreement meant that Iceland would have to take over the bulk of the acts referred to in Chapter I of Annex I, which would allow the import of animal products into Iceland. Therefore, much like the other cases explored in this book, this case also highlights the ability of the EU to ensure that its policies are made part of the EEA Agreement, notwithstanding considerable delays. However, it is not enough for acts to be incorporated into the EEA Agreement in order for them to take effect. They must also be transposed into national legislation and implemented appropriately. As noted, in this case, the downloading process proved to be far from straightforward.

Adoption at the national level

The Food Law Package was adopted by the EEA Joint Committee on 26 October 2007, five years after it came into effect at the EU level. However, it did not enter into force in the EFTA states at that time as both Iceland and Norway had constitutional requirements meaning that a change of national law was necessary in order for them to implement the package. According to Article 103 of the EEA Agreement, the EFTA states have six months to adapt their legislation to Joint Committee Decisions, so in this case the deadline was 26 April 2008. As noted in Chapter 3, similar to Article 102, which relates to the incorporation of acts into the EEA Agreement, Article 103 also contains a clause stating that, if they fail to notify on time, the relevant parts of the EEA Agreement can be provisionally suspended.[23] Despite this, the Icelandic legislation was not adopted until December 2009, more than two years after the incorporation of the package into the Agreement.

Legislative proposals to transpose the package were introduced to the Icelandic Parliament several times, failing to gain support on each occasion. During this time, Iceland frequently updated its EFTA partners and the EU on the status of the national debate, as they grew increasingly impatient with the delay. At a meeting of the Joint Veterinary Working Group on 18 April 2008, the EFTA Secretariat noted that Iceland and Norway should make sure that the package would enter into force by 1 July 2008 in order to ensure their participation in the European Food Safety Authority (EFSA) in 2008. Both the Norwegian and Icelandic delegations indicated that they would strive to fulfil parliamentary procedures by the end of May. The EU asked to be notified as soon as the parliamentary procedures had been fulfilled.[24]

By June 2008 Norway had fulfilled its constitutional requirements. Iceland, on the other hand, noted that a legislative proposal transposing the package had been submitted for first reading in the Parliament during the spring, but that it would not be passed before the summer recess, and so discussions would resume in the autumn. This meant that the EFTA states would not be able to participate in EFSA in 2008, as the cut-off date for participation in the budget was in July.[25] By November 2008, the bill had not yet been reintroduced to the Parliament, although Iceland informed its EFTA partners that it hoped this would be done by the end of the year.[26] It is, however, important to note that the autumn of 2008 was not a run-of-the-mill period in Icelandic politics, as the country's banking system collapsed in October that year. Therefore, it is perhaps unsurprising that there were other more pressing items on the Parliament's agenda at the time.

In the summer of 2009, Iceland hinted that the bill to implement the Food Law Package and related *acquis* might be passed by the Parliament during the summer session. However, this was not to be, and the bill was not reintroduced until 13 October 2009. On 27 October, Iceland reassured the other parties to the EEA Agreement that the package was being dealt with as a matter of the highest priority in the Icelandic Parliament and was being considered by the Fisheries and Agriculture Committee.[27] The bill finally passed through second reading on 15 December and was adopted on 18 December 2009 (Act no. 143/2009).

The Food Law Package contained framework legislation, along with various related amendments and implementing acts. Since the adoption of the package into the EEA Agreement, a large number of legal acts had been adopted by the EU which amended or depended on the acts in the Food Law Package. These acts could not enter into force before the framework legislation. The delay by Iceland therefore led to a large backlog of acts in the food and veterinary area that were taken into the EEA Agreement but were not adopted at the national level, as they were dependent on the entry into force of the Food Law Package. Thus, the content of the EEA Agreement did not correspond to the legal situation at the national level, which made it somewhat unclear which legislation was applicable in the EEA.[28]

In the spring of 2009 the EU refused to incorporate any new relevant acts in this area into the Agreement until the package had come into effect, meaning that the full backlog was even more extensive (Store 2009). This meant that a large part of the food and veterinary legislation applicable in the EU was different from that of the EFTA states, which is contrary to the aim of homogeneity in the EEA and potentially causes problems for the placing of products from the EFTA member states on the internal market. This case thus shows how the delays in adopting a particular piece of legislation can have much broader consequences for the whole policy area.

During the transposition process, the EU side underlined the importance and urgency of finalizing constitutional procedures in Iceland and voiced concern about the growing gap between the rules that applied in the EU and those that applied in the EEA Agreement.[29] They felt that a point had been reached where some might question whether the EEA Agreement was functioning properly and even suggested that further delays could cause problems for Iceland's exports of fish to the EU.[30] Despite formally taking a tough stance in meetings, the EU was relatively lenient in some ways. For example, experts from the EFTA states were allowed to participate in the scientific panels of EFSA, even though the legislation was not yet in place. Furthermore, despite a delay of over two years in adopting the act, the suspension clause allowed for in Article 103 was not invoked. Perhaps their patience was to some extent due to the chaotic situation in Iceland in light of the financial crisis which erupted in October 2008. At a meeting of the EEA Joint Committee on 25 September 2009, the EU representative said that he recognized that the Icelandic parliamentary and administrative systems had faced considerable challenges over the past year.[31]

The language of the EU did, however, become sharper as time wore on, warning of the seriousness of the matter and the consequences that might arise from the delays. At the same meeting of the Joint Committee on 25 September, the EU official even cautioned that the suspension procedure could potentially be initiated if delays continued. He noted that it was unfortunate that parliamentary procedures had postponed the entry into force of the Food Law Package, especially since the adoption of the package into the EEA Agreement had been a long and difficult process resulting in a 'finely balanced' compromise. He also mentioned the problems related to the ever-increasing backlog and growing gap between the EU and the EEA. Therefore, it was essential to ensure a swift finalization of the Icelandic parliamentary procedures. Finally the official expressed hope that Iceland would be able to provide more precise information on the status of parliamentary procedures at the next meeting of the Joint Committee.[32]

In addition to the EU, there was also some degree of pressure from Norway on Iceland to download the package at the national level. As noted by a Norwegian official:

> The delay from Iceland meant that the legislation in the package could not enter into force in Norway either. For Norway it was a matter of high importance to have this legislation in place in the EEA context. At various internal EFTA meetings, Norway expressed its concerns regarding the delays.[33]

The Food Law Package was finally transposed into national legislation on 18 December 2009. As noted, failure to notify the fulfilment of constitutional requirements can lead to a partial suspension of the EEA Agreement, and so the EFTA states have never refused to incorporate legislation into the EEA Agreement or transpose it at the national level. The end result in this case also seems to underline the relative strength of the EU's leverage, although the processes of both incorporation and transposition were significantly delayed in this case. However, Iceland's notification did not signify the end of the controversy surrounding the Food Law Package. Despite having notified fulfilment of constitutional requirements, it is highly debatable whether the contents of the legislation actually complied with EU requirements. The following section looks in greater detail at the debate at the national level and the substance of the national legislation which supposedly transposed the package.

The national debate and content of the implementing legislation

The adoption of the Food Law Package implied that Iceland would participate fully in the internal market as regards animal products, and could no longer apply national legislation concerning these products. As outlined in the previous section, Iceland was under considerable pressure from the EU and also to some extent from Norway to adopt these measures. The EU had also threatened to invoke Article 103, which could have led to a partial suspension of the EEA Agreement. This posed a significant dilemma for Jon Bjarnason, the Eurosceptic Minister of Agriculture and Fisheries, who took office in May 2009 as part of a centre-left coalition.[34] He was one of the staunchest opponents of the Food Law Package due to his strong ties with the agricultural community, which lobbied extensively against the adoption of the package. In fact, while he was in opposition he had argued fervently against the adoption of the package.

Before the new government took office, Bjarnason's Conservative predecessors had attempted to pass legislation more or less in compliance with the EU initiatives. However, when the new Left Green Minister took office he decided on a change of tactic, i.e. adopting the legislation to appease the EU, while still imposing measures to restrict the import of raw animal products. An explanatory note attached to the proposal submitted to Althingi on 13 October 2009 states:

> This legislation implements the changes which are necessary because of the incorporation into the EEA Agreement of the Food Law Package. These changes comply with the relevant EEA Joint Committee Decisions, with the exception that the ban on the import of raw meat and raw eggs remains in place. The same applies to non-disinfected skins and hides, and certain types of fertilizer. Import of these items will not be allowed. This is done with the aim of maintaining protection against diseases, especially considering the long-term isolation of Icelandic animals which makes them particularly susceptible to disease. The new legislation will

ensure that Iceland adopts the same health requirements in the production of food products as other states in the EEA and the same rules will apply with respect to food product surveillance and inspection.

The wording of the explanations attached to the proposal made it fairly clear that the legislation was being adopted against the will of the Minister. They noted that the proposal overturned Iceland's exemption with respect to Chapter I, Annex I of the EEA Agreement, which was decided by the EEA Joint Committee on Iceland's behalf, but still required the approval of Althingi. In various places, the explanations stated that it was 'necessary' to make certain changes in order to comply with the EU regulations or that it was 'impossible' not to make these adjustments because of EU requirements. Nevertheless, raw animal products would be excluded from the scope of the proposal. Although the Minister officially used risk of disease as the reason for maintaining the ban on imported animal products, it is likely that the real motivation had far more to do with protecting the interests of Icelandic farmers and producers. Whereas there is a high risk of spreading disease with import of live animals (from which Iceland has an exemption), this risk is fairly minute with respect to raw animal products, especially as the EU's new food safety requirements are very strict and comprehensive.[35]

As noted in Chapter 3, domestic mobilization in society can in some cases work to hinder compliance with EU rules. Through the years farmers have been a strong force in Icelandic civil society. Although their influence has arguably dwindled in recent years as the sector has decreased in size, they have a long history of political participation and close ties with government. In this case, it is clear that the Icelandic Farmers Association played a key role during the domestic implementation of the Food Law Package. As noted by a representative of the organization: 'During the implementation process of the EU's Food law the Farmers Association fought very hard so that imports of fresh meats would be banned, and we had quite some success.'[36] The Minister has close links with the agricultural community and was in constant contact with the Association throughout the formulation of the proposal.

During the parliamentary debate on 13 October 2009, various MPs were sceptical of the Minister's proposal. He was asked by Olof Nordal, a Conservative MP, whether he really believed that a proposal which completely contradicted the purpose of the EU legislation would be accepted by Brussels. In response the Minister said that he would like to remind the MP that they were in the Icelandic Parliament, not in Brussels. Furthermore, his proposal did not undermine the EEA Agreement because Article 13 of that Agreement stated that the contracting parties could maintain restrictions on the import of goods for reasons related to the protection of health and life of humans, animals or plants, among other things.[37] Ms Nordal again enquired whether the Minister was saying that, whenever he felt like it, he could set different laws from those that were agreed in Brussels. The Minister replied that he was slightly concerned by how much importance the MP attached to Brussels. The government had agreed that the proposal should maintain the ban on raw animal products and that they were in the Icelandic legislature setting Icelandic laws. If anyone had a problem with the new legislation they could pursue it with the courts.

Another Conservative MP, Ragnheidur E. Arnadottir, expressed relief that the proposal was finally being discussed, particularly because of trade interests for Icelandic fisheries. However, despite what the Minister said, she thought the measures regarding the import ban on raw products were only a delaying tactic which could not be maintained. Furthermore, the MP alleged that this was most likely a plot by the Minister to ensure that Iceland's EU membership application process would be a slow and difficult one. This was quite a serious matter as it also put the EEA Agreement in danger. The Minister, however, insisted that his decision to maintain the ban was unconnected to the EU accession negotiations. Furthermore, the ban was not a delaying tactic, but should be maintained for the foreseeable future. If surveillance bodies disagreed, Iceland would meet their criticisms head on. It was also important to bear in mind that the Food Law Package involved a lot more than the import of raw products and that all of the health and safety aspects of the package were included in the proposal.

In response to the Minister's arguments, Sigurdur Ingi Johannsson, an opposition MP from the Progressive Party,[38] noted that if Iceland were allowed to maintain its ban on raw products this would have been stated in the Joint Committee Decision incorporating the package into the EEA Agreement. The Conservatives again took the floor with Jon Gunnarsson saying that he felt sorry for the Minister to have to propose legislation which he so strongly opposed. However, it was necessary to adopt this legislation to get some peace and be able to continue the EEA cooperation. It was common knowledge that the Minister's proposal to maintain a ban on raw goods would be impossible. The main mistake had been lowering tolls on such products.

Atli Gislason, a member of the Minister's own Left Green Party and the Head of the Committee on Agriculture and Fisheries, repeated the Minister's arguments for maintaining the ban due to the susceptibility of Icelandic livestock to disease. He also emphasized that Article 13 of the EEA Agreement allowed this. He further touched upon the 'real' reason for his party's opposition to imports, noting that it was important to ensure that Iceland was self-sufficient in food production and that people in the Icelandic food industry kept their jobs. He said that one of the previous proposals to transpose this legislation, submitted by the Conservative Party when they were in office, allowed import of raw animal products. The Left Green Movement had fought against this and he was proud of their success. He was not worried about the EU or the EFTA Surveillance Authority, as vital national interests were at stake. ESA, he said, would be on Iceland's side once they had understood the grave danger posed to Icelandic stocks.

Anna Margret Gudjonsdottir, a member of the Social Democratic senior coalition partner in the centre-left government, pointed out that the package contained many useful rules in the area of food health and safety. She shared the concern of those who feared for the well-being of livestocks and thought that this should be made a priority in Iceland's negotiations with the EU. However, if Iceland joined the EU, it might be necessary to adopt some things that might not be ideal.

During the debate, Ragnheidur E. Arnadottir enquired whether the Minister had consulted with Norwegian colleagues or colleagues from any of the other EFTA or EU states while drafting the proposal and whether they had approved the bill. The Minister replied that they had certainly conferred with various respected experts on European law, who agreed with the government's interpretation. Regarding whether or not they had asked the opinion of foreign experts, the Minister said he thought the Icelandic government was perfectly capable of setting its own laws. He did, however, say he had spoken to the Norwegian Minister of Agriculture, who was mainly concerned that Iceland should notify the EU of fulfilment of constitutional requirements as soon as possible, so that the legislation could come into effect in the EEA. The contents of the Icelandic legislation did not appear to be the main issue. The Minister concluded by saying that everyone should join together in support of this proposal in order to protect Icelandic interests.

The Fisheries and Agriculture Committee of the Icelandic Parliament issued its opinion on the transposition of the Food Law Package into Icelandic law on 4 December 2009. The opinion noted that the main aim of the package was to harmonize rules on trade in agricultural products in the EEA, based on health and safety rules, ensure food safety and increase surveillance. It further stated that the proposal being put before the Icelandic Parliament was in accordance with the Joint Committee Decisions incorporating the package into the EEA Agreement, taking into account Article 13 of the Agreement which would allow the current ban on imports to be maintained in order to protect animals and humans against disease. The proposal had therefore changed substantially since it first came forward, as it maintained a ban on the import of raw meat and fertilizer, raw eggs and unsterilized skins and hides.

The proposal was adopted on 18 December 2009. Towards the end of the year officials at the EFTA Secretariat and within the Norwegian administration were following the debate closely, hoping that Iceland would adopt the legislation and notify fulfilment of constitutional requirements before Christmas. This would have meant that the legislation could come into effect in the EEA on 1 February 2010, as EEA Joint Committee Decisions generally enter into force on the first day of the second month following the last notification concerning fulfilment of constitutional requirements. However, it soon became clear that the process would be further delayed as the Icelandic Parliament decided that the new legislation would not come into effect until 1 March 2010. Accordingly, Iceland could not notify fulfilment of constitutional requirements until then, which meant that the legislation could not enter into force in the EEA until 1 May. This was most likely a delaying tactic to prolong Iceland's 18-month adaptation period.

Needless to say, Norway was disappointed by this turn of events, as it delayed the coming into effect of the package even further. In the New Year a flurry of exchanges between the EFTA states ensued, leading to a compromise involving a new solution by which Iceland submitted a 'provisional notification'. In other words, the relevant Joint Committee Decisions could be applied provisionally in the EEA from 1 March, while it was agreed that a formal notification would be submitted following the entry into force of the new legislation in Iceland providing for the full entry into force of the decisions as of 1 May 2010. This meant that Norway could implement the Food Law Package from 1 March, but Iceland would only begin the countdown for its 18-month adaptation period from 1 May. Iceland formally notified the fulfilment of constitutional requirements concerning the Food Law Package on 17 March 2010 (EFTA Secretariat 2010). Nonetheless, although legislation was adopted which provides a legal basis for implementing the Food Law Package, it still maintains a ban on imports of raw animal products into Iceland, which is contrary to the aims of the package. This arguably shows that, although the mechanisms in the EEA framework are generally strong enough to ensure incorporation of acts into the EEA Agreement and transposition at the national level, there is some scope to resist domestic adaptation though incorrect legislative transposition. Here it is important to keep in mind that only an outright refusal to adopt acts can incur a suspension of the EEA Agreement, while incorrect adaptation is subject to comparatively milder infringement procedures.

At the time of writing, this thorny issue had yet to be resolved. Iceland's 18-month adaptation period had recently come to an end, yet the clauses in the legislation concerning the ban on the import of raw animal products had not been revised. At the beginning of December 2011, the Icelandic Federation of Trade and Services (SVTH) sent a formal complaint both to the EFTA Surveillance Authority and the Parliament's Ombudsman because of the import ban on fresh meat, arguing that it was an infringement of the EEA Agreement (*Visir* 2011). The Minister of Fisheries and Agriculture responded by stating that he would not make any changes to the laws, pointing out that the Parliament had been in favour of these limitations and that the Federation was under an obligation to obey Icelandic laws (Rikisutvarpid 2011).

According to an EFTA official, at a meeting of the EFTA Working Group on Veterinary Matters in December 2011, the Icelandic authorities informed the Commission that they would maintain prohibitions on all imports of fresh meat and meat products based on Article 13 of the EEA Agreement. The Commission representative expressed doubt as to whether such a broad measure could be taken based on Article 13. Furthermore, the ESA representative informed the group that a letter had already been sent to the Icelandic government asking for information on how the ban on imports was being enforced and the scientific justification for such a ban.[39] It remains to be seen whether ESA will take further action against Iceland as a consequence of its investigation. In the meantime, a reshuffling of the Icelandic government took place on New Year's Eve 2011, resulting in fewer ministries. One of the main changes was that Jon Bjarnason, Minister of Fisheries and Agriculture, was relieved of his duties in favour of the leader of the Left Green Party, Steingrimur J. Sigfusson, who was placed in charge of economic affairs, trade, fisheries and agriculture. This change may produce some policy revisions in this area.

Conclusions and potential next steps

The Food Law case involved a considerable expansion of EU *acquis* into the Icelandic legislative framework, which was strongly resisted by the Icelandic government. Prior to the adoption of the Food Law Package, Iceland was exempt from most legislation in this area. However, the EU's new comprehensive method of legislating meant that it adopted new horizontal framework legislation for the entire food and veterinary area and thus it was no longer viable for Iceland to only implement legislation related to fisheries and aquaculture products. The EU, therefore, insisted that Iceland should align its legal framework to EU Food Law requirements.

During the prolonged negotiation process leading up to the incorporation of the package into the EEA Agreement, Iceland was able to secure considerable adaptations. It was allowed to maintain a ban on importing live animals into Iceland and to continue feeding fishmeal to ruminants. Iceland also received an 18-month transition period in order to implement the necessary legislation. Therefore, Iceland was able to upload some of its preferences before having to adopt the legislation. Nevertheless, the implications of incorporating the package into the EEA Agreement were that Iceland would have to allow trade in animal products, a situation which Icelandic authorities wished to avoid, mainly in order to protect Icelandic farmers from competition from the continent. Accordingly, the transposition of the package into national legislation was also subject to considerable delays. This meant that the content of the EEA Agreement did not correspond to the legal situation at the national level, and a large backlog of acts built up, which could not be adopted as they were dependent on the implementation of the original package, leaving a large gap between the legislation applicable in the EU and the EEA.

Articles 102 and 103 of the EEA Agreement allow for a partial suspension of the EEA Agreement if the EFTA states refuse to incorporate acts into the Agreement or adopt them at the national level. The suspension procedure does not happen automatically, but must be invoked by the EU. So far, it has been used both rarely and cautiously. Even in this case it was not officially invoked, although hints were given, despite serious delays during the downloading process, both in the incorporation of the legislation into the EEA Agreement and transposition at the national level. Nevertheless, the threat of a potential suspension does appear to have some impact, as legislation which has been incorporated into the EEA Agreement has never been rejected outright by the national parliaments of the EFTA states. In this case it appears that Iceland's strategy, spearheaded by a staunchly Eurosceptic Minister in close collaboration with the farmers' lobby, was to deliberately adopt legislation which did not comply with EU requirements, rather than to refuse to adopt the package. The threat of suspension does not apply to incorrect transposition or implementation. However, the EFTA Surveillance Authority can issue infringement proceedings which can culminate in a case before the EFTA Court. At the time of writing the full extent of the measures taken by monitoring bodies to remedy the situation were still unknown.

The potential follow-up to this case must also be seen in conjunction with Iceland's application for EU membership. In light of the application, the Commission has set up a representation in Reykjavik and is actively following events there. On 24 February 2010 the Commission issued a Communication to the Parliament and the Council on its opinion on Iceland's application for membership of the EU. The opinion, among other things, stated that, overall, Iceland had a satisfactory track record in implementing its EEA obligations. However, one of the shortfalls which would have to be addressed at an early stage was the area of food safety. In this area, and others, the Commission noted that Iceland would need to make serious efforts to align its legislation with the *acquis* and/or to implement and enforce it effectively in order to meet the accession criteria (European Commission 2010b).

It is therefore clear that this is one of the focus areas of the accession negotiations, and it is unlikely that Iceland will be able to maintain an indefinite ban on the import of raw meats if it wishes to conclude the negotiations successfully. Furthermore, Iceland will most likely be under pressure from ESA to adapt its legislative framework in accordance with EU requirements now that the 18-month adaptation period has expired. One official summed up the situation as follows: 'The legislation we have adopted is incorrect. We should have lifted the ban. We might get in trouble after the adaptation period. It also depends on the EU accession negotiations and what the EU wants us to do.'[40]

As argued in Chapter 3, ESA infringement procedures appear to be relatively effective, despite the fact that the threat of suspension no longer applies at this stage of the process. This may be due to the fact that, although the EU does not have direct control over the EFTA states, the Commission is generally closely involved in the work of ESA, and the EFTA states do not want to give an impression that the EEA Agreement is not functioning properly. Therefore, it is likely that the ban on imports of raw agricultural products will be revoked at some stage, either in the wake of the accession negotiations or ESA's infringement procedures. The fact that a new minister has been placed in charge of this policy area may also facilitate this process. However, this case does generally seem to be one of inertia or extreme resistance to change, showing that, if domestic opposition to EU requirements is strong, downloading can be severely delayed and obstructed.

8 Review of key findings

Iceland and the other EFTA states have largely been left out of the Europeanization debate, which to date has favoured existing EU member states or non-members such as candidate countries or neighbours to the east. This study has sought to fill this gap in the literature to some extent by exploring Iceland's participation in the EU policy process through the EEA Agreement. This volume has adopted a relatively traditional Europeanization framework and applied it to a state which has a relationship with the EU that is quite distinct from that of a member state yet also very different to a candidate or ENP country. The focus on Iceland thus aims to add new insights to the study of Europeanization, which can potentially lay the groundwork for subsequent studies. This chapter begins by reviewing the general assumptions, research questions and hypotheses posed at the beginning of the book and goes on to evaluate and analyze the key findings from the previous chapters. In general the findings confirm the asymmetrical nature of the EU's relations with non-member states, both in terms of uploading and downloading. In other words, the results of the case studies indicate that Iceland may be both less likely to upload its preferences and more likely to download EU policies than EU member states. Nonetheless, domestic conditions also appear to play an important role when it comes to the full national-level implementation of EU rules, and downloading can be subject to significant delays.

Analytical framework, research questions and hypotheses

Europeanization studies focus on the impact of the EU on the domestic sphere or the adaptation of national structures, processes and policies in response to the demands of the EU (Bache 2008: 10; Wong 2006: 15). They typically examine different dimensions of domestic adaptation to EU requirements within a single state or on one policy sector across a number of countries. Empirical work has demonstrated that the EU can induce significant domestic change (Borzel and Risse 2003: 75). However, an equally important finding is that Europeanization should not be assumed to entail convergence or harmonization (Vink and Graziano 2007: 10). In other words, the impact of the EU varies across states. Domestic political systems have tended to adapt to EU pressures while retaining key national characteristics and traditions (Bache 2008: 10). Academic research has also shown that actors actively attempt to have an input into EU policy-making in order to avoid having to adopt inconvenient policies at the national level, and so this is now seen as an important aspect of the Europeanization process. Therefore, in line with many recent Europeanization studies, this study has explored top-down domestic adaptation to EU requirements in Iceland, while also taking into account the two-way relationship between national actors and the EU.

In order to capture the interactive nature of Europeanization, it was defined as the process whereby a state, in this case Iceland, becomes a participant in the EU's policy process both at the policy-making stage at the EU level and the implementation stage at the national level. Through this involvement key actors learn the rules of the game and develop machinery and strategies for uploading their preferences and downloading EU requirements. Accordingly, the organization and behaviour of the Icelandic government administration was examined as it responded to EU policy requirements, both in terms of uploading, or projecting its preferences at the EU level, and downloading, i.e. adopting EU policy at the national level, and the resulting domestic change. EU policy initiatives were considered to be the independent variable, while domestic responses to these initiatives were seen as the dependent variable. In Iceland's case, the EEA Agreement is the key intervening variable which determines the framework through which domestic actors participate in the EU policy process.

The first research question posed in this volume is related to Iceland's uploading capacity, asking whether a non-member state, such as Iceland, could have an input into EU policy-making. Attributing uploading capacity to a non-member state is a rather new notion in the Europeanization literature, as previous studies have generally assumed that non-member states have no impact on the European policies that they adopt. Nonetheless, it was hypothesized that an interactive dynamic between Iceland and the EU would be found. However, it was also argued that, because of its small size and lack of membership status, Iceland's ability to project its preferences would be significantly less developed than in the larger EU member states.

The second research question is linked to the downloading side of the Europeanization process, exploring the likelihood of domestic adaptation to EU requirements in Iceland and asking whether the EU's leverage is sufficiently strong to ensure domestic change or whether pre-existing domestic institutions and practices are resilient to external incentives for change. It was hypothesized that Iceland would most likely have relatively strong incentives for domestic change in compliance with EU policies, for example in comparison to EU member states.

This hypothesis was based on a rationalist assumption of rule adoption, i.e. that the benefits of adopting EU rules outweighed the disadvantages, as Iceland is highly dependent on its access to the internal market, which the EEA Agreement grants. The EEA Agreement can also relatively easily be revised in

Review of key findings   149

comparison to membership agreements, through Article 102. The uneven power relationship between Iceland and the EU and the threat of partial exclusion from the internal market could thus mean that domestic actors in Iceland are unlikely to oppose or delay the implementation of EU legislation even though it is incompatible with domestic arrangements. This can be compared with the EU's relations with other non-member states, as the EU has sought to impose change upon candidate and ENP countries through mechanisms of conditionality and leverage.

There is, however, another type of mechanism for change which is based on a logic of appropriateness, rather than a logic of consequentialism. In this way states undergo a process of socialization whereby they internalize EU norms. As this study is based on a historical institutionalist approach, the analysis took into account the potential impact of socialization as well as rational cost/benefit calculations. Iceland is allowed to participate in the preparatory work of the Commission when new legislation is being drawn up as well as in EFTA working groups and committees. Nonetheless, Iceland is far less exposed to the EU's rules, norms, practices and structures than the member states and thus perhaps less likely to be socialized into EU ways of doing things. So, according to the logic of appropriateness, socialization might be considered less likely to have an impact on domestic actors in Iceland than in the member states.

The two logics of consequentialism and appropriateness thus led to differing assumptions. Iceland has a relatively strong incentive to comply with EU policy requirements according to the logic of consequentialism, but a fairly weak incentive following the logic of appropriateness. The likelihood of rule adoption was therefore thought to depend largely on the structure of the EEA Agreement and the extent to which it provides a favourable platform through which the EU can channel its leverage. Other intervening factors were also thought to play a role in the process of domestic change, such as such as domestic mobilization in support of or opposition to EU policy, administrative capacity and the extent to which a 'compliance culture' exists in Iceland.

In order to answer the research questions, Chapters 2 and 3 provided background analysis of the institutional setting within which Iceland participates in the EU policy process through the EEA Agreement in terms of uploading and downloading, respectively. Chapters 4 to 7 then looked in detail at these processes by focusing on four specific cases. According to academic literature on Europeanization, policy mismatch, whereby EU requirements clash in some way with pre-existing domestic conditions, is a necessary condition for domestic change. Therefore EU policies in the areas of electricity, citizenship or free movement of persons, environmental policy and food law, which were each deemed to have a high degree of mismatch with the national level, were selected for analysis. In other words, EU obligations in each of these areas were in conflict with existing policies and institutions and prescribed a new model to which domestic arrangements had to be adjusted. This is important, as mismatch between EU requirements and

150 *Review of key findings*

domestic conditions gives states an incentive to upload their preferences to the EU level and also means that EU requirements can impose challenges for states when it comes to downloading them.

In terms of mismatch, the Electricity Directive was designed with much larger electricity systems than Iceland's in mind and is geared towards enabling cross-border trade within Europe, which does not apply to Iceland as it is an isolated system. Thus, from the beginning it was clear that implementation of the Directive would involve extensive and costly changes with respect to the organization of the Icelandic electricity sector. The Citizenship (or Free Movement) Directive arguably expanded the scope of the EEA Agreement beyond its internal market focus to an area that had not previously been included, which Iceland strongly opposed. Regarding the Emissions Trading Scheme, Iceland's participation clashed with its international obligations as it is an independent signatory of the Kyoto Protocol. Furthermore, the EU ETS was extended to include aviation activities, which was problematic for Iceland as its aviation emissions are considerably greater than those of countries on or closer to the mainland. Finally, the Food Law Package revoked Iceland's exemption from legislation related to veterinary and phytosanitary measures, obliging Iceland to adopt most acts in this field. This implied that Iceland would need to allow trade in animal products, a situation which the Icelandic authorities wished to avoid, mainly in order to protect Icelandic farmers from competition from the continent. Therefore, in all of the cases a high degree of mismatch between the EU and national levels was observed.

Each of the case study chapters proceeded along similar lines, attempting to shed light on the same questions. As policy mismatch was considered a necessary condition for domestic change, the chapters explained how and why the EU legislation in question diverged from pre-existing national ways of doing things. Viewing Europeanization as an interactive process, they looked at Iceland's response to EU policy requirements, in terms of uploading, i.e. was Iceland able to upload its preferences to the European level, which strategies did it use and how successful was it? Next, the extent to which each of the EU requirements had been downloaded at the national level was established. Downloading was operationalized as the domestic transposition and implementation or practical application of EU policies. In the Icelandic case, an important aspect of the downloading process also involves negotiations between the EFTA and EU sides for the incorporation of the relevant act(s) into the EEA Agreement. Indeed, this can be seen both as the last stage of the uploading process, as the EFTA states can in some cases obtain certain exemptions and adaptations, and the first stage of the downloading process, as it involves the initial incorporation of acts into the EEA Agreement, which then obliges Iceland and the other EFTA states to make the relevant changes at the national level.

In each chapter, the degree of domestic change resulting from participation in the EU policy process was evaluated and grouped into one of three categories based loosely on a taxonomy developed by Radaelli (2003). According to the taxonomy, inertia, or lack of change, takes the form of lack of participation at the formulation stage at the EU level, lags and delays in the transposition of directives and sheer resistance to EU-induced change. Accommodation is when domestic institutions and organizations show a mixture of resiliency and flexibility, absorbing certain non-fundamental changes, but maintaining their core. Finally, transformation occurs when the fundamental logic of political behaviour changes. Existing policies, processes and institutions have been replaced by new substantially different ones or altered to the extent that their essential features are fundamentally changed (Borzel and Risse 2003: 69–70; Radaelli 2003: 38). Taking a qualitative stance, the chapters also aimed to gauge the incentives and reasons behind Iceland's reactions, for example, whether they were linked to the threat of exclusion or a feeling of responsibility.

As noted, all of the four cases chosen for analysis in some way presented a challenge to the Icelandic government due to a high degree of mismatch between the EU and national levels. Yet they each varied considerably in terms of the obligations they posed, the domestic conditions through which they were adopted and the outcomes that were observed. The following sections of this chapter review and analyze the key findings from each of the cases. First, the results of each case with respect to uploading are examined, and then the outcome of the downloading process in each case is reviewed.

Is Iceland a decision-shaper?

The question as to whether or not Iceland has developed any noticeable uploading capacity is an intriguing one. As mentioned above, it has generally been taken as a given that third countries undergo a unilateral adjustment to EU policy requirements, with uploading capacity being seen as a phenomenon unique to EU member states. Furthermore, the democratic deficit or lack of representation granted to the EFTA states in EU decision-making bodies has been considered the key drawback of the EEA Agreement (EEA Review Committee 2012). Yet, as Iceland adopts the majority of EU legislation, it has a clear incentive to make its voice heard and attempt to influence the policies it is required to adopt, as do other non-member states adopting EU requirements. However, Iceland, like other non-member states, does not have a seat at the table and is therefore largely left out of the EU decision-making process. In addition to non-member status, Iceland's small size also presents an obstacle to uploading, as larger and more powerful states have traditionally had more success at uploading than smaller and new member states.

Chapter 2 examined how the EEA structure constrains the choices and strategies available to Icelandic actors in terms of getting their views across during policy formulation at the EU level, taking into account the small size of the Icelandic administration as well as its lack of access to the decision-making institutions. Chapter 2 indicated that Iceland was involved to some extent in the decision-shaping process at the EU level, despite being at a disadvantage as it lacks resources and does not have a seat at the table. As noted in Chapter 2, the EFTA states somewhat optimistically refer to their participation in the EU policy process as 'decision-shaping' as opposed to decision-making (EFTA Secretariat 2009: 20). The case study chapters set out to explore whether this was an accurate description or whether the rather more gloomy term of 'policy-taker' was more appropriate.

Taking into account the EEA framework, Iceland's attempts to leave its mark on four diverse policy areas were examined. The cases showed that Iceland could in some instances have an impact on the content of the legislation it adopts, although this was fairly limited. Its primary target appeared to be the Commission and its EFTA partners, and the aim was generally to gain an adaptation in the EEA Joint Committee. The cases demonstrated a few examples of success in negotiating exemptions or adaptations prior to incorporating acts into the EEA Agreement. In fact, this is where Iceland's impact appeared to be the most measurable and concrete. For example, in the case of the Electricity Directive Iceland was able to secure an adaptation period and the right to apply for an exemption from certain aspects of the Directive. This was based on the argument that conditions in Iceland merited special consideration because of the small size and isolation of its electricity system. The food law case can also be interpreted as a partial uploading success. In this case, Iceland was not able to extend its overall exemption from veterinary legislation. However, it was able to maintain a ban on the import of live animals and the right to be allowed to use fishmeal in animal feed. Iceland also received a transitional period of 18 months from the entry into force of the package in order to comply fully with the provisions it was required to implement. As hypothesized, these cases, therefore, showed some degree of interaction between Iceland and the EU at the European level before policies were downloaded.

Iceland was not, however, always successful in its uploading attempts. For example, it was not able to gain support for the view that the Citizenship Directive overstepped the legal boundaries of the EEA Agreement and that various aspects of it, namely those dealing with immigration law, should not be considered EEA-relevant. Furthermore, in the ETS case Iceland's argument that the scheme infringed upon its pre-existing international agreements under the Kyoto Protocol was unsuccessful, and the ETS Directive was incorporated into the EEA Agreement. When aviation activities were added to the scheme, Iceland decided not to apply for any exemptions or adaptations for ultra-peripheral regions. A key reason for this was that it was unlikely to be granted any special consideration as none of the EU states had received any adaptations for their ultra-peripheral regions. On the whole, the EFTA states have found it difficult to negotiate adaptations if similar requests have been made by EU member states and refused. Furthermore, the general rule of the EU is not to grant adaptations, although each case is examined individually. Therefore, although the EEA Joint Committee can be an important venue for adjusting EU policies to fit with Icelandic preferences, Iceland

Review of key findings   153

seems to have become aware that it only helps it to secure its interests to a certain extent.

Interview evidence suggested that, rather than attempting to negotiate exemptions, Icelandic officials generally considered it to be a better strategy to try to influence EU policy early in the decision-making process, before it had been adopted by the EU institutions. Accordingly, Iceland's efforts seemed to have become more sophisticated over time, focusing on the earlier stages of the policy process and relying on a mixture of EEA-granted access points and more informal lobbying tactics, which are in some ways similar to those used by small EU member states. Indeed, one Icelandic official noted that if the Electricity Directive had come up a few years later the government would have done things differently and used more complicated tactics, for example, contacting other countries with similar interests or making use of contacts within the EP.[1]

In the ETS case, Iceland attempted to gain support for a special clause on ultra-peripheral regions while the Directive was still being debated by the Council and the Parliament. Iceland actively lobbied the EU institutions to include a clause on ultra-peripheral regions in the Directive, and this case demonstrated that Iceland's lobbying techniques had become more extensive. Although the EFTA states do not have any formal access to the Council or the EP, Iceland has gradually begun to put into practice a range of more informal methods of making its voice heard within these institutions: for example, by engaging in strategic partnerships with EU member states that have similar interests, as well as making use of regional cooperation with the Nordic and Baltic members through pre-Council meetings, and by focusing its attentions on key MEPs and parliamentary committees. However, lack of resources is clearly a hurdle, particularly in light of the financial crisis.

In addition to demonstrating new tactics, the ETS case showed that the success of a non-member state depended not only on its ability to engage with EU institutions and the member states but also on its ability to get its views accepted by these actors. The argument that Iceland should not have to pay fully for its aviation emissions was probably not a popular one when all other countries in Europe were striving to combat their emissions over a wide range of industrial sectors. Furthermore, Iceland was not able to gain the support of its Nordic allies due to their commitment to environmental protection. The final Directive did not grant special consideration to ultra-peripheral regions, which generally fits with findings that small states are most likely to be successful when they have an argument which they are able to promote as being in the interests of the Union as a whole (Arter 2000: 679).

By and large, the electricity and food law cases can be interpreted as partial success stories. In these two cases, Iceland was able to demonstrate that conditions in Iceland were different to those in other EU states and gain certain exemptions. Iceland was not, however, able to upload its preferences in the citizenship or ETS cases. The uploading chapter and the four case studies show that Iceland is not generally an agenda-setter at the EU level. Its uploading attempts often appear to be limited to minimizing the negative consequences of EU policies by lobbying for exemptions or adaptations during the incorporation of acts into the EEA Agreement. Iceland also faces many hurdles when it comes to uploading due to its small size and non-member status. The Icelandic administration is and will always be considerably smaller than those of other EU member states, which, in addition to the limitations of the EEA Agreement, places some constraints on Iceland's ability to present its case at the EU level (Thorhallsson and Ellertsdottir 2004: 91). Therefore, as one would expect, Iceland is not always successful in uploading, even when it applies itself with full force.

Arguably, the chances of uploading success are fairly slim in comparison to EU member states. However, one of the aims of this book has been to give some insight into the larger question of whether an interactive model of Europeanization is appropriate for non-member states such as Iceland. Although uploading success is far from guaranteed, the findings from previous chapters show that Iceland is playing the EU game and has developed some identifiable, albeit fairly weak, uploading capacity as a result of its participation in the EEA.

How likely is domestic adaptation in Iceland?

As noted in the previous section, Iceland was either unable or only partially able to secure its preferences during the uploading stage of the policy process in each of the cases. This means that the downloading of EU policies is potentially challenging or problematic. The second key aim of this book was to explore what happens under such conditions. In other words, do domestic actors in Iceland have sufficient incentives to put EU policy into practice when it conflicts with pre-existing conditions or do they resist domestic change? The institutionalist literature assumes that there will be domestic resistance to change if there is a high degree of mismatch between EU policy requirements and existing structures and practices. Europeanization literature has found that EU member states are frequently reluctant to adopt EU policies in these cases. On the other hand, studies on candidate countries have highlighted the effectiveness of membership conditionality, noting that these states generally appear to be willing to adopt EU requirements even though they clash with pre-existing arrangements. Countries included in the Neighbourhood Policy that have not been offered the carrot of membership are, on the other hand, less disposed to making costly changes. The question of why and to what extent Iceland effectively downloads EU rules through the EEA Agreement, even when they impose costly changes, is thus pivotal to the Europeanization debate.

Chapter 3 explored downloading in the institutional context of the EEA Agreement, attempting to show how adaptation pressure stemming from the EU manifested itself in the EEA. The chapter also touched upon domestic intervening variables which, according to previous research, have been found to facilitate or hinder downloading, such as mobilization in society, administrative capacity, a particular culture of compliance and the existence of veto points within the political system. The findings indicated that domestic conditions in Iceland were generally favourable to change. The EEA framework also appeared to be fairly conducive to domestic adaptation because of the asymmetrical nature of the relationship between Iceland and the EU, and clauses which allow for a partial suspension of the Agreement if the EFTA states refuse to incorporate legislation into the Agreement or transpose it at the national level. On the whole, Chapter 3 observed that Iceland did seem to experience significant pressure to incorporate EU legislation into the EEA Agreement and transpose it at the national level, as it has never overtly refused to do so.

It is, however, important to note that the threat of exclusion from the internal market only applies to the incorporation of acts into the EEA Agreement and transposition by national parliaments, but not to ground-level application, where EFTA infringement procedures apply. These are fairly similar to the mechanisms for monitoring compliance in EU member states, which previous Europeanization studies have often found to be ineffective. Furthermore, the fact that the EFTA states monitor themselves means that these mechanisms appear rather weak at first glance. Nonetheless, the interview evidence compiled in Chapter 3 suggests that they function fairly well. This was partly explained by the fact that the EFTA states have their own institutions increases the legitimacy of the EEA Agreement. Furthermore, each EFTA state is subject to control from its partners, not just its own officials. Finally, the EFTA bodies are in close contact with the EU throughout the monitoring process, and so and the EFTA states are aware of the potential danger in allowing the EU to perceive that the EEA Agreement is not functioning well. Therefore, in practice, the EFTA states may even feel stronger pressure to adapt to EU requirements than EU member states, which could be interpreted as slightly ironic, as one of the reasons they have not joined the EU is reluctance to relinquish their autonomy. One could even argue that their relations with the EU were in some ways more akin to those of candidate countries.

Along with Chapter 2, which focused on uploading, Chapter 3 on downloading provided the necessary backdrop for the case study chapters, in which the processes of both uploading and downloading were examined in depth. These cases were discussed in the previous section with respect to uploading, noting that Iceland had had some success when it came to uploading, but also some failure. On the downloading side, the results also varied considerably. As mentioned above, domestic adaptation can be categorized into three main groups according to Radaelli's (2003) taxonomy, namely inertia, accommodation or transformation. The Electricity Directive was the only case in which transformation occurred. The Citizenship and ETS Directives were considered examples of accommodation, while the Food Law Package was deemed to be a case of inertia. As noted, all cases entailed considerable mismatch between the EU and national levels, which begs the question why change occurred in some cases but not in others. As will be explained, the level of domestic support, or at least lack of domestic opposition, within civil society appeared to play a key role. Domestic political change was also a relevant factor.

As mentioned in the previous section, Iceland was able to secure the right to apply for exemptions from certain aspects of the Electricity Directive, based on its small size and isolated location. Nonetheless, this possibility was not used by the Icelandic government. Rather, the implementing legislation fulfils the aims of the Directive and in some cases even goes beyond the EU requirements. These obligations also seem to have been conscientiously put into practice. Although these changes were initiated at the EU level, in this case the main impetus for change appeared to be at the domestic level. The Directive corresponded with the centre-right government's policy of liberalization and marketization, and larger electricity buyers were also keen to be able to choose their suppliers. Therefore, in this case, the Directive was implemented at the national level without external pressure through the EEA Agreement being put to the test.

The Citizenship Directive proved to be a bone of contention between the EFTA states, particularly Iceland and Liechtenstein, and the EU when negotiating its incorporation into the EEA Agreement, almost causing a suspension of certain parts of the Agreement. However, after a long struggle it was incorporated into the Agreement, which highlights the EU's leverage over the EFTA states and the strength of Article 102 and the threat of suspension as an incentive for EU rule adoption. The results of this case suggest that the EFTA states do not have any sort of real veto power over the incorporation of acts into the EEA Agreement.

Although the Icelandic government strongly opposed the incorporation of the Citizenship Directive into the EEA Agreement, the necessary changes were made to Iceland's legislative framework to download the Directive at the national level. This is interesting, as incorrect transposition and implementation failure incur relatively mild sanctions compared to the threat of suspension. Again, the importance of domestic factors appears to be a key explanation. Iceland opposed the incorporation of the Directive primarily on principle as it did not want to set a precedent for the expansion of the EEA Agreement. The measures required by the Directive were not, however, highly controversial or politically inflammatory within civil society, although they were perhaps in some ways slightly inconvenient for the government. Therefore, there was limited domestic resistance to change once the Directive had been incorporated into the Agreement.

Iceland also opposed the incorporation of the ETS Directive into the EEA Agreement, arguing that it infringed upon its pre-existing international agreements under the Kyoto Protocol. However, the EU threatened to invoke Article 102, and so Iceland had little choice but to agree to the incorporation of the Directive into the EEA Agreement, although the process was protracted, much like in the Citizenship case. The ETS was incorporated into the

EEA Agreement in 2007 and was meant to be transposed into Icelandic law by early 2008. However, after some discussions within the Icelandic Parliament it was decided that legislative change would not be necessary to transpose the Directive. This conclusion is debatable, as arrangements should arguably have been made in the legal framework to allow trade in emissions allowances on the internal market. Therefore, in this case both the incorporation of the Directive into the EEA Agreement and its national application were significantly delayed. Nonetheless, Iceland began actively preparing for the implementation of the ETS once it had been expanded to include more industries which are relevant to Iceland such as aviation and aluminium smelting. In all likelihood an important factor here is governmental change, as a new centre-left government with green aspirations took over in 2009. Furthermore, it later appeared that including aviation in the scheme would not have as drastic an impact as originally feared. This case again highlights the strength of the EEA framework in ensuring the incorporation of acts into the EEA Agreement through the threat of suspension. With respect to adoption at the national level, domestic factors, i.e. the election of a greener government, seem to have played a key role.

In the food law case Iceland fought unsuccessfully to maintain its exemption from veterinary legislation. During the prolonged negotiation process leading up to the incorporation of the package into the EEA Agreement, Iceland was able to secure considerable adaptations. However, the implications of incorporating the package into the EEA Agreement were that Iceland would become part of the internal market with respect to trade in animal products. Like Article 102, Article 103 of the EEA Agreement allows for a partial suspension of the Agreement if the EFTA states refuse to transpose acts into national legislation. This threat appears to have a considerable impact, as EU acts have never been rejected outright by the national parliaments of the EFTA states, as this case also demonstrates. Rather, Iceland's strategy, coordinated by a staunchly Eurosceptic minister with a rural background and close ties to the agricultural lobby, was to deliberately adopt legislation which did not comply with EU requirements rather than refuse to adopt the package and risk a partial suspension of the Agreement.

After much delay, the legislation was finally adopted by the Icelandic Parliament. However, it stated that Iceland would continue to ban the import of raw meats, eggs and related products. This was the only case in which national measures clearly and intentionally defied the aims of the EU legislation and can therefore be categorized as one of inertia or extreme resistance to change. As argued in Chapter 3, EFTA infringement proceedings appear to be relatively effective, despite the fact that the threat of suspension no longer applies at this stage of the downloading process. At the time of writing it remained to be seen whether these would be put into practice in the food law case. However, this case shows that, if domestic opposition to EU requirements was strong within government and civil society, adaptation could be severely delayed or even obstructed.

Overall, it is important to note that in this volume only legislation which was somehow incongruent with domestic conditions was selected for analysis. In most cases, EU legislation corresponds relatively well with pre-existing domestic arrangements in Iceland and does not require much change to the national legal framework. State actors may also often feel that EU policy poses an effective solution to domestic needs and challenges. Therefore, Iceland willingly adopts the majority of the EU legislation which it is required to take on board through the EEA Agreement.[2] Consequently, the picture of EEA cooperation drawn up by this study is somewhat skewed, as it has highlighted controversial cases, while ignoring the bulk of issues which are non-controversial. Yet, in Iceland, as in all states adopting EU rules, situations arise where EU requirements effectively clash with domestic policies or preferences and it is important to explore how these are handled in different contexts.

In general, the findings of this book show that Iceland has become a participant in the EU's policy process through the EEA Agreement at both the policy-making and implementation stages, which has had a substantial impact on the content of public policy in Iceland as well as the structure and behaviour of political and administrative organizations. This expands on previous academic findings which demonstrate that the EU's impact is not confined only to its member states, but is also felt in a range of non-member states within its sphere of influence. It was hypothesized that the EU had had a significant and increasing impact on the policy processes in Iceland and that institutions and organizations had developed both uploading and downloading capacity. However, it was also thought that their receptive capacity would be stronger than their projective capacity because of their small size and limited access to EU institutions due to non-membership status. These hypotheses have generally been confirmed throughout this volume. Iceland has developed some capacity to upload its preferences to the EU level before downloading them at ground level, although this is rather weak. Furthermore, when it comes to downloading, the threat of partial suspension of the EEA Agreement was found to provide a strong incentive for EU rule adoption. However, the cases also show that, if domestic opposition is very fervent, significant delays may be experienced throughout the downloading process, and even outright defiance in terms of putting the relevant requirements into practice at the national level.

The right to veto EU legislation was considered extremely important when the EEA Agreement was being ratified by the Icelandic Parliament.[3] Because of concerns over sovereignty, legislation adopted by the EU does not automatically become part of the EEA Agreement but must be agreed in the EEA Joint Committee. The results of the cases would, however, seem to indicate that this is a mere formality, as the EFTA states have never yet refused the incorporation of any piece of legislation into the Agreement. The Norwegian threat to veto the Third Postal Services Directive may turn out to be a first in this respect, following the decision of the Norwegian Labour Party's National Convention not to implement the Directive (Hillion 2011: 13). However, at the time of writing, negotiations between Norway and the EU were still ongoing.

As the EFTA states are very dependent on their access to the internal market, it is perhaps not surprising that they have never before risked the consequences of suspending the Agreement. True, in some cases the incorporation of legislation has been significantly delayed, and the EFTA states have also been able to negotiate exemptions or adaptations. However, whether or not these are granted is at the discretion of the EU. This generally augments the findings of studies focusing on candidate countries which highlight the strength of the EU's leverage. This is interesting in light of the fact that the general academic literature assumes that domestic change in non-member states can only be successfully promoted through the carrot of EU membership. Iceland's relations with the EU through the EEA would seem to tell a different story.

As the EU expands its sphere of influence, the question of third states' participation in the EU policy process has become increasingly relevant. As noted, the general perception is that third countries have no impact on the policies they adopt and that uploading capacity is a phenomenon reserved solely for the fully-fledged members of the club. This volume has challenged this assumption by looking at Iceland's attempts to influence EU policy and found some evidence of an interactive process. It has also found that the EU can relatively successfully induce domestic change in Iceland through the EEA Agreement. The next and final chapter of this volume further explores the broader consequences of the findings of this study.

9 The EEA: Challenges and future scenarios

'The life of the EEA Agreement may be but a short one because it may be overtaken by an even further degree of integration, through accession of the countries concerned to the Community' (Norberg et al. 1993). These words can be attributed to Claus D. Ehlermann, Director-General for Competition at the Commission of the European Communities in June 1993, six months before the EEA Agreement entered into force. It is true that, out of the seven EFTA states for which the EEA Agreement was originally intended, in 2012 only three are EFTA parties to the Agreement and, out of those three, one is also a candidate for EU membership. Nonetheless, the Agreement has proved more resilient than was originally anticipated.

Using a Europeanization framework, this book has aimed to shed some light on the functioning of this comprehensive Agreement. The results indicate that the EEA works relatively well in the sense that there is some, albeit quite limited, scope for uploading, and downloading seems to take place even in cases where there is a high degree of mismatch between the EU and national levels, though this process can be subject to delays. Indeed, at the end of 2010 the European Council adopted conclusions on its relations with the EFTA states praising the EEA Agreement and noting that the EEA countries had demonstrated 'an excellent record of proper and regular incorporation of the *acquis* into their own legislation' (Council of the European Union 2010).

Recent findings from the EFTA states also show that EEA membership has had a substantial impact on their legal orders. A study conducted in Liechtenstein during the period 2001–09 found that 49.3 per cent of laws adopted there originated in the EU. Unsurprisingly, areas that were particularly 'Europeanized' were those relevant to the four freedoms (Frommelt and Gstohl 2011: 22). An extensive review of Norway's relations with the EU estimated that Norway had incorporated approximately three-quarters of all EU legislative acts into Norwegian legislation and implemented them more effectively than many of the EU member states. Although this figure includes all Norway's agreements with the EU, not only the EEA, the EEA is by far the most far-reaching. The report also concluded that in practice the EEA Agreement had worked far better than many had expected (EEA Review Committee 2012: 6).

Importantly, the EFTA states have also generally found the changes brought about by the EEA Agreement to be beneficial. Indeed, it has not always been the EU putting pressure on the EFTA states to adopt legislation. In some cases the EFTA states have been eager to incorporate acts as it has allowed them to participate in various EU initiatives. A report from the Icelandic Minister of Foreign Affairs noted that the EEA Agreement was a cornerstone of Icelandic foreign policy, that it had made Icelandic companies competitive on the internal market, opened up opportunities for Icelandic workers and students and set the basis for flourishing operations in the area of research and development. The report also expressed the view that Iceland was well prepared for its membership negotiations with the EU due to its close cooperation with the Union through the EEA and that Iceland enjoyed goodwill and there was an understanding of its strong position as a European partner because of the Agreement (Skarphedinsson 2010: 4).

The Norwegian review also indicated that the EEA Agreement had many advantages for Norway and that on the whole it had safeguarded Norwegian interests and values. Although oil and gas activities have played a large role in Norway's economic success over the past 20 years, the report noted that 'the EEA Agreement had provided a stable and relatively predictable framework for almost all aspects of Norway's economic relations with the EU member states, which together constitute Norway's most important economic partner by far'. According to the review, the EEA Agreement has also played a part in the general modernization of Norway's economy and employment and working conditions, while at the same time allowing the Norwegian social model to be preserved and further developed (EEA Review Committee 2012: 7).

A report on Liechtenstein's experience of the EEA stated that, overall, Liechtenstein's economy had greatly benefited from EEA membership. The report further noted that the government had concluded that Liechtenstein had successfully maintained, if not improved, its location attractiveness because of the EEA. Furthermore, due to its small size, access to the EU's internal market, diversification and internationalization were essential conditions for Liechtenstein's prosperity (Frommelt and Gstohl 2011: 17).

In sum, the EEA Agreement appears to work reasonably well and, for the most part, the contracting parties have found it to be advantageous. Indeed, in the words of Maresceau, the EEA constitutes 'a real intellectual masterpiece of legal thinking on integration' (Hillion 2011: 10). This undeniably leads to optimism about its future role. A question thus arises as to whether it is, in fact, a viable long-term alternative rather than a mere stepping-stone towards EU membership as originally foreseen. If this is true, is it also a relevant model for other associated states? However, before addressing these questions, it is important to note that, despite the aforementioned praise of the EEA, there are several factors which may give some cause for concern regarding the overall long-term viability of the Agreement. Most notably, the issue of the democratic deficit inherent in the EEA, as well as challenges which have emerged in relation to the evolution of the EU and Iceland's candidacy for EU membership. These will be explored in the following section, before speculation about the EEA's future.

Challenges in the EEA

The democratic deficit

The democratic deficit is probably the most highly criticized aspect of the EEA Agreement. Given that the EFTA states incorporate a large bulk of EU legislation into the Agreement without access to the EU's decision-making institutions, they have been likened to colonies of the EU which have no influence on the legislation they are required to adopt. This is of course one of the key questions which has been explored in this book, i.e. does uploading occur in the EEA? The results generally indicate that, although some uploading does take place within the context of the EEA, this is fairly limited. Furthermore, the fact remains that the EFTA states do not have a seat at the table where the actual decisions are taken, which may weaken the legitimacy of EU rule adoption. This situation has been described as a 'fax democracy', although perhaps a more apt description today would be an 'email democracy'.

The report of the Norwegian review committee noted that 'the most problematic aspect of Norway's form of association with the EU was the fact that Norway was in practice bound to adopt EU policies and rules on a broad range of issues without being a member and without voting rights'. According to the report, this raises democratic problems, as Norway is not represented in decision-making processes that have direct consequences for Norway (EEA Review Committee 2012: 7). The report measured democracy based on four indicators: representation, accountability, discourse and awareness, and rule of law. The findings showed that the EEA Agreement was severely lacking with respect to the first three factors (Sejersted and Sverdrup 2012). The report noted that the nature of the EEA dampened political engagement and debate and made it difficult to monitor the government and hold it accountable (EEA Review Committee 2012: 7).

This is not a surprising finding. The democratic deficit has been a well-known aspect of the EEA Agreement from the start. It is the price which the EFTA states agreed to pay for enjoying many of the benefits of European integration without being full members of the club and without being bound to participate in some of the areas they considered less attractive. However, the Norwegian report argues that the democratic deficit has been increasing since the EEA first came into effect. An unexpected outcome of the review was how extensive Norway's association with the EU actually is, and how many aspects of society have been affected (EEA Review Committee 2012: 6). Therefore, according to the authors, the price of non-membership has gone up (Sejersted and Sverdrup 2012).

The results of the cases studied in this volume also confirm that the EEA has been slowly extending into new areas which were perhaps not foreseen at the outset. Another reason why the democratic deficit may be said to have increased is the fact that the Parliament and the Council have gained more say in the EU legislative process over the past two decades at the expense of the Commission. The EEA Agreement, on the other hand, only grants formal access to the Commission's committees and expert groups.

Following the publication of the Norwegian report, Icelandic Foreign Minister Ossur Skarphedinsson, a staunch supporter of Iceland's membership of the EU, voiced agreement with the report's critique of the democratic deficit stating that, 18 years ago, when the Agreement first came into force, it was 'close to violating the constitution', but now 'we have gone beyond that'. He further noted that it was 'humiliating' for the Icelandic Parliament to receive EU legislation every week without having had any say about it, this being a major argument for Iceland to join the EU (Rikisutvarpid 2012).

As discussed in previous chapters, in order to counter the EFTA states' lack of access to EU decision-making institutions, the EEA Agreement contains various clauses to formally protect them against loss of sovereignty. For example, legislation does not automatically become part of the EFTA states' legal orders, and a two-pillar system was set up whereby the EFTA states have their own Surveillance Authority and Court. Nonetheless, there are various indications that the EEA Agreement functions as a supranational agreement in practice.

One of the main arguments in this respect is that, at the time of writing, the EFTA states had never refused to incorporate any of the thousands of acts which have been made part of the EEA Agreement since its inception. The right to 'veto' EU legislation was considered extremely important when the EEA Agreement was negotiated. Nonetheless, as it has never been used, many would argue that it is a mere formality. In fact, it can be said that the EFTA states do not have any 'real veto power', as they do not have the right to refuse without considerable consequences, i.e. the suspension of the relevant part of the Agreement. As they are highly dependent on their access to the internal market, it is perhaps not surprising that they have never risked a refusal, although the first such case may be on the horizon with Norwegian plans to reject the Third Postal Services Directive.

It is generally assumed that third countries have no impact on the EU policies they are required to adopt. One of the aims of this volume has been to challenge this assumption, and indeed some evidence of an interactive process was found. While the veto has never been used, the EFTA states have sometimes been able to gain certain exemptions and adaptations during the incorporation of legislation into the EEA Agreement. Furthermore, as discussed in Chapter 2, the EFTA states may in some cases have been able to influence EU decision-making from the outside, though this is difficult to measure. Therefore, with respect to the democratic deficit, it is perhaps overly simplistic to say that the EFTA states have *no* influence over the decisions they are required to adopt through the EEA Agreement, although their impact is undoubtedly limited.

An important aspect of this debate is how much would change, in practical terms, with EU membership. If the EFTAns joined the EU they would officially pool their sovereignty with other EU member states, EU acts would have direct effect in their legal systems and the CJEU would be able to take decisions which are binding on them. However, they would be represented in the EU decision-making bodies. Although this would signify a rather large formal change in status, in practice the change may not be quite as noticeable (Jonsdottir 2009).

In this respect the difference in size between the EFTA states is a significant factor. If Iceland joined the EU, it would be the smallest member of the Union in terms of population. Therefore, it would not receive a large portion of the vote in the Council or a large number of seats in the Parliament. It is also likely that lack of resources would continue to pose a problem, particularly for the smaller EFTA states. Because of its small size, Iceland would undoubtedly need to carry on using methods which it has already begun to use in the context of the EEA Agreement, such as prioritization and coalition-building, in order to have an impact, though these methods might be more effective from the inside.

Liechtenstein is even smaller than Iceland. Although Iceland is quite a small state, it is of a comparable size to EU member states such as Luxembourg and Malta. Liechtenstein is almost ten times smaller. Questions have even been raised as to whether membership of an organization such as the EU is possible for such a small state. However, research has found that, at least from a legal perspective, the option of membership should not be excluded (Breuss 2011). Nonetheless, membership of the EU would pose some practical challenges for Liechtenstein due to its small size, and flexible solutions would have to be found for its representation in the Union's organs (Frommelt and Gstohl 2011: 10).

Norway is by far the largest of the EFTA states and, therefore, membership of the EU might make the biggest difference in terms of influence. However, although Norway is large in the EFTA context, it would still be a relatively small state within a growing EU. It is important to note that just being on the inside is no guarantee of uploading success for any state, large or small. However, having an official seat at the table can certainly make a difference, as many decisions are taken by consensus. This is also unquestionably important from a legitimacy perspective and may make adopting EU *acquis* more palatable. Nonetheless, it may be unwise to over-estimate the increase in actual influence which would be gained by membership (Jonsdottir 2009: 82). Whether or not the EFTA states feel that the democratic deficit within the EEA is acceptable in the long run is a question that they will each have to answer for themselves. If not, whether they choose to remedy it by joining or pulling away from the EU is also something they will have to decide on. Until now, it seems that they have felt that the benefits of EEA membership outweigh the democratic costs.

An evolving EU versus a static EEA

The democratic deficit is not the only challenging feature of the EEA. The EU has not remained stagnant since the Agreement was negotiated. Among other things, it has seen three Treaty revisions. As a result of the latest Treaty of Lisbon, DG RELEX, the traditional counterpart of the EFTA states, has been replaced by the European External Action Service and the pillar structure of the EU no longer exists. The EU's methods of legislating have also evolved over time, with more comprehensive acts being adopted which can span over different policy areas. An increasing focus on democracy and citizenship can be observed, which is sometimes difficult to reconcile with the internal market focus of the EEA. Criminal sanctions are being imposed for breach of internal market legislation, which raises concerns in the EEA context. Furthermore, as the EU's competences increase, questions have come up regarding the ability of the EFTA states to participate in various EU initiatives without giving the EU institutions undue authority over their national systems.

It has been noted that, even though the EEA is constantly being moulded to emulate the regulatory changes within the EU, it has not followed the operational and institutional changes of the Union, which has led to a widening gap between the rapid development of the EU and the more stagnant mechanisms of the EEA (Bergmann 2011: 12). Indeed, a research project at the Liechtenstein-Institut shows that the number of acts being incorporated into the EEA Agreement which require adaptations in order to reconcile EU legislation with the so-called two-pillar system of the EEA has increased over time. These institutional adaptations allocate competences between the Commission, the EFTA Surveillance Authority and the authorities of the member states. The necessity for such adaptations can delay the adoption and implementation of new EU rules and arguably weaken the homogeneity of EEA law (Frommelt and Gstohl 2011: 48). Nevertheless, it is important to keep in mind that most adaptations in the EEA are of a technical nature and, out of all acts incorporated into the Agreement, it is not a large number which have required such extensive adaptations.

In addition to questions related to fact that the EEA is administered by separate bodies on the EU and EFTA sides, Hillion (2011: 17) has observed that the discontinuation of the pillar structure within the EU has made the determination of which acts should be incorporated into the EEA Agreement less predictable and more contentious. According to Hillion, the fact that it is no longer possible to use pillar I as a potential indicator of 'EEA-relevance' may increase uncertainty, hamper the homogenous implementation of new norms within the EEA and lead to additional delays in the implementation of the *acquis*. Hillion also expects that, as a result, the EFTA states may be prone to adopt a 'pick-and-choose' approach of selective incorporation of new EU legislation and acknowledge only the EEA-relevance of parts of legislative measures.

In general it can be said that it is perhaps not the discontinuation of the pillar structure as such which has made the determination of EEA-relevance more challenging. Prior to Lisbon, not all pillar I acts were considered EEA-relevant, and the legal base and content of the act in question can still be used as an indicator. However, it is true that the question of EEA-relevance has become increasingly ambiguous as EU legislation has become more extensive, often covering larger areas. Therefore, in many cases some elements of an act may be EEA-relevant while others are not. Based on the results of this study, the extent to which the EU will accept a pick-and-choose approach from the EFTA states in these cases is questionable. Indeed, perhaps a more likely scenario is that cases where EEA-relevance is controversial will lead to an expansion of the scope of the EEA into new areas which were not foreseen when the Agreement first came into effect, at least when the EU attaches importance to their adoption by the EFTA states. The case study chapter on the 'Citizenship' or 'Free Movement' Directive examined the dilemma of EEA-relevance in detail, showing that the scope of EEA Agreement was growing beyond what was originally envisioned, while the EFTA states had limited power to stop it. Indeed the impact of expanding the scope of the EEA due to questions of EEA-relevance should be examined further.

Another trend related to the scope of the EEA which has been unveiled by this study is that the EEA Agreement appears in some cases to infringe upon the EFTA states' right to conclude international agreements, as evidenced by the ETS case in Chapter 6. In this case the EU adopted legislation related to international obligations which it had negotiated on behalf of its member states. The EU's international agreements should not be considered EEA-relevant. However, if the EU transforms its agreements into legislation and insists that these measures are related to the internal market and should be incorporated into the EEA Agreement, it appears that these international agreements can indirectly influence the EFTA states, as shown in the ETS case. Adopting the ETS legislation arguably meant a surrender of Iceland's right to conclude international agreements to a certain extent. This takes us back to the sovereignty debate, as the right to negotiate international agreements with other states can be seen an important aspect of sovereignty. EU member states have officially pooled their sovereignty, while the EFTA states have not. The extent to which the EU can be said to infringe on this aspect sovereignty through the EEA Agreement is therefore a question which merits further attention.

Although, by and large, cooperation among the EFTA states has been good and they have supported each other's positions vis-à-vis the EU, questions of which acts should be incorporated into the EEA Agreement can be a source of tension between the three, given their diverse interests (Frommelt and Gstohl 2011: 49). Furthermore, as noted, it is not always the EU which puts pressure on the EFTA states to adopt its legislation. For example, Liechtenstein had a great interest in adopting new legal acts on financial supervision which were originally not considered EEA-relevant by the EU (Frommelt and Gstohl 2011: 33). The fact that EEA-relevance is sometimes not clear from the beginning can impede the participation of the EFTA states in the relevant decision-shaping process, particularly if they are unaware at the outset that an act will be incorporated into the EEA Agreement (Frommelt and Gstohl 2011: 48). This highlights the growing need for the EFTA states to be attentive with respect to new legislation and come to an early conclusion regarding EEA-relevance, which in some cases may not be that simple. In sum, the EU has evolved considerably over the past two decades, which can pose challenges in relation to both the two-pillar structure and the scope of the EEA. To date, such questions have been met with incremental solutions. However, in order for the EEA to function in the long term, a more comprehensive and coordinated approach towards these challenges may need to be adopted.

Dwindling numbers on the EFTA side

Since the coming into force of the Agreement, three rounds of enlargement have taken place, changing the ratio of states on the EU side versus the EFTA side of the EEA from 12:6 to 27:3. As a result, it has been argued that the political significance of the Agreement is declining and that the EFTA states have been shifted onto the sidelines of European collaboration (Bergmann 2011: 19). The growing asymmetry between the EFTA and EU sides of the EEA undoubtedly means that the EFTA states must work harder to ensure that their rights are observed. However, arguably the larger challenge caused by diminishing numbers on the EFTA side relates to the institutional set up of the EEA. As discussed in Chapter 3, the EEA Agreement follows a two-pillar structure by which the EFTA Surveillance Authority and the EFTA Court have a similar monitoring role towards the EFTA states as that of the Commission and the Court of Justice of the EU in relation to EU member states. It is unusual that third countries are entrusted with the task of monitoring themselves, and this set-up is most likely a relic of the comparative importance of the EFTA block when negotiations for the Agreement were conducted.

The fact that the EFTA states formally monitor themselves means that the infringement mechanisms may appear rather weak at first glance. Nonetheless, this study has found that they seem to function relatively well. As has been noted in previous chapters, this can most likely be traced to a number of factors. Having their own institutions may serve to increase the legitimacy of the Agreement. The EFTA institutions also remain in close contact with the EU throughout the monitoring process and the EFTA states are aware of the asymmetry of power and the potential danger involved should the EU perceive that the EEA Agreement was not functioning well. However, one of the main reasons that the system functions is probably the fact that each EFTA state is also subject to monitoring and control, not only by its own officials, but also by officials from its EFTA partners. For this reason Iceland's potential membership of the EU would give rise to some concern, although, as discussed in the introduction, Iceland's accession is far from guaranteed.

Currently, the EFTA partners are three. They each have one member on the ESA College and one judge in the EFTA Court. Given the odd number, the EFTA Court and ESA are able to take their decisions by simple majority. With only two EFTA states, a solution would have to be found to avoid deadlocks. Moreover, with a population of approximately 35,000 as opposed to a population of 5 million, Liechtenstein and Norway would be highly unequal partners. As noted by Hillion (2011: 18):

> an ESA and EFTA Court that would be essentially composed of Norwegians might make the whole institutional framework look fairly artificial, if not awkward. In effect, the ESA and EFTA Court agreements would appear to be agreements of Norwegians for Norwegians (and some Liechtensteiner ...).

Thus there is reason to believe that the EU might question the legitimacy of the EEA two-pillar system if any further reductions in EFTA membership took place. The recent Norwegian review of the EEA also reached the conclusion that, if Iceland's accession to the EU went through, the Agreement might need to be renegotiated (EEA Review Committee 2012: 9).

On the whole it can be said that, although the EEA Agreement functions reasonably well in practice and has yielded tangible benefits for its signatories, it is not without its challenges. The democratic deficit along with the evolution of the EU's institutional structure, methods of legislating and competences are posing certain challenges for EEA cooperation, especially given the rather static, internal market focus of the Agreement. In addition, Iceland's membership of the EU could present a structural problem within the EEA if indeed Iceland (or any of the other EFTA states) did join the Union or leave EFTA. These challenges are in all likelihood not insurmountable, but the future of the EEA will depend largely on the reactions of the EFTA states to them as time moves on. Therefore, any deliberations into the future will need to take these questions into account. In the following section several potential scenarios related to the future of the Agreement are discussed.

Future of the EEA

What does the future have in store for the EEA? Could there be a substantial revision of the Agreement extending it beyond its current boundaries, or is more likely to collapse altogether? Arguably, there are four potential scenarios which merit attention. The first is of course that Iceland will not join the EU, and the EEA will continue with business as usual for the foreseeable future. This may indeed be the most likely way forward. However, given that the main aim of this volume has been to assess how the EEA Agreement currently functions, this alternative will not be discussed in greater detail here. It suffices to say that, if this did turn out to be the case, some of the challenges identified in the previous section would need to be addressed more rigorously, particularly those related to the evolving nature of the EU versus the static nature of the EEA. This might require some renegotiation of the structure and scope of the Agreement.

The second scenario is that Iceland would join the EU and that Norway and Liechtenstein would continue their cooperation with the EU through the EEA, albeit with certain institutional modifications and potential revisions of content. A third alternative is that, if Iceland joined the EU, Norway and Liechtenstein would opt to go their own separate ways, whether they followed Iceland into the Union or established bilateral forms of cooperation with the EU. This option would result in the discontinuation of the EEA Agreement as such. A final option is that the EEA would be substantially renegotiated (and expanded) in terms of membership, and potentially also content. These scenarios are discussed in greater detail below.

And then there were two?

As noted in the previous section, Iceland's accession to the EU would pose certain challenges with respect to the institutional framework of the EEA Agreement. This does not, however, mean that the two remaining EFTA partners would be unable to continue their cooperation with the EU through the EEA. Rather, this would depend to a large extent on the political will within both countries as well as the EU. For Norway and Liechtenstein there are arguably three conceivable forms of association with the EU: the current EEA model, full membership or a looser form of bilateral association. There is reason to believe that, even in the event of Iceland's departure, the EEA would still be the most politically viable option for these two states.

The EEA Agreement is often considered a political compromise in Norway. While it is not generally the first choice of most political parties, all of the parties have in the past been able to live with this form of association and it has provided a basis for stable coalition governments (EEA Review Committee 2012: 8). Following Norway's review of its relations with the EU, Fredrik Sejersted, head of the Norwegian Review Committee, indicated to the press that there were official signals from both the EU and Norway that the Agreement would continue even if Iceland joined the EU (Tolbaru 2012b).

It is not unlikely that Liechtenstein would also favour an institutional adaptation of the EEA, should Iceland join the EU. As noted by Frommelt and Gstohl (2011: 14), there is a 'political consensus that Liechtenstein should in the future avoid a "step back" and "at least keep the level of integration already achieved". Yet both the current foreign minister and the reigning prince are against EU membership.'

Thus it appears that both Norway and Liechtenstein, at least officially, favour a continuation of the EEA, even if Iceland were to join the EU. This would, however, imply a certain amount of institutional adjustment, particularly in relation to ESA and the EFTA Court. For example, the ESA College and the EFTA Court might still have three members each to avoid deadlock, but not necessarily of different nationalities. In order to strengthen credibility, another option would be to allow individuals from EU member states to sit in these institutions (Frommelt and Gstohl 2011: 52). With respect to the EFTA Court, Article 28 of the Surveillance and Court Agreement does not prohibit the appointment of two judges of the same nationality, nor does it specify that all judges must be citizens of an EFTA state (Hillion 2011: 18). In the case of ESA, Article 7 of the same Agreement foresees that two out of three members of the College should be EFTA nationals. However, that does leave scope for a member of a different nationality. Therefore, there are options available to Norway and Liechtenstein if they did decide to continue with the EEA. However, they would need to consider how the credibility of the institutions would be affected if their members were only composed of their own nationals, particularly bearing in mind the difference in size between the two states. Alternatively, if they did allow non-EFTA nationals to sit in these bodies, they would need to contemplate whether and how such a move would coincide with considerations of sovereignty and the two-pillar nature of the EEA Agreement.

EEA no more?

Although both Norway and Liechtenstein have indicated an interest in continuing their cooperation with the EU through the EEA in the event that Iceland joined the EU, there is also a possibility that the two states would decide to go their own separate ways. In some ways the EFTA partners make strange bedfellows and, as noted by the authors of the Norwegian review, it is an accident of history that they ended up together in the EEA. There are great differences in interests, capacity and internal procedures between the EFTA partners (Sejersted and Sverdrup 2012). To a certain extent Iceland, with its Nordic history and small size, represents a middle ground between Norway and Liechtenstein. Norway may in particular face the temptation to act alone as it has the necessary resources to do so. Therefore, the possibility exists that the EEA would be discontinued, while Norway and Liechtenstein sought their own solutions either by following Iceland into the Union or forming bilateral relations with the EU.

The Norwegian report noted that a new, fundamental debate in Norway on its relations with the EU could result in renewed authority and legitimacy for the EEA model, but it could also entail a loss of support (EEA Review Committee 2012: 9). It has arguably become a fairly unlikely scenario that Norway would, under the present circumstances join the EU. Figures in 2011 varied considerably as to what the Norwegian population wanted. According to one poll, 50 per cent of the population was either in favour of joining the EU or continuing with the EEA, while 29 per cent preferred a two-sided trade agreement between Norway and the EU; the remaining one in five respondents were uncertain (Aale 2012). Another poll conducted for the No to the EU movement showed that a majority of 52 per cent of Norwegian voters wanted to replace the EEA Agreement with a bilateral trade agreement with the EU (Dagens Naeringsliv 2011). A general trend appeared to be that Norwegians were becoming more negative towards the EEA Agreement. At the end of 2011, 38 per cent said they would vote 'no' in a referendum on the Agreement tomorrow, compared with 22.3 per cent in December of 2010 (Dypvik 2011b).

The public debate in Norway suggests that at the beginning of 2012 support for EU membership was at an all time low and that support for EEA membership was dwindling. Criticism of the EEA came from all angles, and the dominant Labour Party appeared to be under considerable pressure to review its positive stance towards the EEA, even from its coalition partners. A spokesperson for fiscal policy of the Socialist Left Party, forming part of the governing coalition, demanded that the government reconsider its position towards the entire EEA Agreement calling it a 'sacred cow' that no one has dared to touch but that now it's time to kill it (Thorenfeldt 2011). The other junior coalition partner, the Centre Party, also voiced the opinion that it was realistic that Norway would soon leave the EEA and that the party had launched a campaign on this topic (Hornburg 2011). Another criticism was the lack of use of the veto. The leader of the opposition Christian Democratic Party said that he was dissatisfied with the government not being willing to use this option and that the time had come for a broader discussion of the EEA Agreement (Dypvik 2011a).

Despite mounting opposition, high-level officials within the Norwegian Labour Party have rejected the idea that a discontinuation of the Agreement could be on the cards. Jonas Gahr Store, Minister of Foreign Affairs, has been particularly vocal on the topic saying that the EEA Agreement was possibly more important for Norway than ever before and that the business sector was dependent on access to European markets and the legal protection included in the EEA Agreement (Brox 2011). Those in favour of the EEA have argued that it is unrealistic that Norway would be able to secure looser bilateral agreements with the EU which would adequately serve its interests (Dagens Naeringsliv 2011). This has been referred to as a Swiss-type model. Based on the Swiss experience, there is concern that such a solution would be more bureaucratic and slower than the EEA (Tolbaru 2012a). Furthermore, the EU has not been very enthusiastic towards such arrangements, as it does not consider them to function well (Council of the European Union 2010). In allowing extensive bilateral agreements, the EU might also be concerned about setting a precedent for other countries, in particular those belonging to the ENP (Frommelt and Gstohl 2011: 53). Despite support within the dominant Labour Party and some sectors of Norwegian society, as well as a lack of a viable alternative, the government may in the future be faced with increasing public pressure to reconsider Norway's relations with the EU. This will be particularly true if Iceland joins the EU, necessitating a renegotiation of some aspects of the Agreement.

As noted in the previous section, Liechtenstein has indicated that it would like to retain the EEA despite Iceland's accession to the EU, but the feasibility of this option will most likely be determined by Norway's reaction. If Norway lost interest in the EEA, Liechtenstein would be faced with the question of whether to opt for a bilateral association or full or partial EU membership. The practical aspects of these options would need to be negotiated and subjected to a public referendum (Frommelt and Gstöhl 2011: 55). Having already been 'Europeanized' so extensively through the EEA, Norway and Liechtenstein might find it difficult to take a step back. Such a move would undoubtedly call for an interesting study on de-Europeanization. All in all, the direction taken by the EFTA states will depend not only on their internal political considerations but also on developments on the EU side.

Expansion of the Agreement?

The final, and perhaps most interesting, scenario would involve a substantial revision of the EEA in terms of both membership and content. To date, the EEA has not been a model that has been replicated elsewhere; the closest exception might be Puerto Rico's relations with the USA. As noted by the authors of the Norwegian review, the EEA has often been considered a second-best solution, both by those who favour EU membership and those who would prefer looser ties with the EU. It has been seen as a compromise that most people can live with, but no one loves. Other states have generally not found this to be an attractive model, and no other state has so far seriously made an effort to join EFTA and become part of the EEA (Sejersted and Sverdrup 2012).

Yet the 2010 European Council conclusions on the EFTA states openly suggest the possibility of 'developments in the membership of the EEA' (Council of the European Union 2010: 5). Already a member of EFTA, an obvious candidate for joining the EEA is Switzerland. Other potential members, as hinted at in the Council conclusions, include small western European states such as Andorra, San Marino and Monaco. In other contexts, significantly larger countries such as the Eastern Partnership states have been mentioned. Finally, with forecasts of a two-tier Europe predicting a widening gap between an outer core and an inner core, current EU members, particularly the UK, have been named in this debate.

In his book, *The Future of Europe: Towards a Two-Speed EU?*, Jean-Claude Piris reaches the conclusion that the solution to the current economic and political climate is to permit 'two-speed' development: allowing an inner core to move towards closer economic and political union (Piris 2011). Michael van Hulten, a former Dutch MEP, has also detailed what a two-layer Europe might look like. 'The outer layer would be an overarching, less intrusive and more inclusive framework for European cooperation: a European Area of Freedom, Security and Prosperity (EFSP). This would comprise all EU and EFTA member states, as well as all existing EU candidate countries, including Turkey. It could be expanded eastward to all European countries, including Russia, if and when the Copenhagen accession criteria (or similar) were met' (Korski 2011).

In addition to suggestions which would expand the EEA to a wide range of states, there is also the issue of an increasing gap between developments in the EU and the EEA due to the fairly static nature of the Agreement, as described in the previous section. As noted by Frommelt and Gstohl (2011: 49), this problem could be tackled by a deepening and/or broadening of the EEA. This would potentially imply more (quasi-) supranationality and new areas being integrated into the Agreement. Such revisions could take into account the EU's Treaty revisions since the Treaty of Maastricht, as well as new policy fields that were originally left out of the EEA. Such a comprehensive agreement could, for example, encompass areas such as Schengen and the CFSP (Sejersted and Sverdrup 2012). Furthermore, the establishment of the EEAS has provided an occasion for the EU to examine its current external arrangements, with the aim of rationalizing and optimalizing them. It has been suggested that the current EEA institutional framework is too formal and cumbersome in view of its actual functions in the administration of the Agreement (Hillion 2011: 17). Such considerations could be addressed in any revision of the EEA.

Thus, there has been no lack of suggestions as to how EFTA and the EEA could be revised and restructured. But how likely is a widening and deepening of the EEA? Key questions in this debate are whether the current EFTA states would agree to such an expansion and whether other states would want to sign up to such an Agreement. Norway has strongly resisted any suggestions to expand the EEA model to other states (EEA Review Committee 2012: 6), and some would argue that the EEA is likely neither to widen its membership, unless Switzerland reconsidered its policy, nor to deepen its integration (Frommelt and Gstohl 2011: 55). Assuming that a substantial revision of the content of the EEA would be coupled with a widening of its membership, this section examines some of the candidates which have been proposed as potential members of the EEA.

Switzerland, as a current member of EFTA, is generally the first to be named as a potential EEA candidate. Switzerland originally intended to join the EEA, but the public rejected membership in a referendum on 6 December 1992. Since then it has structured its relations with the EU through a series of bilateral agreements. In recent years the EU appears to have become weary of these agreements. In its conclusions on EU relations with the EFTA countries, the European Council noted that:

> while the present system of bilateral agreements has worked well in the past, the challenge of the coming years will be to go beyond this complex system, which is creating legal uncertainty and has become unwieldy to manage and has clearly reached its limits.
> (Council of the European Union 2010)

174 *The EEA: Challenges and future scenarios*

The constant updating of the EEA Agreement ensures continued homogeneity within the EEA. This is generally lacking in other association agreements, including the EU's bilateral agreements with Switzerland. Indeed, it is the 'lack of efficient arrangements for the take-over of new EU *acquis*' which constitutes the main EU critique regarding its relations with Switzerland (Hillion 2011: 11).

There was fairly little movement in negotiations between Switzerland and the EU in 2011 owing to the Swiss federal elections. Thus, one of the key tasks of the new Swiss government was to define the relationship between Switzerland and the EU. Yet Switzerland has not been particularly enthusiastic towards any renegotiation of its agreements with the EU. In its report on the assessment of Swiss European policy in 2010, the Federal Council concluded that the bilateral way was still the most suitable choice for Switzerland (Frommelt and Gstohl 2011: 11). The accession of Switzerland to the EEA would arguably largely resolve the deficiencies in EU–Swiss relations. Yet, however logical this option might be, it is doubtful that Switzerland's accession to the EEA would be supported by the Swiss population (Hillion 2011: 19), which is a crucial prerequisite to this option moving forward.

Moving on to a founding member of EFTA, the UK has been frequently named as an EU outsider and potential reverter to EFTA. Indeed, the UK was instrumental in setting up EFTA as a counterbalance to the supranational EEC. Although the UK later decided that membership of the Economic Community better served its interests, it has never been a very enthusiastic member of the European project, preferring to remain outside areas of cooperation such as Schengen and the Eurozone. Indeed, some would argue that distrust of Europe seems inherently British. Although the British do not have a monopoly on Euroscepticism, suspicion towards the European project has arguably existed for longer within the British mainstream than anywhere else (White 2012).

David Cameron's veto of the EU fiscal Treaty in December 2011 reopened the debate on the UK's relationship with the EU, with EFTA being named as a potential alternative to EU membership. In the British media a number of reports suggested that the UK might have something to learn from Norway and Switzerland. As noted in *The Economist*, 'the crisis in the Eurozone and new strains in Britain's relations with France and Germany have prompted interest in two countries that not only refused to join the euro but have stayed outside the European Union' (*The Economist* 2011). One article argued that 'switching from the costly and undemocratic European Union and joining the European Free Trade Association would bring many benefits and job creation is one of them'. Slightly ironically, the article further explained that such a move would mean regaining control over democratic law-making processes and being able to choose the best policies in a host of important areas (Oulds 2011). Another report stated that, if Britain were to withdraw from the Union, but remain in the EEA 'it would neither participate in the much maligned Common Agricultural Policy – nor the equally criticized Common

Fisheries Policy. It would also fall outside of the common foreign and defence policies so detested by some Eurosceptics' (Stares 2011).

Many would, however, argue that a return to EFTA would not work for the UK, not least because the EFTA states are bound by EU rules, but lack access to its decision-making processes. As noted in one article, in comparison to the EFTA states,

> semi-detached status for a larger and more assertive country might well be harder to achieve. And being in with the outs while trading freely in Europe comes at a price. It means paying to administer and police the single market while the in-crowd makes the important decisions about how it works. For a noisy nation accustomed to a place at the table and having its voice heard, that could feel like a very un-splendid isolation.
>
> (*The Economist* 2011)

The adoption of EU acquis by the EFTA states is an inherently asymmetrical process, whereby they adopt legislation which has been decided without their participation. It is unlikely that a country such as the UK would be satisfied with this situation. Therefore, a return to EFTA for the UK might not be such a plausible scenario.

The EU has also indicated that states which are neither former nor current members of EFTA could potentially join the association and become participants in the EEA. The EU appears, in particular, to have an interest in a possible accession of European micro-states to ensure their integration in the internal market. With respect to Andorra, Monaco and San Marino, the European Council conclusions from December 2010 stated that 'their current relations with the EU are extended but fragmented, with large parts of the *acquis* related to the internal market not introduced in their legislation and therefore not applicable' (Council of the European Union 2010: 2).

A report of the Hungarian Presidency on EU relations with Andorra, San Marino and Monaco from June 2011 noted that EU relations with these three countries diverged significantly from one country to the other. However, according to the report, these states, particularly Andorra and San Marino, had shown strong interest in strengthening, extending and possibly restructuring their relations with the EU. San Marino had even expressed openness towards the possibility of EEA membership. The report concluded that a new institutional framework was needed in order to ensure further integration of these countries into the internal market and that the use of existing instruments should not be a priori excluded (Presidency of the European Union 2011). More specific recommendations were due to be made in 2012. From an EU perspective, inclusion of the micro-states in the EEA might be logical, given the EEA's effective mechanisms to ensure homogeneity (Hillion 2011: 19). However, as noted, such an expansion of the EEA would need to be accepted by the pre-existing members of the club, and Norway has so far voiced strong resistance to such a move.

A widening of the EEA could also include the more advanced of the European Neighbourhood Policy states. In particular, Commission initiatives have been aimed at pulling the EU's six post-Soviet neighbours[1] closer to the West and perhaps in the long run including these countries in the internal market (Runner 2008). Indeed, the Eastern Partnership envisages that in the long term a broader regional trade approach could be adopted, perhaps taking inspiration from the EEA (Frommelt and Gstohl 2011: 51). The EEA model has been regularly evoked in EU policy papers on the ENP, and the EEA model has even been presented as a long-term objective of the policy (Hillion 2011: 19).

The EEA has been compared with the ENP in the sense that the EU's relations with the EFTA states are driven by the same fundamental interest as its relations with the ENP countries, 'that of creating an environment as similar as possible to the Union, in legal terms, through the export of its norms' (Hillion 2011: 8). Much like the ENP, the incentives provided in the EEA are not linked to the prospect of EU membership. However, 'contrary to the ENP, EU norm projection is assured by instruments, covering almost the whole range of the Union's activities, and involving unique bodies endowed with compliance control and enforcement powers'. Given the strong legal and institutional tools established to ensure homogeneity, the EEA is, from an EU point of view, a nearly perfect tool of norm projection (Hillion 2011: 13).

Despite the potential benefits which an expansion of the EEA would entail, this also raises certain questions. In relation to the ENP states, there are many factors which need to be considered and which may mean that an EEA-type solution would not function as well for them. The EFTA states are small, relatively rich and highly industrialized democracies, while most of the ENP countries are noticeably below the EU average in economic and political terms. Therefore, most of the ENP countries lack the necessary institutional and administrative capacities for an EEA-like internal market association (Frommelt and Gstohl 2011: 51). As noted in Chapter 3 and confirmed in the case study chapters of this volume, domestic variables are important in the process of Europeanization. Having a fairly efficient administration, a relatively strong 'culture of compliance' and a lack of veto points which could facilitate opposition are all significant factors when it comes to downloading. Moreover, the interests of the current EFTA states and the ENP countries do not always coincide, as the ENP countries generally have a great interest in the Common Agricultural and Fisheries Policies (Frommelt and Gstohl 2011: 51).

Another key question is whether any of these countries want to join the EEA. This research has lent support to the argument that offering states a sufficient carrot alongside credible sanctions is conducive to domestic change. In other words, the results of this volume indicate that an important reason why the EEA works well in practice is that the EFTA states value the Agreement. Would it work so well if it were made up of states which were pressured into joining against their will? Past studies have shown that candidate status offers states a sufficient carrot, while ENP status does not. However, the ENP countries have not expressed any particular desire to become members of EFTA or the EEA (Hillion 2011: 20). For that matter, neither have the micro-states as they may prefer an institutionally less demanding and less expensive form of association with the EU (Frommelt and Gstohl 2011: 51). Therefore, before extending an EEA-type model to these states it is necessary to measure how strong the incentives and threats have to be in order for domestic change to occur in third countries, taking into consideration relevant domestic political conditions.

Furthermore, adding a greater number of states to the EFTA pillar of the EEA would make speaking with one voice more difficult. According to the EEA Agreement, Iceland, Norway and Liechtenstein are meant to harmonize their positions internally and then speak with one voice towards the EU. Although the three EFTA states have generally been able to agree on a common position, this requirement has sometimes led to delays and, on occasion, disagreements. It could thus be argued that an expansion of the EFTA pillar would need to be coupled with institutional reforms in the EEA, given that it might render the decision-making more cumbersome and time-consuming, potentially resulting in extensive delays in the implementation of EU *acquis* (Hillion 2011: 19). However, the extent to which such institutional reforms could coexist with sovereignty considerations is questionable. Therefore, although an increase in EFTA membership could consolidate the EEA Agreement's added value for the EU (Hillion 2011: 18), there are various issues which make this scenario unlikely, at least under the present circumstances.

In conclusion, taking into account various challenges inherent in the EEA Agreement, this chapter has speculated about its future. Various questions have been raised in this context. For example, is the EEA a viable long-term model? Can it function with only two members on the EFTA side? And does it could provide a suitable alternative to a broader range of countries? Twenty years ago most would have guessed that the EEA would serve as a mere stepping-stone towards EU membership. At the time of writing, the economic climate within the EU had perhaps served to decrease the attractiveness of EU membership, particularly for the more economically successful EFTA states. Therefore, the EEA may be here to stay, at least in the medium term. However, it may require some adjustment, particularly if any further decreases in membership on the EFTA side take place. As regards the accession of other countries to EFTA and the EEA, it has been reasoned in this chapter that this is perhaps unlikely for various reasons, at least for the time being. However, this does not mean that the EEA can provide no lessons for the EU's relations with third countries. Previously it has been assumed that the carrot of membership is necessary to promote domestic change in non-member states. Based on the experience of the EEA, this does not appear to be the case. Rather, given that the EEA has generally been found to function well, further research should explore how and to what extent such a model could be further developed.

Whether the EEA continues as it is, whether membership of the EFTA pillar increases or decreases, whether the Agreement's content and structure are revised or whether it ceases to exist at all are questions which will only be answered in the fullness of time. The future of the EEA is of course largely dependent on developments within the EU. While some believe that the Union is about to fall apart, others believe that it will be reinforced and intensified in coming years (EEA Review Committee 2012: 5). In the period of uncertainty which has followed the economic crisis, lessons learned from the Icelandic case can perhaps be important for a wider circle of countries and offer a starting point for further research.

Notes

Introduction

1 Technically, the EU did not come into existence until November 1993 when the Treaty on European Union (TEU) entered into force. Furthermore, before the entry into force of the Treaty on the Functioning of the European Union (TFEU) on 1 December 2009, the term EU was not strictly applicable to legal matters relating to the EC Treaty. Nevertheless, for the sake of simplicity, the term EU will be used throughout this volume even when discussing events before 1993 and policies legally belonging to the EC.
2 Norway applied for EU membership in 1972 and 1994, but on both occasions this was rejected by a rather narrow majority in public referendums.
3 On the initiative of the United Kingdom (UK), EFTA was established in 1960 by Austria, Denmark, Norway, Portugal, Sweden, Switzerland and the UK as an economic counterbalance to the EEC, which then included France, Germany, Italy and the Benelux countries.
4 Liechtenstein became a full member of EFTA in 1991 having previously been linked to EFTA through a special protocol.
5 Although Switzerland is also a member of EFTA, any mention of 'the EFTA states' in this volume will generally refer only to the EFTA parties to the EEA Agreement: Iceland, Norway and Liechtenstein.
6 Croatia's accession would bring this number up to 28.
7 *Acquis* or *acquis communautaire* refers to the cumulative body of EU laws.
8 This view was expressed in several interviews, for example with the Director General of the Directorate for External Trade and Economic Affairs at the Icelandic Ministry for Foreign Affairs on 23 November 2007 in Reykjavik.

1 Europeanization: An analytical framework

1 In their analysis of the impact of the EU on Britain, Bache and Jordan (2006a) define Europeanization as the 'reorientation or reshaping of politics in the domestic arena in ways that reflect policies, practices and preferences advanced through the EU system of governance'. Other examples include Heriter *et al.* (2001: 3), who see Europeanization as 'the process of influence deriving from European decisions and impacting member states' policies and political and administrative structures'; Buller and Gamble (2002: 17), who describe Europeanization as 'a situation where distinct modes of European governance have transformed aspects of domestic politics'; and Haverland (2003: 203) who argues that 'Europeanization can be used to refer to national responses to European integration or national adaptation to EU policies'.

2 Various authors have developed definitions that encapsulate the interactive nature of Europeanization. Laffan and Stubb (2003: 70), for example, have described Europeanization as a two-way process 'whereby national systems (institutions, policies, governments) adapt to EU policies and integration more generally, while also themselves shaping the European Union'. Featherstone and Kazamias (2001a: 6) share this view, defining Europeanization as a process between the domestic and the EU levels, involving both 'top down and bottom up pressures'. Additionally, in their study on Greece, Featherstone and Papadimitriou (2008: 1) argue that: 'It is not only a matter of how the EU impacts on domestic systems but of how national governments seek to shape the agenda of the EU as a whole, inserting their interests and preferences into common policies and understandings. In other words the relationship between member states and the EU flows in both directions, shaping the politics and economics of each other.'
3 The EU has different methods of legislating, which give states varying degrees of flexibility with respect to implementation. The two principal types of legislation, which are directly binding on states, are regulations and directives. Regulations have the most direct impact because they are directly applicable within national legal systems and obligatory in all of their elements. Directives give states more flexibility. They are binding as to the end to be achieved but leave states considerable choice as to how they are implemented. Nevertheless, the objectives which states have to meet are set out in considerable detail and thus directives also have substantial impact. The EU also engages in a variety of non-binding intitiatives, for example through the Open Method of Coordination (OMC) or in the area of Common Foreign and Security Policy.
4 Many scholars refer to incompatibility between EU policy and domestic arrangements as 'misfit', but the terms 'mismatch' or 'incongruence' are generally preferred in this study.
5 Also known as the "logic of expected consequences".
6 The first phase of infringement proceedings involves a 'letter of formal notice', whereby the Commission requests that a member state submit its observations on a particular problem regarding the application of EU law. In the second stage, the Commission can issue a 'reasoned opinion' setting out its position on the infringement and the reasons why it considers the member state in question to have failed to fulfil its obligations. Finally, a referral by the Commission to the Court of Justice opens a litigation procedure against the member state, which can lead to a fine.
7 The OMC was created as part of employment policy but has been expanded to other areas such as social protection and inclusion, education, youth and training which fall under the competence of the member states. Under this intergovernmental method, the member states use various non-binding tools such as benchmarking and peer reviews where they evaluate each other and stimulate good practice through peer pressure.
8 This generally refers to the countries of Central and Eastern Europe (CEECs), from the time that they became credible potential members of the EU in the mid-1990s to the time of their accession in 2004 and 2007.
9 Earlier rounds of accession were not subject to such extensive monitoring.
10 As members, the countries would, for example, have access to the internal market, enjoy the protection of EU rules and gain a voice in EU policy-making (Vachudova 2005: 66).
11 The European Neighbourhood Policy (ENP) applies to the EU's immediate neighbours by land or sea (excluding Russia). These are Algeria, Armenia, Azerbaijan, Belarus, Egypt, Georgia, Israel, Jordan, Lebanon, Libya, Moldova, Morocco, the Palestinian Authority, Syria, Tunisia and Ukraine.
12 A list of the internal EFTA documents referenced can be found in Appendix II.
13 A full list of interviews can be found in Appendix I.

2 Uploading in the EEA

1. This view was expressed in interviews with a number of relevant officials and is also based on the experience of the author having worked at the EFTA Secretariat.
2. The EEA Agreement entails a two-pillar decision-making structure whereby EEA EFTA bodies were established, including a Standing Committee, a Surveillance Authority and a Court, to mirror corresponding institutions on the EU side. Common bodies made up of representatives from both the EEA EFTA States and the EU were also established to take substantive decisions related to the EEA Agreement (See Fig. 3.1). The pillar structure of the EEA should not be confused with the three pillars of the EU that existed prior to the Treaty of Lisbon.
3. Interview with a specialist on the EEA EFTA states at DG RELEX on 12 November 2008 in Brussels.
4. Interview with a Legal Expert in Civil Law Affairs at the Icelandic Ministry of Justice and Ecclesiastical Affairs on 10 June 2008 in Reykjavik.
5. Figures exclude locally employed personnel abroad.
6. The government manifesto of the centre-left coalition which came to power on 10 May 2009 states that severe cuts will have to be made in government spending in order to counter loss of government revenues and accumulation of government debt in the wake of the financial crisis.
7. The embassy in Vienna was opened in conjunction with the establishment of a Permanent Mission to the Organization for Security and Co-operation in Europe (OSCE), while the Embassy in Helsinki also serves the Baltic states and the Ukraine.
8. For example, the Icelandic Confederation of Labour (ASI) and the Confederation of State and Municipal Employees (BSRB) are members of ETUC, while the Confederation of Icelandic Employers (SA) and the Federation of Icelandic Industries (SI) are members of BUSINESSEUROPE.
9. Interview with the Head of Social Affairs at the Icelandic Confederation of Labour on 12 June 2008 in Reykjavik and the Head of Social Policy at the Confederation of Icelandic Employers on 9 September 2008 in Reykjavik.
10. The Council and the Commission must consult the EESC in certain areas related to social policy. On average the EESC delivers 170 advisory documents and opinions a year. Members of the EESC are drawn from economic and social interest groups from each of the member states. The Committee's Employers' Group works in close partnership with the main European employers' and enterprises' organizations, BUSINESSEUROPE, CEEP, EUROCHAMBRES and EUROCOMMERCE, while the Employees' group works in close cooperation with ETUC.
11. Interview with the Head of Social Affairs at the Icelandic Confederation of Labour on 12 June 2008 in Reykjavik.
12. Interviews with the Director of Policymaking and Communications at the Confederation of Icelandic Employers on 9 September 2008 in Reykjavik and the Project Manager in Environmental Matters at the Icelandic Association of Local Authorities on 9 September 2008 in Reykjavik.
13. Nearly 50 interviews have been conducted with various officials. None mentioned any instances of Iceland trying to initiate a piece of legislation at the EU level.
14. According to Article 99 (1) of the EEA Agreement.
15. Interview with the Deputy Secretary General of the EFTA Secretariat on 11 November 2008 in Brussels.
16. This was confirmed in various interviews, for example with the Director of the Department of Civil Law Affairs at the Icelandic Ministry of Justice and Ecclesiastical Affairs on 29 February 2008 in Reykjavik.

182 *Notes*

17 Interview with the Deputy Secretary General of the EFTA Secretariat on 11 November 2008 in Brussels.
18 Interview with the Director of the Department of Civil Law Affairs at the Icelandic Ministry of Justice and Ecclesiastical Affairs on 29 February 2008 in Reykjavik.
19 Based on interviews with representatives of various government ministries, the Icelandic Mission to the EU, the EFTA Secretariat and the Commission.
20 Interview with the Director of the Services, Capital, Persons and Programmes Division of the EFTA Secretariat on 11 November 2008 in Brussels.
21 Interview with the Director of the EEA Coordination Division at the EFTA Secretariat on 11 November 2008 in Brussels.
22 Interview with the Director of the EEA Coordination Division at the EFTA Secretariat on 11 November 2008 in Brussels.
23 Interview with a Legal Expert at the Icelandic Ministry of Business Affairs on 5 September 2008 in Reykjavik.
24 Articles 290 and 291 of the consolidated version of the TFEU.
25 Particular reference is made to the EEA EFTA states in paragraph 95 and the conclusions of the guidelines (SEC(2011)855/1).
26 Interview on 25 February 2008 in Reykjavik.
27 Interview with the former Counsellor for Industry at the Icelandic Mission to the EU (1995–98) on 8 September 2008 in Reykjavik.
28 EFTA report on EU Comitology Committees with EEA EFTA Participation or Relevance.
29 Interview with the Head of Social Affairs at the Icelandic Confederation of Labour on 12 June 2008 in Reykjavik.
30 Interview with the Counsellor for Transport at the Icelandic Mission to the EU on 10 November 2008 in Brussels.
31 Interview with the Director of the Department of Civil Law Affairs at the Icelandic Ministry of Justice and Ecclesiastical Affairs on 29 February 2008 in Reykjavik.
32 Interview with the Deputy Secretary General of the EFTA Secretariat on 11 November 2008 in Brussels.
33 Working Paper by the EFTA Secretariat on the Open Method of Coordination (OMC).
34 Institutionalized cooperation between the Nordic countries has taken place since 1952 in the Nordic Council and since 1971 in the Nordic Council of Ministers. These fora are aimed at increasing intergovernmental and parliamentary collaboration in various policy areas such as the environment, social affairs, culture, and defence and security, as well as promoting Nordic interests abroad.
35 Interviews with the Director of the Department of Civil Law Affairs at the Icelandic Ministry of Justice and Ecclesiastical Affairs on 29 February 2008 in Reykjavik and the Head of Energy Policy at the Icelandic Ministry of Industry, Energy and Tourism on 25 February 2008 in Reykjavik.
36 Interview with a Legal Expert in Civil Law Affairs at the Icelandic Ministry of Justice and Ecclesiastical Affairs on 10 June 2008 in Reykjavik.
37 Interview with the General Director of the Icelandic Environment Agency on 11 June 2008 in Reykjavik.
38 Interview with a Legal Expert at the Icelandic Ministry of Business Affairs on 5 September 2008 in Reykjavik.
39 Interview with the Counsellor for Justice and Home Affairs at the Norwegian Mission to the EU on 12 November 2008 in Brussels.
40 Interviews with the General Director of the Icelandic Environment Agency on 11 June 2008 in Reykjavik and with the Director of Policymaking and Communications at the Confederation of Icelandic Employers on 9 September 2008 in Reykjavik.
41 Interview with the Head of Energy Policy at the Icelandic Ministry of Industry, Energy and Tourism on 25 February 2008 in Reykjavik.

42 Interview with the Deputy Head of the Icelandic Mission to the EU on 29 November 2007 in Brussels.
43 Interview with the Counsellor for Transport at the Icelandic Mission to the EU on 10 November 2008 in Brussels.
44 Together they form the EFTA Parliamentary Committee. Switzerland also participates but does not have a vote on EEA issues.
45 Interview with an MP for the Social Democratic Alliance and leader of the Icelandic delegation to the EFTA Parliamentary Committee on 27 February 2008 in Reykjavik.
46 Interview with the former Minister of Social Affairs (1995–2003) on 5 June 2008 in Reykjavik.
47 Interview with the former Counsellor for Industry at the Icelandic Mission to the EU (1995–98) on 8 September 2008 in Reykjavik.
48 Interview with a Legal Expert at the Icelandic Ministry of Business Affairs on 5 September 2008 in Reykjavik.
49 Ibid.
50 Interview with the Deputy Secretary General of the EFTA Secretariat on 11 November 2008 in Brussels.
51 Interview with the Director of the Services, Capital, Persons and Programmes Division of the EFTA Secretariat on 11 November 2008 in Brussels.
52 Interview with the Director General of the Directorate for External Trade and Economic Affairs at the Icelandic Ministry for Foreign Affairs on 23 November 2007 in Reykjavik.
53 There are four subcommittees, on the free movement of goods, free movement of capital and services, free movement of persons, and horizontal and flanking policies.
54 Prior to the establishment of the External Action Service, DG RELEX had a special office that dealt with the EEA and relations with the EFTA Secretariat and prepared participation in the EEA Joint Committee.
55 Interview with the Director of the EEA Coordination Division at the EFTA Secretariat on 11 November 2008 in Brussels.
56 This figure does not cover amending law or adaptations that have been made for all EEA EFTA states due to the two-pillar structure of the EEA Agreement.
57 Interview with the Deputy Head of the Icelandic Mission to the EU on 29 November 2007 in Brussels.
58 Interview with the Deputy Secretary General of the EFTA Secretariat on 11 November 2008 in Brussels.
59 Interview with a specialist on the EEA EFTA states at DG RELEX on 12 November 2008 in Brussels.
60 Interview with officials at the EEA Coordination Unit in Liechtenstein on 7 July 2008 in Vaduz.
61 Interview with a specialist on the EEA EFTA states at DG RELEX on 12 November 2008 in Brussels.
62 Article 102 of the EEA Agreement states that 'If, at the end of the time limit set out in paragraph 4, the EEA Joint Committee has not taken a decision on an amendment of an Annex to this Agreement, the affected part thereof, as determined in accordance with paragraph 2, is regarded as provisionally suspended, subject to a decision to the contrary by the EEA Joint Committee.'
63 Interview with the Director General of the Directorate for External Trade and Economic Affairs at the Icelandic Ministry for Foreign Affairs on 23 November 2007 in Reykjavik.
64 Interview with the former Counsellor for Industry at the Icelandic Mission to the EU (1995–98) on 8 September 2008 in Reykjavik.
65 Interview with the Director of the EEA Coordination Division at the EFTA Secretariat on 11 November 2008 in Brussels.

184 Notes

66 Interview with the former Counsellor for Industry at the Icelandic Mission to the EU (1995–98) on 8 September 2008 in Reykjavik.

3 Downloading in the EEA

1. Schimmelfennig and Sedelmeier (2005a: 20–22) refer to this type of rule transfer as 'lesson-drawing'. In these instances, adoption of EU rules is domestically driven and the activities of the EU, i.e. the rewards that it attaches to the adoption of particular rules or its persuasion abilities, are not the decisive factor in the decision of states to adopt EU rules. Rather, states take the initiative to import EU rules voluntarily as the result of perceived domestic utility.
2. Based on interviews with various high-ranking officials at the Icelandic Mission to the EU and the Ministry of Foreign Affairs.
3. Iceland scored 89.6 in 1996, 97.2 in 1998, 98.1 in 2000, 96.7 in 2002, 100 in 2003, 98.6 in 2004, 100 in 2005, 98.1 in 2006, 97.6 in 2007 and 91.5 in 2008.
4. Interview with the Head of Environmental Affairs at the Federation of Icelandic Industries on 4 September 2008 in Reykjavik.
5. Interview with a Legal Expert at the Icelandic Ministry of Business Affairs on 5 September 2008 in Reykjavik.
6. Interview with a Legal Expert in Civil Law Affairs at the Icelandic Ministry of Justice and Ecclesiastical Affairs on 10 June 2008 in Reykjavik.
7. Interview with First Secretaries at the Department for European Affairs at the Icelandic Ministry of Foreign Affairs on 10 June 2008 in Reykjavik.
8. Interview with the Counsellor for Environmental Affairs at the Icelandic Mission to the EU on 14 November 2008 in Brussels.
9. Interview with the General Director of the Icelandic Environment Agency on 11 June 2008 in Reykjavik.
10. Regulations are not directly applicable in Iceland through the EEA Agreement and so they need to be translated and adopted through domestic procedures.
11. Interview with a Legal Expert at the Icelandic Ministry of Business Affairs on 5 September 2008 in Reykjavik.
12. Interview with First Secretaries at the Department for European Affairs at the Icelandic Ministry of Foreign Affairs on 10 June 2008 in Reykjavik.
13. Ibid.
14. Interview with the General Director of the Icelandic Environment Agency on 11 June 2008 in Reykjavik.
15. Interview with the Head of Energy Policy at the Icelandic Ministry of Industry, Energy and Tourism on 25 February 2008 in Reykjavik.
16. Interview with the former Minister of Social Affairs (1995–2003) on 5 June 2008 in Reykjavik.
17. Interview with the Director of the EEA Coordination Division at the EFTA Secretariat on 11 November 2008 in Brussels.
18. Interview with the Head Legal Adviser in Employment Policy at the Confederation of Icelandic Employers on 9 September 2008 in Reykjavik.
19. Interviews with First Secretaries at the Department for European Affairs at the Icelandic Ministry of Foreign Affairs on 10 June 2008 in Reykjavik and with the Counsellor for Transport at the Icelandic Mission to the EU on 10 November 2008 in Brussels.
20. Interview with the Director of Policymaking and Communications at the Confederation of Icelandic Employers on 9 September 2008 in Reykjavik.
21. The New Approach, defined in a Council Resolution (85/C 136/01), has the purpose of ensuring that products that meet certain harmonized standards have free market access to the entire internal market in line with the principle of mutual recognition.

22 At the time of negotiation the EFTA side included Austria, Finland and Sweden, which joined the EU soon after the EEA Agreement came into effect, and Switzerland, which rejected the EEA Agreement in a referendum and structures its relations with the EU through bilateral agreements.
23 The Czech Republic, Estonia, Hungary, Latvia, Lithuania, Poland, Slovakia, Slovenia, Malta and Cyprus joined the EU in 2004, and Bulgaria and Romania became members in 2007.
24 Interview with the Deputy Secretary General of the EFTA Secretariat on 11 November 2008 in Brussels.
25 Interview with the General Director of the Icelandic Environment Agency on 11 June 2008 in Reykjavik.
26 Interview with a specialist on the EEA EFTA states at DG RELEX on 12 November 2008 in Brussels.
27 Interview with the Director of the EEA Coordination Division at the EFTA Secretariat on 11 November 2008 in Brussels.
28 Interview with the Head of International Affairs at the Icelandic Federation of State and Municipal Employees on 11 June 2008 in Reykjavik.
29 Interview with the Director of the EEA Coordination Division at the EFTA Secretariat on 11 November 2008 in Brussels.
30 Interview with officials at the EEA Coordination Unit in Liechtenstein on 7 July 2008 in Vaduz.
31 Interview with the Director of the EEA Coordination Division at the EFTA Secretariat on 11 November 2008 in Brussels.
32 Interview with the Deputy Secretary General of the EFTA Secretariat on 11 November 2008 in Brussels.
33 Interview with the Head of Energy Policy at the Icelandic Ministry of Industry, Energy and Tourism on 25 February 2008 in Reykjavik.
34 According to Article 103(2) of the EEA Agreement.
35 Formerly the European Court of Justice.
36 The EFTA Court is also responsible for the settlement of disputes between two or more EFTA states, for appeals concerning decisions taken by the EFTA Surveillance Authority and for giving advisory opinions to courts in EFTA states on the interpretation of EEA rules.
37 Interview with a Legal Expert in Civil Law Affairs at the Icelandic Ministry of Justice and Ecclesiastical Affairs on 10 June 2008 in Reykjavik.
38 Interview with a Director at the Icelandic Ministry of Social Affairs and Social Security on 25 February 2008 in Reykjavik.
39 Interview with the General Director of the Icelandic Environment Agency on 11 June 2008 in Reykjavik.
40 Interview with the Counsellor for Environmental Affairs at the Icelandic Mission to the EU on 14 November 2008 in Brussels.
41 Interview with a Legal Expert at the Icelandic Ministry of Business Affairs on 5 September 2008 in Reykjavik.
42 Interview with officials at the EEA Coordination Unit in Liechtenstein on 7 July 2008 in Vaduz.
43 Interview with a specialist on the EEA EFTA states at DG RELEX on 12 November 2008 in Brussels.
44 Interview with the Head of Social Affairs at the Icelandic Confederation of Labour on 12 June 2008 in Reykjavik.
45 Interview with the Counsellor for Environmental Affairs at the Icelandic Mission to the EU on 14 November 2008 in Brussels.
46 Interview with a Legal Expert at the Department of Equality and Labour at the Icelandic Ministry of Social Affairs on 28 February 2008 in Reykjavik.

47 Interview with the Head of Energy Policy at the Icelandic Ministry of Industry, Energy and Tourism on 25 February 2008 in Reykjavik.
48 Seminar at the EFTA Court on 24 November 2009.
49 The EFTA Court has jurisdiction to give 'advisory opinions' on the interpretation of the EEA Agreement. This procedure is modelled on Article 234 EC where the ECJ (now CJEU) has jurisdiction to give preliminary rulings concerning the interpretation of community law. The main differences between the two procedures are that the EFTA states are never under any obligation to bring matters before the EFTA Court and the EFTA Court's opinions are not legally binding.
50 The case of Erla Maria Sveinbjornsdottir (E-9/97) is an important example. In this case Ms. Sveinbjornsdottir brought an action for compensation against the Icelandic government claiming that it was liable for damages for not having adjusted the Insolvency Act correctly to a directive incorporated into the EEA Agreement. In response, the Reykjavik City Court submitted a request to the EFTA Court for an advisory opinion on the matter. The Court's opinion was that the relevant EU directive had not been transposed correctly into Icelandic law and that the Icelandic government should be obliged to provide for compensation for loss and damage caused to an individual due to incorrect implementation of the directive.
51 Interview with the Director of the EEA Coordination Division at the EFTA Secretariat on 11 November 2008 in Brussels.
52 Ibid.
53 Interview with the Counsellor for Transport at the Icelandic Mission to the EU on 10 November 2008 in Brussels.
54 Seminar at the EFTA Surveillance Authority on 1 September 2009.
55 Ibid.

4 Market competition in the electricity sector

1 Interview with the former Counsellor for Industry at the Icelandic Mission to the EU (1995–98) on 8 September 2008 in Reykjavik.
2 The specific provisions and arrangements concerning energy are listed in Annex IV to the EEA Agreement, as provided for by Article 24 of the Agreement.
3 EDF is one of the largest electricity producers in the world, primarily from nuclear power. It was founded in 1946 and owned by the French government. Prior to adoption of the First Electricity Directive, EDF held a monopoly on the distribution of electricity in France.
4 Interviews with the Counsellor for Industry at the Icelandic Mission to the EU on 14 November 2008 in Brussels and with the Head of Energy Policy at the Icelandic Ministry of Industry, Energy and Tourism on 25 February 2008 in Reykjavik.
5 Interview with the Head of Energy Policy at the Icelandic Ministry of Industry, Energy and Tourism on 25 February 2008 in Reykjavik.
6 Interview with the Counsellor for Industry at the Icelandic Mission to the EU on 14 November 2008 in Brussels.
7 Interviews with the Deputy Head of the Icelandic Mission to the EU on 29 November 2007 in Brussels, the Head of Energy Policy at the Icelandic Ministry of Industry, Energy and Tourism on 25 February 2008 in Reykjavik and the Head of Corporate Communications at Landsvirkjun on 27 February 2008 in Reykjavik.
8 Interview with the Head of Energy Policy at the Icelandic Ministry of Industry, Energy and Tourism on 25 February 2008 in Reykjavik.
9 Ibid.
10 Ibid.
11 Interviews with the Deputy Head of the Icelandic Mission to the EU on 29 November 2007 in Brussels, the Head of Energy Policy at the Icelandic Ministry of

Notes 187

  Industry, Energy and Tourism on 25 February 2008 in Reykjavik and the Head of Corporate Communications at Landsvirkjun on 27 February 2008 in Reykjavik.
12 Interview with the Head of Energy Policy at the Icelandic Ministry of Industry, Energy and Tourism on 25 February 2008 in Reykjavik.
13 Interviews with the Head of Corporate Communications at Orkuveita Reykjavikur on 4 March 2008 in Reykjavik, the Head of Corporate Communications at Landsvirkjun on 27 February 2008 in Reykjavik and the Head of Energy Policy at the Icelandic Ministry of Industry, Energy and Tourism on 25 February 2008.
14 Interview with the former Counsellor for Industry at the Icelandic Mission to the EU (1995–98) on 8 September 2008 in Reykjavik.
15 Article 24 of Directive 96/92/EC allows the Commission to agree to derogations in some cases from chapters IV, V, VI and VII on Transmission, Distribution, Unbundling and transparency of accounts and VII on Organisation of access to the system. It does not permit derogation from Chapter III on Generation, but rather gives states a choice between an authorization procedure or a tendering procedure for the construction of new generating capacity.
16 Interview with the Head of Energy Policy at the Icelandic Ministry of Industry, Energy and Tourism on 25 February 2008 in Reykjavik and the former Counsellor for Industry and the Environment at the Icelandic Mission to the EU (1995–98) on 8 September 2008 in Reykjavik.
17 Ibid.
18 As noted in Chapter 2, EFTA working groups form an important venue for the EFTA states to share information and make their views known to each other and to the Commission. The energy working group is particularly active. It meets approximately five or six times per year. Often meetings are only attended by Iceland and Norway, while Liechtenstein does not send a representative. Norway generally sends approximately 10–12 representatives, but Iceland often only sends one. Norway always chairs these meetings because of its oil and gas resources (Interview with the former Counsellor for Industry at the Icelandic Mission to the EU (1995–98) on 8 September 2008 in Reykjavik).
19 Interviews with the Head of Energy Policy at the Icelandic Ministry of Industry, Energy and Tourism on 25 February 2008 in Reykjavik and the former Counsellor for Industry at the Icelandic Mission to the EU (1995–98) on 8 September 2008 in Reykjavik.
20 Interview with the former Counsellor for Industry and the Environment at the Icelandic Mission to the EU (1995–98) on 8 September 2008 in Reykjavik.
21 Interview with the Counsellor for Commerce and Industry at the Icelandic Mission to the EU (2006–8) on 5 September 2008 in Reykjavik.
22 Ibid.
23 Interview with the Head of Energy Policy at the Icelandic Ministry of Industry, Energy and Tourism on 25 February 2008 in Reykjavik.
24 Usage of electricity per capita is higher in Iceland than in any other OECD country, probably due mainly to the large amount of electricity produced for heavy industry, but also because electricity is relatively inexpensive in Iceland, the standard of living is high and the climate is cold.
25 Interview with the Head of Energy Policy at the Icelandic Ministry of Industry, Energy and Tourism on 25 February 2008 in Reykjavik.
26 Interview with the former Counsellor for Industry and the Environment at the Icelandic Mission to the EU (1995–98) on 8 September 2008 in Reykjavik.
27 Interview with the Head of Energy Policy at the Icelandic Ministry of Industry, Energy and Tourism on 25 February 2008 in Reykjavik.
28 According to the Second Electricity Directive (2003/54/EC), the definition of small isolated systems is changed to those that produced less than 3,000 GWh in 1996 and where less than 5 per cent is from connection with other systems. A new term,

micro isolated system, is also adopted and refers to a system with consumption of less than 500 GWh in 1996 and with no connection with other systems. According to the new Directive, small isolated systems can apply for derogations from the same chapters as before if they can demonstrate substantial problems in implementing the Directive. Micro isolated systems can additionally apply for derogations from Chapter III on generation. Iceland still falls outside the scope of this definition of small isolated systems.

29 Interview with the Head of Energy Policy at the Icelandic Ministry of Industry, Energy and Tourism on 25 February 2008 in Reykjavik.
30 Ibid.
31 The electricity market in Liechtenstein is sufficiently small, although it is not sufficiently isolated.
32 Speech by the former Minister of Foreign Affairs, Ingibjorg Solrun Gisladottir, to the Icelandic Parliament on 27 November 2007.
33 Eight countries applied for transitional regimes, the UK, France, Luxembourg, Germany, Austria, the Netherlands, Spain and Denmark. Only Germany was granted a transitional regime from the relevant provisions of Chapter VII.
34 Both Malta and Cyprus qualified as small isolated systems as their consumption was less than 3,000 GWh in 1996, and less than 5 per cent of their annual consumption was obtained through interconnections with other systems.
35 Interview with the Head of Energy Policy at the Icelandic Ministry of Industry, Energy and Tourism on 25 February 2008 in Reykjavik.
36 Interview with the CEO of Hitaveita Sudurnesja on 3 March 2008 in Reykjanesbaer, Iceland.
37 Interview with the Head of Corporate Communications at Landsvirkjun on 27 February 2008 in Reykjavik.
38 Interview with the former Counsellor for Industry at the Icelandic Mission to the EU (1995–98) on 8 September 2008 in Reykjavik.
39 Interview with the Head of Corporate Communications at Landsvirkjun on 27 February 2008 in Reykjavik.
40 Interview with the Manager of the Electricity Division at the Federation of Icelandic Energy and Utilities on 4 March 2008 in Reykjavik.
41 Interview with the former Counsellor for Industry at the Icelandic Mission to the EU (1995–98) on 8 September 2008 in Reykjavik.
42 Interview with the Head of Energy Policy at the Icelandic Ministry of Industry, Energy and Tourism on 25 February 2008 in Reykjavik.
43 Interview with the Head of Corporate Communications at Orkuveita Reykjavikur on 4 March 2008 in Reykjavik.
44 Interview with the Manager of the Electricity Division at the Federation of Icelandic Energy and Utilities on 4 March 2008 in Reykjavik.
45 Interview with the former Counsellor for Industry at the Icelandic Mission to the EU (1995–98) on 8 September 2008 in Reykjavik.
46 Interview with the CEO of Hitaveita Sudurnesja on 3 March 2008 in Reykjanesbaer, Iceland.
47 Interview with the Manager of the Electricity Division at the Federation of Icelandic Energy and Utilities on 4 March 2008 in Reykjavik.
48 Interview with the Head of Energy Policy at the Icelandic Ministry of Industry, Energy and Tourism on 25 February 2008 in Reykjavik.
49 Acts no. 89/2004, 149/2004 and 30/2008. Various regulations have also been adopted based on the Electricity Act: 466/2003, 513/2003, 1048/2004, 1050/2004 and 1040/2005.
50 Article 4 of the Electricity Act no. 65/2003.
51 Article 15 of Directive 2003/54/EC.

Notes 189

52 Interview with the Deputy Director General of the National Energy Authority in Reykjavik on 5 March 2008.
53 The EFTA Surveillance Authority launched an energy sector inquiry, parallel to the European Commission's inquiry, on 22 June 2005. The focus was to examine how competition was functioning in the wholesale electricity markets of the EFTA States with the objective of identifying possible distortions or restrictions of competition.
54 According to figures from Landsvirkjun, in 2004 the company produced 84 per cent of the total electricity generated in Iceland. In 2007, its share had decreased to 72 per cent.
55 Interview with the Deputy Director General of the National Energy Authority in Reykjavik on 5 March 2008.
56 Interview with the Manager of the Electricity Division at the Federation of Icelandic Energy and Utilities on 4 March 2008 in Reykjavik.
57 Interview with the Head of Corporate Communications at Orkuveita Reykjavikur on 4 March 2008 in Reykjavik.
58 According to the Act on Landsvirkjun (no. 43/1983).
59 Interview with the CEO of Hitaveita Sudurnesja on 3 March 2008 in Reykjanesbaer, Iceland.
60 The most significant ownership change that has occurred since the legislation came into effect is that a Canadian company, Magma Energy, bought over 98 per cent of the production arm of HS (HS Orka), a deal which sparked a great deal of controversy as many in Iceland were reluctant to allow foreign ownership in the energy sector.
61 Interview with the Head of Corporate Communications at Landsvirkjun on 27 February 2008 in Reykjavik.
62 Interview with the Head of Corporate Communications at Orkuveita Reykjavikur on 4 March 2008 in Reykjavik.
63 Interview with the Manager of the Electricity Division at the Federation of Icelandic Energy and Utilities on 4 March 2008 in Reykjavik.
64 Interview with the Manager of the Electricity Division at the Federation of Icelandic Energy and Utilities on 4 March 2008 in Reykjavik.
65 Interview with the former Counsellor for Industry at the Icelandic Mission to the EU (1995–98) on 8 September 2008 in Reykjavik.

5 European citizenship and free movement of persons

1 Interview with the Deputy Secretary General of the EFTA Secretariat on 11 November 2008 in Brussels.
2 Interviews with a specialist on the EEA EFTA states at DG RELEX on 12 November 2008 in Brussels and with the Director of the EEA Coordination Division at the EFTA Secretariat on 11 November 2008 in Brussels.
3 Interview with the Director of the Department of Civil Law Affairs at the Icelandic Ministry of Justice and Ecclesiastical Affairs on 29 February 2008 in Reykjavik.
4 Interviews with First Secretaries at the Department for European Affairs at the Icelandic Ministry of Foreign Affairs on 10 June 2008 in Reykjavik and with a specialist on the EEA EFTA states at DG RELEX on 12 November 2008 in Brussels.
5 Interview with the Director of the Department of Civil Law Affairs at the Icelandic Ministry of Justice and Ecclesiastical Affairs on 29 February 2008 in Reykjavik.
6 Article 17(1) TEC states: 'Citizenship of the Union is hereby established. Every person holding the nationality of a Member State shall be a citizen of the Union. Citizenship of the Union shall complement and not replace national citizenship.'
7 Article 18(1) TEC states: 'Every citizen of the Union shall have the right to move and reside freely within the territory of the Member States, subject to the

limitations and conditions laid down in this Treaty and by the measures adopted to give it effect.'
8 Articles 19–21 of the EC Treaty.
9 The primary objective of the Schengen Convention was to eliminate border controls between participating states, which also necessitates various compensatory measures designed to increase security such as harmonized controls at external borders and a common visa and asylum policy, as well as extensive police and judicial cooperation.
10 Four major judgments have been given on the interpretation of Directives 93/96, 90/364 et 90/365 (Cases C-456/02; C-200/02; C-209/03 and C-157/03). According to these judgements, the right to reside in the territory of an EU member state is conferred directly on every citizen of the Union by Article 18(1) EC, and citizenship of the Union is destined to be a fundamental status of nationals of EU member states.
11 Directive 2004/38/EC amends Regulation (EEC) No 1612/68 and repeals Directives 64/221/EEC, 68/360/EEC, 72/194/EEC, 73/148/EEC, 75/34/EEC, 75/35/EEC, 90/364/EEC, 90/365/EEC and 93/96/EEC.
12 Directives 93/96, 90/364 and 90/365 sought to extend the scope of Community law to encompass welfare assitance to non-economically active citizens.
13 Family members who can enjoy rights under Community law include the spouse, minor (under 21) or dependent children and dependent ascendants, though in the case of students only the spouse and dependent children enjoy this right.
14 Interview with a specialist on the EEA EFTA states at DG RELEX on 12 November 2008 in Brussels.
15 Interview with the Counsellor for Justice and Home Affairs at the Icelandic Mission to the EU on 10 November 2008 in Brussels.
16 Ibid.
17 Interview with the Director of the Department of Civil Law Affairs at the Icelandic Ministry of Justice and Ecclesiastical Affairs on 29 February 2008 in Reykjavik.
18 Interview with the Counsellor for Justice and Home Affairs at the Icelandic Mission to the EU on 10 November 2008 in Brussels.
19 Interview with a Legal Expert at the Department of Equality and Labour at the Icelandic Ministry of Social Affairs on 28 February 2008 in Reykjavik.
20 Interview with the Director of the Services, Capital, Persons and Programmes Division of the EFTA Secretariat on 11 November 2008 in Brussels.
21 Interview with the Director of the Department of Civil Law Affairs at the Icelandic Ministry of Justice and Ecclesiastical Affairs on 29 February 2008 in Reykjavik.
22 Interview with First Secretaries at the Department for European Affairs at the Icelandic Ministry of Foreign Affairs on 10 June 2008 in Reykjavik.
23 Interview with the Counsellor for Justice and Home Affairs at the Icelandic Mission to the EU on 10 November 2008 in Brussels.
24 Interview with First Secretaries at the Department for European Affairs at the Icelandic Ministry of Foreign Affairs on 10 June 2008 in Reykjavik.
25 Interview with the Counsellor for Justice and Home Affairs at the Icelandic Mission to the EU on 10 November 2008 in Brussels.
26 Interview with a Legal Expert in Civil Law Affairs at the Icelandic Ministry of Justice and Ecclesiastical Affairs on 10 June 2008 in Reykjavik.
27 Interview with First Secretaries at the Department for European Affairs at the Icelandic Ministry of Foreign Affairs on 10 June 2008 in Reykjavik.
28 Interview with the Deputy Secretary General of the EFTA Secretariat on 11 November 2008 in Brussels.
29 Interview with officials at the EEA Coordination Unit in Liechtenstein on 7 July 2008 in Vaduz.

Notes 191

30 Interview with the Director of the Department of Civil Law Affairs at the Icelandic Ministry of Justice and Ecclesiastical Affairs on 29 February 2008 in Reykjavik.
31 Interview with First Secretaries at the Department for European Affairs at the Icelandic Ministry of Foreign Affairs on 10 June 2008 in Reykjavik.
32 Interview with a specialist on the EEA EFTA states at DG RELEX on 12 November 2008 in Brussels.
33 Interview with the Director of the Services, Capital, Persons and Programmes Division of the EFTA Secretariat on 11 November 2008 in Brussels.
34 Interview with officials at the EEA Coordination Unit in Liechtenstein on 7 July 2008 in Vaduz.
35 Interview with the Counsellor for Justice and Home Affairs at the Icelandic Mission to the EU on 10 November 2008 in Brussels.
36 Interview with the Director of the Services, Capital, Persons and Programmes Division of the EFTA Secretariat on 11 November 2008 in Brussels.
37 Interview with officials at the EEA Coordination Unit in Liechtenstein on 7 July 2008 in Vaduz.
38 Interview with the Director of the EEA Coordination Division at the EFTA Secretariat on 11 November 2008 in Brussels.
39 Interview with the Counsellor for Justice and Home Affairs at the Icelandic Mission to the EU on 10 November 2008 in Brussels.
40 Interview with officials at the EEA Coordination Unit in Liechtenstein on 7 July 2008 in Vaduz.
41 Interview with the Director of the EEA Coordination Division at the EFTA Secretariat on 11 November 2008 in Brussels.
42 Ibid.
43 Interviews with officials at the EEA Coordination Unit in Liechtenstein on 7 July 2008 in Vaduz and with the Director of the Services, Capital, Persons and Programmes Division of the EFTA Secretariat on 11 November 2008 in Brussels.
44 Interview with the Deputy Secretary General of the EFTA Secretariat on 11 November 2008 in Brussels.
45 Interview with the Director of the EEA Coordination Division at the EFTA Secretariat on 11 November 2008 in Brussels.
46 Interview with the Director of the Services, Capital, Persons and Programmes Division of the EFTA Secretariat on 11 November 2008 in Brussels.
47 Interview with First Secretaries at the Department for European Affairs at the Icelandic Ministry of Foreign Affairs on 10 June 2008 in Reykjavik.
48 Interview with the Director of the Department of Civil Law Affairs at the Icelandic Ministry of Justice and Ecclesiastical Affairs on 29 February 2008 in Reykjavik.
49 Interview with a specialist on the EEA EFTA states at DG RELEX on 12 November 2008 in Brussels.
50 Interview with the Director of the Services, Capital, Persons and Programmes Division of the EFTA Secretariat on 11 November 2008 in Brussels.
51 Interview with a specialist on the EEA EFTA states at DG RELEX on 12 November 2008 in Brussels.
52 Interview with the Deputy Secretary General of the EFTA Secretariat on 11 November 2008 in Brussels.
53 Interview with the Director of the Services, Capital, Persons and Programmes Division of the EFTA Secretariat on 11 November 2008 in Brussels.
54 Interview with the Counsellor for Justice and Home Affairs at the Icelandic Mission to the EU on 10 November 2008 in Brussels.
55 Interview with the Counsellor for Justice and Home Affairs at the Icelandic Mission to the EU on 10 November 2008 in Brussels.
56 Interview with officials at the EEA Coordination Unit in Liechtenstein on 7 July 2008 in Vaduz.

192 *Notes*

57 Interview with the Director of the Department of Civil Law Affairs at the Icelandic Ministry of Justice and Ecclesiastical Affairs on 29 February 2008 in Reykjavik.
58 Interview with First Secretaries at the Department for European Affairs at the Icelandic Ministry of Foreign Affairs on 10 June 2008 in Reykjavik.
59 Interview with the Director of the Services, Capital, Persons and Programmes Division of the EFTA Secretariat on 11 November 2008 in Brussels.
60 Interview with the Counsellor for Justice and Home Affairs at the Icelandic Mission to the EU on 10 November 2008 in Brussels.
61 Interview with officials at the EEA Coordination Unit in Liechtenstein on 7 July 2008 in Vaduz.
62 Interview with the Deputy Secretary General of the EFTA Secretariat on 11 November 2008 in Brussels.
63 Ibid.
64 Interview with the Director of the EEA Coordination Division at the EFTA Secretariat on 11 November 2008 in Brussels.
65 Ibid.
66 Ibid.
67 Interview with a specialist on the EEA EFTA states at DG RELEX on 12 November 2008 in Brussels.
68 Interview with the Director of the Services, Capital, Persons and Programmes Division of the EFTA Secretariat on 11 November 2008 in Brussels.
69 Interview with the Director of the EEA Coordination Division at the EFTA Secretariat on 11 November 2008 in Brussels.
70 Interviews with officials at the EEA Coordination Unit in Liechtenstein on 7 July 2008 in Vaduz and with the Counsellor for Justice and Home Affairs at the Icelandic Mission to the EU on 10 November 2008 in Brussels.
71 Interview with a Legal Expert in Civil Law Affairs at the Icelandic Ministry of Justice and Ecclesiastical Affairs on 10 June 2008 in Reykjavik.
72 Interview with the Counsellor for Justice and Home Affairs at the Icelandic Mission to the EU on 10 November 2008 in Brussels.
73 Interview with the Director of the Department of Civil Law Affairs at the Icelandic Ministry of Justice and Ecclesiastical Affairs on 29 February 2008 in Reykjavik.
74 Interview with a Legal Expert in Civil Law Affairs at the Icelandic Ministry of Justice and Ecclesiastical Affairs on 10 June 2008 in Reykjavik.
75 Interview with the Counsellor for Justice and Home Affairs at the Icelandic Mission to the EU on 10 November 2008 in Brussels.
76 Interview with the Deputy Secretary General of the EFTA Secretariat on 11 November 2008 in Brussels.

6 The Emissions Trading Scheme

1 Conservation of natural habitats, i.e. the Natura Directives, is one of the few areas of Environmental policy which is not considered EEA-relevant.
2 Interview with the Counsellor for Environmental Affairs at the Icelandic Mission to the EU on 14 November 2008 in Brussels.
3 Interview with the General Director of the Icelandic Environment Agency on 11 June 2008 in Reykjavik.
4 Each allowance gives the right to emit one tonne of CO_2 or the equivalent of another GHG.
5 The United Nations Framework Convention on Climate Change (UNFCC) was adopted in Rio de Janeiro in 1992 and took effect on 21 March 1994. The Kyoto Protocol to the UNFCC, which contains binding targets, was adopted in 1997 but did not take effect until 16 February 2005 as the ratification process was slow and difficult. The aim is to prevent GHG emissions from causing long-lasting and

dangerous damage to the environment so as to ensure that the eco-system can stabilize itself and promote sustainable development.
6 For the period beginning on 1 January 2013 the total quantity of allowances allocated to aircraft operators shall be equivalent to 95 per cent of the historical aviation emissions multiplied by the number of years in the period (Article 3.c).
7 The European Council of March 2007 made a firm commitment to reduce the overall greenhouse gas emissions of the Community by at least 20 per cent below 1990 levels by 2020 and by 30 per cent if other developed countries commit themselves to comparable reductions and more economically advanced developing countries contribute adequately according to their responsibilities and respective capabilities.
8 Interview with the Director of Policymaking and Communications at the Confederation of Icelandic Employers on 9 September 2008 in Reykjavik.
9 Interview with a specialist on the EEA–EFTA states at DG RELEX on 12 November 2008 in Brussels.
10 Interviews with the Head of Energy Policy at the Icelandic Ministry of Industry, Energy and Tourism on 25 February 2008 in Reykjavik and with the Counsellor for Environmental Affairs at the Icelandic Mission to the EU on 14 November 2008 in Brussels.
11 Interview with a specialist on the EEA–EFTA states at DG RELEX on 12 November 2008 in Brussels.
12 Interview with the Deputy Head of the Icelandic Mission to the EU on 29 November 2007 in Brussels.
13 Interview with a specialist on the EEA–EFTA states at DG RELEX on 12 November 2008 in Brussels.
14 Interview with officials at the EEA Coordination Unit in Liechtenstein on 7 July 2008 in Vaduz.
15 Interview with a specialist on the EEA–EFTA states at DG RELEX on 12 November 2008 in Brussels.
16 Interviews with the Head of Energy Policy at the Icelandic Ministry of Industry, Energy and Tourism on 25 February 2008 in Reykjavik and with the Counsellor for Environmental Affairs at the Icelandic Mission to the EU on 14 November 2008 in Brussels.
17 Interview with the Deputy Secretary General of the EFTA Secretariat on 11 November 2008 in Brussels.
18 Interview with the Head of Energy Policy at the Icelandic Ministry of Industry, Energy and Tourism on 25 February 2008 in Reykjavik.
19 Interview with the General Director of the Icelandic Environment Agency on 11 June 2008 in Reykjavik.
20 Interview with the Head of Energy Policy at the Icelandic Ministry of Industry, Energy and Tourism on 25 February 2008 in Reykjavik.
21 Interview with the Deputy Secretary General of the EFTA Secretariat on 11 November 2008 in Brussels.
22 Interview with the Counsellor for Environmental Affairs at the Icelandic Mission to the EU on 14 November 2008 in Brussels.
23 According to Appendix B of the Kyoto Protocol, most states were required to considerably reduce their emissions of GHGs. However, three states were allowed to maintain the same level of emissions as 1990: New Zealand, Russia and Ukraine. A few states were allowed to increase their emissions from the 1990 level: Norway by 1 per cent, Australia by 8 per cent and Iceland by 10 per cent.
24 Although this decision is often called the 'Icelandic clause', it does not apply uniquely to Iceland, but to all states which emitted less than 0.05 per cent of total emissions by all states listed in Appendix I in 1990.
25 Althingi 2001–02, 127th session of the Parliamnet, document no. 1100, p. 5119.

26 Interview with the Counsellor for Environmental Affairs at the Icelandic Mission to the EU on 14 November 2008 in Brussels.
27 Interview with the Head of Energy Policy at the Icelandic Ministry of Industry, Energy and Tourism on 25 February 2008 in Reykjavik.
28 Interview with the Deputy Secretary General of the EFTA Secretariat on 11 November 2008 in Brussels.
29 Interview with the Officer for the Environment at the EFTA Secretariat on 11 November 2008 in Brussels.
30 Interview with officials at the EEA Coordination Unit in Liechtenstein on 7 July 2008 in Vaduz.
31 Interview with a specialist on the EEA–EFTA states at DG RELEX on 12 November 2008 in Brussels.
32 Interview with the Head of Energy Policy at the Icelandic Ministry of Industry, Energy and Tourism on 25 February 2008 in Reykjavik.
33 Interview with the Deputy Head of the Icelandic Mission to the EU on 29 November 2007 in Brussels.
34 It was agreed that the EFTA states should submit their NAPs to ESA for approval instead of to the Commission, although ESA reviews the NAPs in close collaboration with the Commission.
35 Interview with the Head of Energy Policy at the Icelandic Ministry of Industry, Energy and Tourism on 25 February 2008 in Reykjavik.
36 See Appendix to JCD no. 146/2007.
37 Interview with the General Director of the Icelandic Environment Agency on 11 June 2008 in Reykjavik.
38 Interview with First Secretaries at the Department for European Affairs at the Icelandic Ministry of Foreign Affairs on 10 June 2008 in Reykjavik.
39 Interview with the Director of Policymaking and Communications at the Confederation of Icelandic Employers on 9 September 2008 in Reykjavik.
40 Communication of 27 September 2005 to the Council, the EP, the EESC and the Committee of the Regions entitled, 'Reducing the Climate Change Impact of Aviation'.
41 Interview with the Deputy Head of the Icelandic Mission to the EU on 29 November 2007 in Brussels.
42 Interview with the Director of Policymaking and Communications at the Confederation of Icelandic Employers on 9 September 2008 in Reykjavik.
43 Annex I of the EP's position at first reading states that 'From 1 January 2011, all flights which arrive at or depart from an airport situated in the territory of a Member State to which the Treaty applies shall be included, *taking into account the special situation of the flights between ultra-peripheral regions and the European Continental zone.*'
44 Interview with the Officer for the Environment at the EFTA Secretariat on 11 November 2008 in Brussels.
45 Interview with the Counsellor for Transport at the Icelandic Mission to the EU on 10 November 2008 in Brussels.
46 Interviews with the Deputy Head of the Icelandic Mission to the EU on 29 November 2007 in Brussels and with the Counsellor for Transport at the Icelandic Mission to the EU on 10 November 2008 in Brussels.
47 Interview with First Secretaries at the Department for European Affairs at the Icelandic Ministry of Foreign Affairs on 10 June 2008 in Reykjavik.
48 Interview with the Counsellor for Transport at the Icelandic Mission to the EU on 10 November 2008 in Brussels.
49 Interview with the Counsellor for Environmental Affairs at the Icelandic Mission to the EU on 14 November 2008 in Brussels.

50 Interview with a Legal Expert at the Icelandic Ministry of Business Affairs on 5 September 2008 in Reykjavik.
51 Interview with the Counsellor for Commerce and Industry at the Icelandic Mission to the EU (2006–08) on 5 September 2008 in Reykjavik.
52 Interview with the Counsellor for Environmental Affairs at the Icelandic Mission to the EU on 14 November 2008 in Brussels.
53 Interview with the Counsellor for Transport at the Icelandic Mission to the EU on 10 November 2008 in Brussels.
54 Interview with the Leader of the Icelandic delegation to the EFTA Parliamentary Committee on 27 February 2008 in Reykjavik.
55 Interview with the Director of Policymaking and Communications at the Confederation of Icelandic Employers on 9 September 2008 in Reykjavik.
56 Interview with First Secretaries at the Department for European Affairs at the Icelandic Ministry of Foreign Affairs on 10 June 2008 in Reykjavik.
57 Interview with the Counsellor for Environmental Affairs at the Icelandic Mission to the EU on 14 November 2008 in Brussels.
58 Interview with a Legal Expert at the Icelandic Ministry of Business Affairs on 5 September 2008 in Reykjavik.
59 Interview with the Director of Policymaking and Communications at the Confederation of Icelandic Employers on 9 September 2008 in Reykjavik.
60 Interview with a Legal Expert at the Icelandic Ministry of Business Affairs on 5 September 2008 in Reykjavik.
61 Interview with the Director of Policymaking and Communications at the Confederation of Icelandic Employers on 9 September 2008 in Reykjavik.
62 Interview with the Officer for the Environment at the EFTA Secretariat on 11 November 2008 in Brussels.
63 Interview with the Deputy Secretary General of the EFTA Secretariat on 11 November 2008 in Brussels.
64 Interview with the Head of Energy Policy at the Icelandic Ministry of Industry, Energy and Tourism on 25 February 2008 in Reykjavik.
65 Interview with a specialist on the EEA–EFTA States at DG RELEX on 12 November 2008 in Brussels.
66 Interview with the Counsellor for Environmental Affairs at the Icelandic Mission to the EU on 14 November 2008 in Brussels.
67 Personnal communication from the Officer for the Environment at the EFTA Secretariat on 23 March 2010.
68 Personal communication from Hrafnhildur Bragadottir on 16 June 2008.

7 The Food Law Package

1 Regulations (EC) nos 852/2004, 853/2004, 854/2004, 882/2004 and 183/2005 and Directive 2004/41/EC.
2 Regulation (EC) no. 1774/2002 and Directive 2002/33/EC.
3 Decision of the EEA Joint Committee no. 133/2007 from 26 October 2007 states that: 'The Contracting Parties have reviewed the situation for Iceland and decided that Iceland will take over the acts referred to in Chapter I of Annex I, except for the provisions that concern live animals, other than fish and aquaculture animals, and animal products such as ova, embryo and semen.'
4 Telephone interview with the Chief Veterinary Officer at the Icelandic Food and Veterinary Authority on 24 February 2010.
5 Ibid.
6 Annual Report on the functioning of the EEA Agreement in 1998.
7 Telephone interview with the Chief Veterinary Officer at the Icelandic Food and Veterinary Authority on 24 February 2010.

196 *Notes*

8 Telephone interview with the Chief Veterinary Officer at the Icelandic Food and Veterinary Authority on 24 February 2010.
9 Chapter 2, Part II of the EEA Agreement lays down the rules applicable to fisheries and agricultural products.
10 Report from a meeting of the Joint Working Group on Veterinary Matters on 11 September 1998.
11 Report from a meeting of the Joint Working Group on Veterinary Matters on 14 November 2000.
12 Telephone interview with the Chief Veterinary Officer at the Icelandic Food and Veterinary Authority on 24 February 2010.
13 Report from a meeting of the EEA Joint Committee on 25 September 2009.
14 Telephone interview with the Chief Veterinary Officer at the Icelandic Food and Veterinary Authority on 24 February 2010.
15 Report from a meeting of the Standing Committee of the EFTA States on 7 June 2007.
16 Report from a meeting of the EEA Joint Committee on 25 September 2009.
17 Telephone interview with the Chief Veterinary Officer at the Icelandic Food and Veterinary Authority on 24 February 2010.
18 Report from a meeting of the Joint Veterinary Working group on 18 April 2008.
19 Decision of the EEA Joint Committee no. 133/2007 states that, 'due to the specific situation in Iceland as regards climate, geographical localization and nature of resources available, the feeding of fishmeal to ruminants may be accepted. This authorisation takes into account the absence of production and importation of meat and bone meal in Iceland.'
20 Report from a meeting of the Joint Working Group on Veterinary Matters on 24 March 2004.
21 Report from a meeting of the EEA Joint Committee on 8 June 2007.
22 Report from a meeting of the Joint Working Group on Veterinary Matters on 7 September 2006.
23 Article 103(2) reads: 'If upon the expiry of a period of six months after the decision of the EEA Joint Committee such a notification has not taken place, the decision of the EEA Joint Committee shall be applied provisionally pending the fulfilment of the constitutional requirements unless a Contracting Party notifies that such a provisional application cannot take place. In the latter case, or if a Contracting Party notifies the non-ratification of a decision of the EEA Joint Committee, the suspension provided for in Article 102 (5) shall take effect one month after such a notification but in no event earlier than the date on which the corresponding EC act is implemented in the Community.'
24 Report from a meeting of the Joint Veterinary Working Group on 18 April 2008.
25 Report from a meeting of the Working Group on Feedingstuffs on 4 June 2008.
26 Report from a meeting of the Working Group on Feedingstuffs on 26 November 2008.
27 Report from a meeting of the Working Group on Feedingstuffs on 27 October 2009.
28 In early 2010, the consolidated version of Annex I of the EEA Agreement contained a large number of acts which were marked 'entry into force pending' as Iceland had not yet fulfiled its constitutional requirements.
29 Report from a meeting of the EEA Joint Committee on 25 September 2009.
30 Telephone interview with the Chief Veterinary Officer at the Icelandic Food and Veterinary Authority on 24 February 2010.
31 Report from a meeting of the EEA Joint Committee on 25 September 2009.
32 Report from a meeting of the EEA Joint Committee on 25 September 2009.
33 Personal Communication from the Deputy Head of the Norwegian Mission to the EU on 6 April 2010.

34 Jon Bjarnason was the only member of the centre-left coalition government to vote against Iceland's application for EU membership.
35 Telephone interviews with the Chief Veterinary Officer at the Icelandic Food and Veterinary Authority, Head of Division at the Icelandic Ministry of Fisheries and Agriculture and Deputy Director of the Division for Food Safety at the EFTA Surveillance Authority on 24 February 2010.
36 Personal Communication from the Chief Economist of the Farmers Association of Iceland, 9 September 2010.
37 Article 13 states: 'The provisions of Articles 11 and 12 shall not preclude prohibitions or restrictions on imports, exports or goods in transit justified on grounds of public morality, public policy or public security; the protection of health and life of humans, animals or plants; the protection of national treasures possessing artistic, historic or archaeological value; or the protection of industrial and commercial property. Such prohibitions or restrictions shall not, however, constitute a means of arbitrary discrimination or a disguised restriction on trade between the Contracting Parties.'
38 This is a centrist party, with traditionally strong support from rural areas.
39 Interview with the Officer for Veterinary, Phytosanitary and Food Safety Policies at the EFTA Secretariat on 1 February 2012 in Brussels.
40 Telephone interview with Head of Division at the Icelandic Ministry of Fisheries and Agriculture on 24 February 2010.

8 Review of key findings

1 Interview with the former Counsellor for Industry at the Icelandic Mission to the EU (1995–98) on 8 September 2008 in Reykjavik.
2 Based on interviews with various high-ranking officials at the Icelandic Mission to the EU and the Ministry of Foreign Affairs.
3 Interview with the Deputy Secretary General of the EFTA Secretariat on 11 November 2008 in Brussels.

9 The EEA: Challenges and future scenarios

1 Belarus, Moldova, Ukraine, Georgia, Armenia and Azerbaijan.

Appendix I: Interviews

Table A1

Title	Date interviewed	Place
Director General of the Directorate for External Trade and Economic Affairs	23-Nov-07	Reykjavik
Deputy Head of the Icelandic Mission to the EU	29-Nov-07	Brussels
Head of Energy Policy at the Icelandic Ministry of Industry, Energy and Tourism	25-Feb-08	Reykjavik
Director at the Icelandic Ministry of Social Affairs and Social Security	25-Feb-08	Reykjavik
MP for the Social Democratic Alliance and Leader of the Icelandic delegation to the EFTA Parliamentary Committee	27-Feb-08	Reykjavik
Head of Corporate Communications at Landsvirkjun	27-Feb-08	Reykjavik
Legal Expert at the Department of Equality and Labour at the Icelandic Ministry of Social Affairs	28-Feb-08	Reykjavik
Director of the Department of Civil Law Affairs at the Icelandic Ministry of Justice and Ecclesiastical Affairs	29-Feb-08	Reykjavik
CEO of Hitaveita Sudurnesja	03-Mar-08	Reykjanesbaer
Head of Corporate Communications at Orkuveita Reykjavikur	04-Mar-08	Reykjavik
Manager of the Electricity Division at the Federation of Icelandic Energy and Utilities	04-Mar-08	Reykjavik
Deputy Director General of the National Energy Authority	05-Mar-08	Reykjavik
Former Minister of Social Affairs (1995–2003)	05-Jun-08	Reykjavik
Managing Director at the Federation of Icelandic Industries	10-Jun-08	Reykjavik
First Secretaries at the Department for European Affairs	10-Jun-08	Reykjavik

Table A1 (continued)

Title	Date interviewed	Place
Legal Expert in Civil Law Affairs at the Icelandic Ministry of Justice and Ecclesiastical Affairs	10-Jun-08	Reykjavik
General Director of the Icelandic Environment Agency	11-Jun-08	Reykjavik
Head of International Affairs at the Icelandic Federation of State and Municipal Employees	11-Jun-08	Reykjavik
Head of International Affairs at the Icelandic Association of Local Authorities	12-Jun-08	Reykjavik
Professor of Sociology at the University of Iceland	12-Jun-08	Reykjavik
Head of Social Affairs at the Icelandic Confederation of Labour	12-Jun-08	Reykjavik
Head of the Department of Development and Inspection of the Icelandic Administration of Occupational Safety and Health	12-Jun-08	Reykjavik
Officials at the EEA Coordination Unit in Liechtenstein	07-Jul-08	Vaduz
Head of Environmental Affairs at the Federation of Icelandic Industries	04-Sep-08	Reykjavik
Legal Expert at the Icelandic Ministry of Business Affairs	05-Sep-08	Reykjavik
Counsellor for Industry at the Icelandic Mission to the EU (1995–98)	08-Sep-08	Reykjavik
Head Legal Adviser in Employment Policy at the Confederation of Icelandic Employers	09-Sep-08	Reykjavik
Project Manager in Environmental Matters at the Icelandic Association of Local Authorities	09-Sep-08	Reykjavik
Director of Policymaking and Communications at the Confederation of Icelandic Employers	09-Sep-08	Reykjavik
Counsellor for Justice and Home Affairs at the Icelandic Mission to the EU	10-Nov-08	Brussels
Counsellor for Transport at the Icelandic Mission to the EU	10-Nov-08	Brussels
Director of the Services, Capital, Persons and Programmes Division of the EFTA Secretariat	11-Nov-08	Brussels
Deputy Secretary General of the EFTA Secretariat	11-Nov-08	Brussels
Counsellor for Labour and Social Affairs at the Norwegian Mission to the EU	11-Nov-08	Brussels
Officer for free movement of workers, equal treatment for men and women, labour law, health and safety at work at the EFTA Surveillance Authority	11-Nov-08	Brussels

Table A1 (continued)

Title	Date interviewed	Place
Director of the EEA Coordination Division at the EFTA Secretariat	11-Nov-08	Brussels
Officer for the Environment at the EFTA Secretariat	11-Nov-08	Brussels
Counsellor for Justice and Home Affairs at the Norwegian Mission to the EU	12-Nov-08	Brussels
Specialist on the EEA EFTA states at DG RELEX	12-Nov-08	Brussels
Head of Sector – Borders at DG Justice and Home Affairs	12-Nov-08	Brussels
Officer for Environment, Energy and DTR at the EFTA Surveillance Authority	13-Nov-08	Brussels
Counsellor for Industry at the Icelandic Mission to the EU	14-Nov-08	Brussels
Counsellor for Environmental Affairs at the Icelandic Mission to the EU	14-Nov-08	Brussels
Head of Division at the Icelandic Ministry of Fisheries and Agriculture	24-Feb-10	By phone
Chief Veterinary Officer at the Icelandic Food and Veterinary Authority	24-Feb-10	By phone
Deputy Director of the Division for Food Safety at the EFTA Surveillance Authority	24-Feb-10	By phone
Deputy Head of the Norwegian Mission to the EU	6-Apr-10	By email
Chief Economist of the Farmers' Association of Iceland	9-Sept-10	By email
Officer for Veterinary, Phytosanitary and Food Safety Policies at the EFTA Secretariat	1-Feb-12	Brussels

Appendix II: Internal EFTA documents

- EFTA review on EU Comitology Committees with EEA EFTA Participation or Relevance
- Report from the EEA Joint Committee, 8 June 2007
- Report from the EEA Joint Committee, 25 September 2009
- Report from the Joint Working Group on Veterinary Matters, 11 September 1998
- Report from the Joint Working Group on Veterinary Matters, 14 November 2000
- Report from the Joint Working Group on Veterinary Matters, 24 March 2004
- Report from the Joint Working Group on Veterinary Matters, 7 September 2006
- Report from the Joint Working Group on Veterinary Matters, 18 April 2008
- Report from the Standing Committee of the EFTA States, 7 June 2007
- Report from the Working Group on Feedingstuffs, 4 June 2008
- Report from the Working Group on Feedingstuffs, 26 November 2008
- Report from the Working Group on Feedingstuffs, 27 October 2009
- Working Paper by the EFTA Secretariat on the Open Method of Coordination (OMC).

Bibliography

Aale, Per Kristian (2012), 'Rapport: EOS-avtalen er en demokratisk fiasko for Norge' www.aftenposten.no/nyheter/iriks/politikk/Rapport-EOS-avtalen-er-en-demokratisk-fiasko-for-Norge-6742382.html, *Aftenposten*, accessed 1 February 2012.
Arter, David (2000), 'Small State Influence Within the EU: The Case of Finland's Northern Dimension Initiative', *Journal of Common Market Studies*, 38 (5), 677–97.
Asgeirsdottir, Olafia Dogg (2008), 'Ahrif Evropusambandsins a stefnumotun islenska raforkumarkadarins' (University of Iceland).
Bache, Ian (2006), 'The Europeanization of Higher Education: Markets, Politics or Learning?', *Journal of Common Market Studies*, 44 (2), 231–48.
—— (2008), *Europeanization and Multilevel Governance: Cohesion Policy in the European Union and Britain* (Lanham, MD: Rowman & Littlefield Publishers, Inc.).
Bache, Ian and Jordan, Andrew (2006a), 'Europeanisation and Domestic Change', in Ian Bache and Andrew Jordan (eds), *The Europeanisation of British Politics* (Basingstoke and New York: Palgrave Macmillan).
—— (eds) (2006b), *The Europeanization of British Politics* (Basingstoke and New York: Palgrave Macmillan).
Bauby, Pierre and Varone, Frederic (2007), 'Europeanization of the French Electricity Policy: Four Paradoxes', *Journal of European Public Policy*, 14 (7), 1048–60.
Baudenbacher, Carl (2012), 'The EFTA Court – The EFTA Judicial System Reaches the Age of Majority – Accomplishments and Problems', presentation given at an *EFTA Seminar on the EEA: Current and Future Challenges* (Brussels).
Berglund, Nina (2011), 'Historic "No" to an EU Directive', *Views and News from Norway* www.newsinenglish.no/2011/05/23/historic-no-to-an-eu-directive/%3E, accessed 30 January 2012.
Berglund, Sarah, Gange, Ieva and van Waarden, Frans (2006), 'Mass Production Law. Routinization in the Transposition of European Directives: A Sociological-institutionalist Account', *Journal of European Public Policy*, 13 (5), 692–716.
Bergmann, Erikur (2011), 'Iceland and the EEA, 1994–2011', *Europautredningen: Utvalget for utredning av Norges avtaler med EU* www.europautredningen.no/wp-content/uploads/2011/04/Rap7-island.pdf%3E, accessed 30 January 2012.
Beyers, Jan (2005), 'Multiple Embeddedness and Socialization in Europe: The Case of Council Officials', *International Organization*, 59 (Fall), 899–936.
Bjorgvinsson, David Thor (2006), *EES-rettur og landsrettur* (Reykjavik: Bokautgafan Codex).
Borgmann-Prebil, Yuri (2008), 'The Rule of Reason in European Citizenship', *European Law Journal*, 14 (3), 328–50.

Borzel, Tanja (2000), 'Why There Is No "Southern Problem": On Environmental Leaders and Laggards in the European Union', *Journal of European Public Policy*, 7 (1), 141–62.
——(2001), 'Non-compliance in the European Union: Pathology or Statistical Artefact?', *Journal of European Public Policy*, 8 (5), 803–24.
——(2002), 'Pace-setting, Foot-Dragging, and Fence-Sitting: Member State Responses to Europeanization', *Journal of Common Market Studies*, 40 (2), 193–214.
Borzel, Tanja and Risse, Thomas (2003), 'Conceptualising the Domestic Impact of Europe', in Kevin Featherstone and Claudio M. Radaelli (eds), *The Politics of Europeanisation* (Oxford: Oxford University Press).
Borzel, Tanja, Sprunk, Carina, Hofmann, Tobias and Panke, Diana (2008), 'To Comply or Not to Comply? Explaining Member State Violations of European Law', *ECPR Joint Sessions* (Rennes).
Bragadottir, Hrafnhildur (2008), 'Losun grodurhusalofttegunda: thjodrettarlegar skuldbindingar og islenskur rettur', LL.M (Haskoli Islands).
Braun, Marcel (2009), 'The Evolution of Emissions Trading in the European Union – The Role of Policy Networks, Knowledge and Policy Entrepreneurs', *Accounting, Organizations and Society*, 34 (3/4).
Bretherton, Charlotte and Vogler, John (2006), *The European Union as a Global Actor* (2nd edn; London: Routledge).
Breuss, Emilia (2011), *Die Zukunft des Kleinstaates in der europäischen Integration: Eine Untersuchung unter besonderer Berücksichtigung des Fürstentums Liechtenstein* (Schaan: Verlag der LAG).
Brox, Johan (2011), 'EØS styrkt av krisa', *Klassekampen* www.klassekampen.no/59546/article/item/null/-eos-styrkt-av-krisa%3E, accessed 2 February 2012.
Buller, Jim and Gamble, Andrew (2002), 'Conceptualising Europeanization', *Public Policy and Administration*, 17 (2), 2–24.
Bulmer, Simon and Burch, Martin (2005), 'The Europeanization of UK Government: From Quiet Revolution to Explicit Step-Change', *Public Administration*, 83 (4), 861–90.
——(2006), 'Central Government', in Ian Bache and Andrew Jordan (eds), *The Europeanization of British Politics* (Basingstoke and New York: Palgrave Macmillan).
Burnham, Peter, Gilland, Karin and Grant, Wyn (2004), *Research Methods in Politics* (Basingstoke and New York: Palgrave Macmillan).
Checkel, Jeffrey T. (2001), 'Why Comply? Social Learning and European Identity Change', *International Organization*, 55 (3), 553–88.
——(2005), 'International Institutions and Socialization in Europe: Introduction and Framework', *International Organization*, 59 (Fall), 801–26.
——(2006), 'Social Construction and Integration', in Mette Eilstrup-Sangiovanni (ed.), *Debates on European Integration* (Basingstoke and New York: Palgrave Macmillan).
Cini, Michelle (2003), 'Implementation', in Michelle Cini (ed.), *European Union Politics* (Oxford: Oxford University Press).
Corbett, Richard, Jacobs, Francis and Shackleton, Michael (2000), *The European Parliament* (4th edn) (London: John Harper Publishing).
Council of the European Union (2010), 'Council Conclusions on EU Relations with EFTA Countries', *3060th General Affairs Council Meeting Brussels, 14 December 2010* www.consilium.europa.eu/uedocs/cms_data/docs/pressdata/EN/foraff/118458.pdf%3E, accessed 31 January 2012.

Bibliography

Dagens Naeringsliv (2011), 'Leder DN: Handelsavtale' www.dn.no/forsiden/kommentarer/article2267001.ece%3E, accessed 2 February 2012.

Det Kongelige Utenriksdepartment (1999), 'Om samtykke til godkjenning av EØS-komiteens beslutning nr 69/98 om endring af EØS-avtalens veglegg I – Veternaere og plantesanitaere forhold'.

Duffin, Simon (2008), 'MEPs Vote to Include Aviation in the EU's Emissions Trading System' www.europarl.org.uk/news/NWScurrentmain.htm%3E, accessed 10 September 2008.

Dypvik, Astrid Sverresdotter (2011a), 'KrF vil diskutere EØS og vetoretten', *Nationen Politikk* www.nationen.no/2011/10/14/politikk/eos/eu/vetorett/krf/6985990/%3E, accessed 2 February 2012.

—— (2011b), 'Undersøking: Motstanden mot EØS-avtalen er dobla på eit år', *Nationen Politikk* www.nationen.no/2011/11/09/politikk/eos/meningsmaling/eu/eos-avtalen/7041165/%3E, accessed 2 February 2012.

—— (2012), 'ESA får godkjend, men EFTA-domstolen får kritikk i Europautredningen', *Nationen Politikk* www.nationen.no/2012/01/20/politikk/esa/eu/efta/efta-domstolen/7201201/%3E, accessed 30 January 2012.

Editorial Comments (2008), 'Two-speed European Citizenship? Can the Lisbon Treaty Help Close the Gap?', *Common Market Law Review*, 45 (1), 1–11.

EEA Review Committee (2012), 'Outside and Inside: Norway's Agreements with the European Union', *Official Norwegian Reports NOU 2012: 2*, Chapter1 www.regjeringen.no/pages/36798821/PDFS/NOU201220120002000EN_PDFS.pdf%3E, accessed 30 January 2012.

EFTA Court (1998), 'Advisory Opinion of the Court: Council Directive 80/987/EEC – Incorrect Implementation of a Directive – Liability of an EFTA State' www.eel.nl/documents/svein.pdf%3E, accessed 26 March 2008.

EFTA Secretariat (2002), 'The European Economic Area: Decision Shaping and Participation in Committees', in Glumur Baldvinsson (ed.), *EFTA Bulletin* (Brussels).

—— (2006), 'EEA Info Kit: An Introduction to the European Economic Area and other EFTA Activities' (EFTA Secretariat), 1–24.

—— (2007), 'EEA Decision-making' http://secretariat.efta.int/Web/InfoKit/Info_Kit/EEAdecisionmaking%3E, accessed 8 November 2007.

—— (2008a), 'EEA Joint Parliamentary Committee' www.efta.int/content/eea/institutions/eea/institutions/eea-joint-parliamentary-committee%3E, accessed 5 September 2008.

—— (2008b), 'EEA Decision-Making' www.efta.int/content/publications/fact-sheets/eea-factsheets/FS_DecMaking/view%3E, accessed 13 March 2008.

—— 'EFTA Surveillance Authority' (2008c), http://secretariat.efta.int/Web/EuropeanEconomicArea/institutions/ESA%3E, accessed 9 February 2008.

—— 'The EFTA Court' (2008d), http://secretariat.efta.int/Web/EuropeanEconomicArea/institutions/EFTACourt%3E, accessed 8 February 2008.

—— (2009), 'Decision Shaping in the European Economic Area', *EFTA Bulletin* www.efta.int/~/media/Files/Publications/Bulletins/eeadecisionshaping-bulletin.pdf%3E, accessed 30 January 2012.

—— (2010), 'The Food Law Package Will Formally Enter into Force on 1 May 2010' www.efta.int/eea/news/food-low-package-enters-into-force.aspx%3E, accessed 6 April 2010.

—— (2011), 'Thirty-sixth Meeting of the EEA Council in Brussels' www.efta.int/eea/eea-news/2011-11-15-eea-council.aspx%3E, accessed 30 January 2012.

——(2012), 'Parliamentary Committee' www.efta.int/advisory-bodies/parliamentary-committee.aspx%3E, accessed 30 January 2012.
EFTA Surveillance Authority (2005), 'Internal Market Scoreboard for the EFTA states – July 2005' www.eftasurv.int/information/internalmarket/dbaFile7443.html%3E, accessed 19 March 2009.
——(2006), 'Energy Sector Inquiry: Preliminary Report' www.eftasurv.int/information/reportsdocuments/competitionreports/dbaFile8617.pdf%3E, accessed 8 June 2009.
——(2008a), 'Infringement Proceedings' www.eftasurv.int/procedures/infringement/%3E, accessed 29 January 2008.
——(2008b), 'Internal Market Scoreboard for the EEA EFTA States – February 2008' www.eftasurv.int/information/internalmarket/dbaFile13338.pdf%3E, accessed 26 March 2008.
——(2008c), 'About the EFTA Surveillance Authority' www.eftasurv.int/about/%3E, accessed 8 February 2008.
Eilstrup-Sangiovanni, Mette (2006), 'Introduction: The Constructivist Turn in European Integration Studies', in Mette Eilstrup-Sangiovanni (ed.), *Debates on European Integration* (Basingstoke and New York: Palgrave Macmillan).
Einarsson, Eirikur Bergmann (2003), *Evropusamruninn og Island* (Reykjavik: Haskolautgafan).
Eiriksson, Stefan (2004), 'Deeply Involved in the European Project: Membership of Schengen', in Baldur Thorhallsson (ed.), *Iceland and European Integration: On the Edge* (London and New York: Routledge).
Europa (2009), 'Right of Union Citizens and Their Family Members To Move and Reside Freely Within the Territory of the Member States', *Summaries of EU Legislation* http://europa.eu/legislation_summaries/education_training_youth/lifelong_learning/l33152_en.htm%3E, accessed 22 July 2009.
European Commission (2005a), 'Questions and Answers on Emissions Trading and National Allocation Plans' (updated 20 June 2005) http://europa.eu/rapid/pressReleasesAction.do?reference=MEMO/05/84&format%3E, accessed 19 August 2009.
——(2005b), 'Annual Report on the Implementation of the Gas and Electricity Internal Market' http://eur-lex.europa.eu/LexUriServ/LexUriServ.do?uri=CELEX:52004DC0863:EN:HTML%3E, accessed 22 July 2009.
——(2006), 'Right To Move and Reside Freely' http://ec.europa.eu/justice_home/fsj/citizenship/movement/fsj_citizenship_movement_en.htm%3E, accessed 22 July 2009.
——(2007), 'Register of Expert Groups' http://ec.europa.eu/transparency/regexpert/index.cfm%3E, accessed 27 April.
——(2008), 'Questions and Answers on the Revised EU Emissions Trading System' (updated 17 December 2008) http://europa.eu/rapid/pressReleasesAction.do?reference=MEMO/08/796%3E, accessed 19 August 2009.
——(2010a), 'General Food Law – Principles' http://ec.europa.eu/food/food/foodlaw/principles/index_en.htm%3E, accessed 26 March 2010.
——(2010b), 'Commission Opinion on Iceland's Application for Membership of the European Union (COM(2010) 62)' http://ec.europa.eu/enlargement/pdf/key_documents/2010/is_opinion_en.pdf%3E, accessed 24 March 2010.
——(2012), 'Extenstion of Aviation in the EU ETS to the EEA EFTA States' http://ec.europa.eu/clima/policies/transport/aviation/eea/index_en.htm%3E, accessed 30 January 2012.
Fairbass, Jenny (2006), 'Organized Interests', in Ian Bache and Andrew Jordan (eds), *The Europeanization of British Politics* (Basingstoke: Palgrave Macmillan).

Falkner, G., Hartlapp, M. and Leiber, S. (2005), *Complying with Europe: EU Harmonisation and Soft Law in the Member States* (Cambridge: Cambridge University Press).

Falkner, Gerda and Treib, Oliver (2008), 'Three Worlds of Compliance or Four? The EU-15 Compared to the New Member States', *Journal of Common Market Studies*, 46 (2), 293–313.

Featherstone, Kevin (2003), 'Introduction: In the Name of Europe', in Kevin Featherstone and Claudio M. Radaelli (eds), *The Politics of Europeanization* (Oxford: Oxford University Press).

Featherstone, Kevin and Kazamias, George (2001a), 'Introduction', in Kevin Featherstone and George Kazamias (eds), *Europeanization and the Southern Periphery* (London and Portland, OR: Frank Cass).

Featherstone, Kevin and Kazamias, George (eds) (2001b), *Europeanization and the Southern Periphery* (London and Portland, OR: Frank Cass).

Featherstone, Kevin and Papadimitriou, Dimitris (2008), *The Limits of Europeanization: Reform Capacity and Policy Conflict in Greece* (Basingstoke and New York: Palgrave Macmillan).

Foreign Affairs Committee of the Icelandic Parliament (2009), 'Committee Report on a Proposal for a Parliamentary Resolution on Application for Membership of the European Union' http://evropa.utanrikisraduneyti.is/media/info/Foreign-Affairs-Committee-report.pdf%3E, accessed 17 May 2010.

Forsaetisraduneytid (2007), 'Tengsl Islands og Evropusambandsins' (Gutenberg).

Forster, Paul (2009), 'What's the Big (Aviation Global) Deal?', *Air Cargo World*, 99 (6).

Frommelt, Christian and Gstohl, Sieglinde (2011), 'Liechtenstein and the EEA: The Europeanization of a (Very) Small State', *Europautredningen: Utvalget for utredning av Norges avtaler med EU* www.europautredningen.no/wp-content/uploads/2011/04/Rap18-Liechtenstein2.pdf%3E, accessed 30 January 2012.

George, Alexander L. (1979), 'Case Studies and Theory Development: The Method of Structured, Focused Comparison', in Paul Gordon Lauren (ed.), *Diplomacy: New Approaches in History, Theory, and Policy* (New York: Free Press).

George, Alexander L. and Bennett, Andrew (2004), *Case Studies and Theory Development in the Social Sciences* (Cambridge, MA and London: MIT Press).

Grabbe, Heather (2000), 'The Sharp Edges of Europe: Extending Schengen Eastwards', *International Affairs*, 76 (3), 519–36.

——(2001), 'How Does Europeanization Affect CEE Governance? Conditionality, Diffusion and Diversity', *Journal of European Public Policy*, 8 (6), 1013–31.

——(2002), 'European Union Conditionality and the Acquis Communautaire', *International Political Science Review*, 23 (3), 249–68.

——(2005), 'Regulating the Flow of People Across Europe', in Frank Schimmelfennig and Ulrich Sedelmeier (eds), *Europeanization of Central and Eastern Europe* (New York: Cornell University Press).

Gudmundsen, Jan Ole (2008), 'New Forms of EU Governance and the EEA', *Decision-Shaping Seminar*, presentation given at the EFTA Secretariat (Brussels).

Gunnarsdottir, Dora S. (2010), 'Markmid nyrrar matvaelaloggjafar', *Morgunbladid*, 26 January.

Haverland, Markus (2003), 'The Impact of the European Union on Environmental Policies', in Kevin Featherstone and Claudio M. Radaelli (eds), *The Politics of Europeanisation* (Oxford and New York: Oxford University Press).

Haverland, Markus and Romeijn, Marleen (2007), 'Do Member States Make European Policies Work? Analysing the EU Transposition Deficit', *Public Administration*, 85 (3), 757–78.

Heritier, Adrienne (2005), 'Europeanization Research East and West: A Comparative Assessment', in Frank Schimmelfennig and Ulrich Sedelmeier (eds), *The Europeanization of Central and Eastern Europe* (Ithaca, NY and London: Cornell University Press).

Heritier, Adrienne, Kerwer, Dieter, Knill, Christoph, Lehmkuhl, Dirk, Teutsch, Michael and Douillet, Anne-Cecile (2001), *Differential Europe: The European Union Impact on National Policymaking* (Lanham, MD: Rowman & Littlefield).

Hill, Christopher (2002), *The Changing Politics of Foreign Policy* (new York and London: Palgrave Macmillan).

Hillion, Christophe (2011), 'Integrating an Outsider: An EU Perspective on Relations with Norway', *Europautredningen: Utvalget for utredning av Norges avtaler med EU* www.europautredningen.no/wp-content/uploads/2011/04/Rap16-E%C3%98S-sett-fra-EU.pdf%3E, accessed 30 January 2012.

Hix, Simon (2005), *The Political System of the European Union* (2nd edn) (Basingstoke: Palgrave Macmillan).

Hix, Simon and Goetz, Klaus H. (2001), 'Introduction: European Integration and National Political Systems', in Klaus H. Goetz and Simon Hix (eds), *Europeanised Politics? European Integration and National Political Systems* (London and Portland, OR: Frank Cass).

Hornburg, Thomas Boe (2011), 'Det går nå opp for folk at de er blitt ført bak lyset', *Aftenposten* www.aftenposten.no/nyheter/iriks/Det-gr-n-opp-for-folk-at-de-er-blitt-frt-bak-lyset-6722086.html –.TyrdOZjA5UQ, accessed 2 February 2012.

Hreinsson, Egill B. (2003), 'Hrod throun i vidskiptaumhverfi, raforku og taekni', *Morgunbladid*, 8 May.

Hughes, James, Sasse, Gwendolyn and Gordon, Claire (2004), 'Conditionality and Compliance in the EU's Eastward Enlargement: Regional Policy and the Reform of Sub-national Government', *Journal of Common Market Studies*, 42 (3), 523–51.

Idnadarraduneytid (2000), 'Framtidarskipulag raforkuflutnings a Islandi' www.idnadarraduneyti.is/media/Acrobat/skyr00_1.PDF%3E, accessed 13 March 2009.

—— (2007a), 'Innleiding raforkutilskipana', internal document (Reykjavik).

—— (2007b), 'Einfoldunaraaetlun' www.idnadarraduneyti.is/media/frettir/Einfoldunaraatlun_idnadarraduneytis–loka.doc%3E, accessed 17 June 2008.

Jachtenfuchs, Markus and Kohler-Koch, Beate (2004), 'Governance and Institutional Development', in Antje Wiener and Thomas Diez (eds), *European Integration Theory* (Oxford: Oxford University Press).

Jonsdottir, Johanna (2009), 'Ahrif adildar ad ESB a fullveldi Islands', *Stjornmal og stjornsysla*, 5 (1).

Jordana, Jacint, Levi-Faur, David and Puig, Imma (2006), 'The Limits of Europeanization: Regulatory Reforms in the Spanish and Portuguese Telecommunications and Electricity Sectors', *Governance: An International Journal of Policy, Administration, and Institutions*, 19 (3), 437–64.

Juliusdottir, Katrin and Wallis, Diana (2007), 'Future Perspectives for the European Economic Area' (Brussels: European Economic Area Joint Parliamentary Committee).

Kelley, Judith (2006), 'New Wine in Old Wineskins: Promoting Political Reforms through the New European Neighbourhood Policy', *Journal of Common Market Studies*, 44 (1), 29–55.

Knill, Christoph (2001), *The Europeanisation of National Administrations: Patterns of Institutional Change and Persistence* (Cambridge: Cambridge University Press).

Korski, Daniel (2011), 'What Kind of Europe?', *The Spectator Blog* www.spectator.co.uk/coffeehouse/7421503/what-kind-of-europe.thtml%3E, accessed 2 February 2012.

Kostakopoulou, Dora (2007), 'European Union Citizenship: Writing the Future', *European Law Journal*, 13 (5), 623–46.

Ladrech, Robert (1994), 'Europeanization of Domestic Politics and Institutions: The Case of France', *Journal of Common Market Studies*, 32 (1), 69–88.

——(2004), 'Europeanisation and the Member States', in Maria Green Cowles and Desmond Dinan (eds), *Developments in the European Union 2* (Basingstoke: Palgrave).

Laergreid, Per, Steinthorsson, Runolfur Smari and Thorhallsson, Baldur (2004), 'Europeanization of Central Government Administration in the Nordic States', *Journal of Common Market Studies*, 42 (2), 347–69.

——(2005), 'Europeanization of Nordic Central Goverments: Towards a Transnational Regulatory State?' (Bergen: Stein Rokkan Centre for Social Studies).

Laffan, Brigid and Stubb, Alexander (2003), 'Member States', in Elizabeth Bomberg and Alexander Stubb (eds), *The European Union: How Does it Work?* (Oxford: Oxford University Press).

Lavenex, Sandra (2004), 'EU External Governance in "Wider Europe"', *Journal of European Public Policy*, 11 (4), 680–700.

Lewis, Jeffrey (2005), 'The Janus Face of Brussels: Socialisation and Everyday Decision-Making in the European Union', *International Organization*, 59 (Fall).

McGowan, Lee (2005), 'Europeanization Unleashed and Rebounding: Assessing the Modernization of EU Cartel Policy', *Journal of European Public Policy*, 12 (6), 986–1004.

Magnusdottir, Asta (2008), 'EU Legislation and the EEA', presentation given at a *Decision-Shaping Seminar* at the EFTA Secretariat (Brussels).

March, James G. and Olsen, Johan P. (1998), 'The Institutional Dynamics of International Political Orders', *International Organization*, 52 (4).

——(2004), 'The Logic of Appropriateness', *Arena Centre for European Studies Working Papers No. 04/09* www.arena.uio.no/publications/wp04_9.pdf%3E, accessed 21 May 2010.

Mbaye, Heather (2001), 'Why National States Comply with Supranational Law', *European Union Politics*, 2 (3).

Mellvang-Berg, Trygve (2011), 'The EFTA Surveillance Authority as the EEA Watchdog', presentation given at an *EFTA Seminar on the EEA and the EU Internal Energy Market* at the EFTA Secretariat (Brussels).

Mendez, Carlos, Wishlade, Fiona and Yuill, Douglas (2006), 'Conditioning and Fine-Tuning Europeanization: Negotiating Regional Policy Maps under the EU's Competition and Cohesion Policies', *Journal of Common Market Studies*, 44 (3), 581–605.

Milieu Ltd and Edinburgh Europa Institute (2008), 'Conformity Studies of Member States' National Implementation Measures Transposing Community Instruments in the Area of Citizenship of the Union', *Horizontal Synthesis Report* (Brussels: European Commission).

Ministry of Foreign Affairs (2012), '33 Chapters of the EU Acquis' http://europe.mfa.is/phase-2—negotiation-process/chapters/%3E, accessed 30 January 2012.

Morgunbladid (2003), 'Orkulog raedd a fundi RARIK', 28 May.

Nationen Politikk (2011), 'Ingen tilnaerming mellom Norge og EU om postdirektivet' www.nationen.no/2011/11/15/politikk/postdirektivet/eu/eu-direktiv/arbeiderpartiet/7053146/%3E, accessed 30 January 2012.

Niemann, Arne (2004), 'Between Communicative Action and Strategic Action: The Article 113 Committee and the Negotiations on the WTO Basic Telecoms Services Agreement', *Journal of European Public Policy*, 11 (3), 379–407.

Norberg, Sven I., Hokborg, Karin, Johansson, Martin, Eliasson, Dan and Dedichen, Lucien (1993), *The European Economic Area – EEA Law – A Commentary on the EEA Agreement* (Stockholm: CE Fritzes AB).

Nordgaard, Lars Erik (2011), 'Policy Shaping in the EEA and the Role of the Secretariat', presentation given at an *EFTA Seminar on the EEA and the EU Internal Energy Market* at the EFTA Secretariat (Brussels).

Nordic Competition Authorities (2007), 'Capacity for Competition: Investing for an Efficient Nordic Electricity Market' www.samkeppni.is/samkeppni/upload/files/skyrs lur/samnorraenar_skyrslur/capacity_for_competition.pdf%3E, accessed 13 May 2009.

Nugent, Neill (2003), *The Government and Politics of the European Union* (5th edn) (Basingstoke: Palgrave).

O'Donnell, Clara (2006), 'The Enlarged EU's Relations with the Ukraine' (University of Cambridge).

Olsen, Espen D. H. (2008), 'The Origins of European Citizenship in the First Two Decades of European integration.', *Journal of European Public Policy*, 15 (1), 40–57.

Olsen, Johan P. (2002), 'The Many Faces of Europeanization', *Journal of Common Market Studies*, 40 (5), 921–52.

Oulds, Robert (2011), 'Time To Leave the EU and Stop Axporting British jobs abroad?', *Public Service Europe* www.publicserviceeurope.com/article/1139/time-to-leave-the-eu-and-stop-exporting-british-jobs-abroad%3E, accessed 2 February 2012.

Padgett, Stephen (2003), 'Between Synthesis and Emulation: EU Policy Transfer in the Power Sector', *Journal of European Public Policy*, 10 (2), 227–45.

Panke, Diana (2007), 'The European Court of Justice as an Agent of Europeanization? Restoring Compliance with EU law', *Journal of European Public Policy*, 14 (6), 847–66.

——(2008), 'Small States in the EU: Coping with Structural Disadvantages', *ECPR Standing Group on the European Union Pan European Conference on EU Politics* (Riga, Latvia).

Pederson, Tomas (1994), *European Union and the EFTA Countries: Enlargement and Integration* (London: Wellington House).

Piris, Jean-Claude (2011), *The Future of Europe: Towards a Two-speed EU?* (Cambridge: Cambridge University Press).

Pollack, Mark A. (2004), 'The New Institutionalisms and European Integration', in Antje Wiener and Thomas Diez (eds), *European Integration Theory* (Oxford: Oxford University Press).

Presidency of the European Union (2011), 'EU Relations with the Principality of Andorra, the Republic of San Marino and the Principality of Monaco', *Report to the Council* http://register.consilium.europa.eu/pdf/en/11/st11/st11466.en11.pdf%3E, accessed 2 February 2012.

Princen, Sebastiaan (2007), 'Agenda-setting in the European Union: A theoretical Exploration and Agenda for Research', *Journal of European Public Policy*, 14 (1), 21–38.

Radaelli, Claudio M. (2003), 'The Europeanisation of Public Policy', in Kevin Featherstone and Claudio M. Radaelli (eds), *The Politics of Europeanisation* (Oxford: Oxford University Press).

RARIK (2009), 'RARIK' www.rarik.is/English%3E, accessed 9 June 2009.
Rikisutvarpid (2011), 'Aetlar ekki ad endurskoda matvaelalog' http://ruv.is/frett/atlar-ekki-ad-endurskoda-matvaelalog%3E, accessed 30 January 2012.
——(2012), 'Framsalid ordid of mikid' www.ruv.is/frett/framsalid-ordid-of-mikid%3E, accessed 31 January 2012.
Risse, Thomas (2004), 'Social Constructivism and European Integration', in Antje Wiener and Thomas Diez (eds), *European Integration Theory* (Oxford: Oxford University Press).
Risse, Thomas, Cowles, Maria Green and Caporaso, James (2001), 'Europeanization and Domestic Change: Introduction', in Maria Green Cowles, James Caporaso and Thomas Risse (eds), *Europeanisation and Domestic Change: Transforming Europe* (Ithaca, NY and London: Cornell University Press).
Rognvaldardottir, Gudrun (2006), 'Stadlar og stjornsysla: Framkvaemd "Nyju adferdarinnar" a Island' (University of Iceland).
Rosamond, Ben (2000), *Theories of European Integration* (New York: St. Martin's Press).
Runner, Philippa (2008), 'Brussels To Recognise "European Aspirations" of Post-Soviet States', *EU Observer*, 24 November.
Schimmelfennig, Frank and Sedelmeier, Ulrich (2004), 'Governance by Conditionality: EU Rule Transfer to the Candidate Countries of Central and Eastern Europe', *Journal of European Public Policy*, 11 (4), 661–70.
——(2005a), 'Conclusions: The Impact of the EU on the Accession Countries', in Frank Schimmelfennig and Ulrich Sedelmeier (eds), *The Europeanization of Central and Eastern Europe* (Ithaca, NY and London: Cornell University Press).
——(2005b), 'Introduction: Conceptualizing the Europeanization of Central and Eastern Europe', in Frank Schimmelfennig and Ulrich Sedelmeier (eds), *The Europeanization of Central and Eastern Europe* (Ithaca, NY and London: Cornell University Press).
Schimmelfennig, Frank and Sedelmeier, Ulrich (eds) (2005c), *The Europeanization of Central and Eastern Europe* (Cornell Studies in Political Economy, Ithaca, NY and London: Cornell University Press).
Schimmelfennig, Frank, Engert, Stefan and Knobel, Heiko (2005), 'The Impact of EU Political Conditionality', in Frank Schimmelfennig and Ulrich Sedelmeier (eds), *The Europeanization of Central and Eastern Europe* (Ithaca, NY and London: Cornell University Press).
Sedelmeier, Ulrich (2008a), 'After Conditionality: Post-accession Compliance in the Postcommunist EU Member States', presentation given at the *ECPR Joint Sessions* (Rennes).
——(2008b), 'After Conditionality: Post-accession Compliance with EU Law in East Central Europe', *Journal of European Public Policy*, 15 (6).
Sejersted, Fredrik and Sverdrup, Ulf (2012), 'The Norwegian EEA Review – Presentation of the Final Report', presentation given at the *EFTA Seminar on the EEA: Current and Future Challenges* (Brussels).
Skarphedinsson, Ossur (2007), 'Skyrsla Ossurar Skarphedinssonar idnadarradherra um raforkumalefni' www.idnadarraduneyti.is/media/frettir/Raforkuskyrsla_2007.pdf %3E, accessed 13 May 2009.
——(2010), 'Iceland's Interests and a Responsible Foreign Policy', *Report of Ossur Skarphedinsson Minister of Foreign Affairs to Althingi the Parliament of Iceland on 14 May 2010* http://europe.mfa.is/media/Skyrslur/Executive-summary.pdf%3E, accessed 31 January 2012.

Skjaerseth, Jon Birgir and Wettestad, Jorgen (2009), 'The Origin, Evolution and Consequences of the EU Emissions Trading System', *Global Environmental Politics*, 9 (2).

Spaventa, Eleanor (2008), 'Seeing the Wood Despite the Trees? On the Scope of Union Citizenship and its Constitutional Effects', *Common Market Law Review*, 45 (1), 13–45.

Standing Committee of the EFTA States (2006), 'EEA EFTA Comment on the Proposal for a Regulation on the Accelerated Phasing-in of the Double-hull or Equivalent Design Requirements for Single-hull Oil Tankers and Repealing Council Regulation (EC) No 2978/94 (COM(2006)111 Final)' (Brussels: EFTA).

Stares, Justin (2011), 'What Exactly Would the UK Gain from Leaving the EU?', *Public Service Europe* www.publicserviceeurope.com/article/1090/what-exactly-would-the-uk-gain-from-leaving-the-eu%3E, accessed 2 February 2012.

Steiner, Josephine, Woods, Lorna and Twigg-Flesner, Christian (2006), *EU Law* (Oxford and New York: Oxford University Press).

Store, Jonas Gahr (2009), 'Redegjørelse av utenriksministeren om viktige EU-og EOS-saker den 17. november 2009' http://stortinget.no/no/Saker-og-publikasjoner/Publikasjoner/Referater/Stortinget/2009–10/091117/2/-a1, accessed 6 April 2010.

Sverdrup, Ulf (2004), 'Compliance and Conflict Management in the European Union: Nordic Exceptionalism', *Scandinavian Political Studies*, 27 (1).

Tallberg, Jonas (2002), 'Paths to Compliance: Enforcement, Management, and the European Union', *International Organization*, 56 (3).

Taverna, Michael A. (2009), 'Caps Off', *Aviation Week & Space Technology*, 170 (20).

The Economist (2011), 'In With the Out Crowd – MPs look to Norway and Switzerland' www.economist.com/node/21541863%3E, accessed 2 February 2012.

Thomassen, Tore N. (2008), 'Two Good(s) Examples of EFTA Cooperation with the EU', *Decision-Shaping Seminar* presentation given at the EFTA Secretariat (Brussels).

Thorenfeldt, Gunnar (2011), 'SV-topp vil slakte regjeringens hellige ku', *Dagbladet.no* www.dagbladet.no/2011/11/15/nyheter/eos/eu/utenriks/politikk/19033466/%3E, accessed 2 February 2012.

Thorhallsson, Baldur (2000), *The Role of Small States in the European Union* (Aldershot: Ashgate).

——(2001), 'Stjornsyslumal', in Eirikur Bergmann Einarsson (ed.), *Island i Evropu* (Reykjavik: Samfylkingin).

——(2004a), 'Towards a New Theoretical Approach', in Baldur Thorhallsson (ed.), *Iceland and European Integration: On the Edge* (London and New York: Routledge).

——(2004b), 'Shackled by Smallness: A weak Administration as a Determinant of Policy Choice', in Baldur Thorhallsson (ed.), *Iceland and European Integration: On the Edge* (London and New York: Routledge).

——(2005), 'What Features Determine Small States' Activities in the International Arena? Iceland's Approach to Foreign Relations until the Mid-1990s', *Stjornmal og stjornsysla*, 1 (1).

——(2006), 'The Size of States in the European Union: Theoretical and Conceptual Perspectives', *European Integration*, 28 (1).

Thorhallsson, Baldur and Ellertsdottir, Elva (2004), 'The Fishmeal Crisis', in Asthildur Elva Bernhardsdottir and Lina Svedin (eds), *Small-State Crisis Management: The Icelandic Way* (Stockholm: The Crisis Management Europe Research Program).

Thorhallsson, Baldur and Vignisson, Hjalti Thor (2004), 'A Controversial Step: Membership of the EEA', in Baldur Thorhallsson (ed.), *Iceland and European Integration: On the Edge* (London and New York: Routledge).

Thorhallsson, Baldur and Wivel, Anders (2006), 'Small States in the European Union: What Do We Know and What Would We Like to Know?', *Cambridge Review of International Affairs*, 19 (4).

Thorhallsson, Baldur, Laergreid, Per and Steinthorsson, Runolfur S. (2002), 'Europeanization of Public Administration: Effects of the EU on the Central Administration in the Nordic States. Working Paper 17–2002', Rokkansenteret, Stein Rokkan Centre for Social Studies, Bergen University Research Foundation.

Tolbaru, Ana-Maria (2012), 'Norway Sparks Debate on Future of EU Relations', *EurActiv* www.euractiv.com/global-europe/norway-sparks-debate-future-eu-relations-news-510204%3E, accessed 2 February 2012.

Umhverfisraduneytid (2008), 'Umhverfismal i EES samstarfinu' www.umhverfisraduneyti.is/frettir/nr/1197%3E, accessed 17 June 2008.

—— (2009), 'Adgerdaaaetlun i loftslagsmalum – 1. drog, des. 2009' www.umhverfisraduneyti.is/media/PDF_skrar/adgerdaraaetlun_i_loftslagsmalum_drog.pdf%3E, accessed 23 March 2010.

Umhverfisstofnun (2010), 'Vidskiptakerfid ESB med losunarheimildir' www.ust.is/Mengunarvarnir/Hnattraenmengun/vidskiptakerfiESB/%3E, accessed 23 March 2010.

UNFCCC (2010a), 'Impact of Single Projects on Emissions in the Commitment Period' http://unfccc.int/methods_and_science/other_methodological_issues/items/1072.php%3E, accessed 22 March 2010.

—— (2010b), 'Kyoto Protocol' http://unfccc.int/kyoto_protocol/items/2830.php%3E, accessed 22 March 2010.

Utanrikisraduneytid (2007), 'Skyrsla utanrikisradherra um Island a innri markadi Evropu' www.althingi.is/altext/135/s/pdf/0590.pdf%3E, accessed 16 June 2008.

—— (2012), 'Islenska utanrikisthjonustan i tolum og samanburdi vid onnur Evropuriki' www.utanrikisraduneyti.is/raduneytid/samantekt/%3E, accessed 30 January 2012.

Vachudova, Milada Anna (2005), *Europe Undivided: Democracy, Leverage and Integration after Communism* (Oxford: Oxford University Press).

Vink, Maarten P. and Graziano, Paolo (2007), 'Challenges of a New Research Agenda', in Paolo Graziano and Maarten P. Vink (eds), *Europeanization: New Research Agendas* (Basingstoke and New York: Palgrave Macmillan).

Visir (2011), 'Telja innflutningsbann stangast a vid EES samninginn' http://visir.is/telja-innflutningsbann-stangast-a-vid-ees-samninginn/article/2011111209088%3E, accessed 30 January 2012.

Vitorino, Antonio (2004), 'Foreword', in *Free Movement and Residence of Union Citizens Within the European Union* (Brussels: European Commission).

Wallace, Helen, Wallace, William and Pollack, Mark A. (2005), 'An Overview', in Helen Wallace, William Wallace and Mark A. Pollack (eds), *Policy-Making in the European Union* (Oxford and New York: Oxford University Press).

Wallis, Diana (2002), *Forgotten Enlargement* (London: Centre for Reform).

Wessels, Wolfgang, Maurer, Andreas and Mittag, Jurgen (2003), 'The European Union and Member States: Analysing Two Arenas Over Time', in Wolfgang Wessels, Andreas Maurer and Jurgen Mittag (eds), *Fifteen into One?* (Manchester and New York: Manchester University Press).

Wettestad, Jorgen (2009), 'European Climate Policy: Toward Centralized Governance', *Review of Policy Research*, 26 (3).

White, Michael (2012), 'Britain, Proud Home of Euroscepticism', *The Guardian* www.guardian.co.uk/world/2012/jan/26/britain-proud-home-euroscepticism?newsfeed=true%3E, accessed 2 February 2012.

Wiedswang, Kjetil (2011), 'På Innsiden: EØS-alternativ', *DN.no* www.dn.no/forsiden/kommentarer/article2271975.ece%3E, accessed 2 February 2012.

Wong, Reuben (2006), *The Europeanization of French Foreign Policy* (Basingstoke and New York: Palgrave Macmillan).

World Bank (2009), 'Governance Matters 2009: Worldwide Governance Indicators 1996–2008' http://info.worldbank.org/governance/wgi/index.asp%3E, accessed 11 March 2010.

Zalewski, Piotr (2008), 'MEPs and Council Presidency Reach Deal on Airline Emissions' www.europarl.europa.eu/news/expert/infopress_page/064-32956-175-06-26-911-20080627IPR32955-23-06-2008-2008-false/default_en.htm%3E, accessed 10 September.

Index

Access to Information Directive 22
accession 23, 167, 168, 169–70
accommodation 31, 151, 155
adaptations
   see exemptions and adaptations
administrations, small
   see small administrations
administrative capacity 58–60
agency/structure 16
aluminium 114
Amsterdam Treaty 98
Andorra 175
animal products 133 *see also*
   aquaculture products; fisheries
   products; fishmeal case
appropriateness, logic of 17–18, 26–27, 149
aquaculture products 131, 135–36
Arnadottir, Ragnheidur E. 142, 143
Article 102
   dispute-settlement clause 107–8
   exemptions and adaptations 50
   invocation 145
   mutually acceptable solution 68
   partial suspension 66–67, 96
   provisional suspension 183n62
   repercussions of 108–10
Article 103 137, 140, 145
Asgrimsson, Halldor 64–65
asymmetries 33–34, 65–66, 148, 167–68
Austria 3
Aviation Directive 125–26, 127–28
aviation sector 116, 120–26, 150

Belgium, diplomatic missions 36
Bjarnason, Jon 140, 145
BSE 133
Bulgaria 24

Cameron, David 174
candidate countries
   decision-making process 7
   EFSP 173
   influence on 1, 7–8, 23–25, 57, 159
   membership conditionality 154
   monitoring compliance 69
carbon dioxide emissions
   see Emissions Trading Scheme (ETS)
Central and Eastern European countries (CEECs) 23–25
citizenship
   concept of 110–11
   exclusivity 101–2
   free movement and 97–101
Citizenship Directive
   accommodation 155
   downloading 51, 152
   EEA-relevance 29–30, 97, 101–4
   free movement and 99–101
   incorporation 4, 105–110, 156
   mismatch 150
   overview 97
   transposition 112
civil society 37–38, 62–64, 141, 149
client states 7
climate change
   see Emissions Trading Scheme (ETS)
coalition-building 46
comitology committees 42–44
Committee of Permanent
   Representatives (COREPER) 44
Common Agricultural Policy (CAP) 3, 134
Common Fisheries Policy (CFP) 5, 47
Common Foreign and Security Policy 5, 180n3
Common Trade Policy 5

complaints 72
compliance *see also* downloading
 culture of 61-62, 149
 EU member states 21-22
 hidden non-compliance 27-28
 monitoring 25, 69, 71-76
 new member states 25-26
 non-member states 22-27
 overview 76-77
Confederation of Employers 63
consequentialism, logic of 17, 26-27, 149
constructivism 19
Court of Justice of the European Union (CJEU) 22, 69, 74, 164
Customs Union 5
Cyprus 87, 124
Czech Republic 23, 25

decision-making process *see also* uploading
 asymmetries 33-34, 65-66, 148, 167-68
 Commission 38-44
 democratic deficit 162-64
 EU member states 21
 exemptions and adaptations 50-53
 intra-EFTA collaboration 48-50
 lobbying 44-46
 lobbying from outside 44-48
 small administrations 34-38
decision-shaping 13, 33-34, 48-50, 152
Delors, Jacques 3
democratic deficit 7, 162-64
Denmark 36, 46, 59-60, 61
deportation 104, 110
derogations 51-52
DG RELEX 165, 183n54
dioxin contamination 133
diplomatic missions 36
directives 180n3
Directorate-Generals 41
domestic change
 see downloading
domestic institutions 17
downloading
 domestic intervening variables 58-64
 domestic utility 184n1
 effectiveness 31, 71-76
 Electricity Directives 81-83, 94
 Europeanization and 14-15
 external pressures 64-71
 levels of 31
 likelihood of 154-59
 mismatch 13-14, 28-29

 non-member states 23
 overview 6-8, 148, 150
 reception and projection 12
 stickiness 21

Eastern Partnership 176
Economic and Monetary Union (EMU) 5
EEA-relevance
 determining 96-97, 108
 evolving EU 165-67
 non-adoption 101-4
 prominence 52
EFTA Court
 advisory opinions 186n49
 ESA and 168, 169-70
 overview 70-71, 73-76
 responsibilities 185n36
EFTA Surveillance Authority (ESA)
 EFTA Court and 168, 169-70
 Electricity Directive 92
 energy sector inquiry 189n53
 imported goods 144
 overview 69-76
Ehlermann, Claus D. 160
Electricity Directive
 exemptions and adaptations 83-87, 153-54, 156
 mismatch 81-83, 94, 150
 origins and objectives 29, 79-81
 over-implementation 90-94
 overview 78-79, 94-95
 terminology 188n28
 transformation 155
 transposition without exemption 86-90
electricity usage 187n24
'EMAS' Regulation 21
embassies 36-37
Emissions Trading Scheme (ETS)
 accommodation 155
 aims 30
 downloading 126-28, 130, 152
 exemptions and adaptations 119-20, 125, 153
 explanation of 114-16
 green-house gases 193n7
 incorporation 67, 117-20, 156-57
 overview 113-14, 129-30, 150
 transposition 157
 ultra-peripheral regions 120-26
Employment Committee (EMCO) 45
Energy Efficiency of Buildings Directive 67
energy policy 81-83 *see also* Electricity Directive

Index

energy working group 187n18
Environmental Impact Assessment (EIA) 22
environmental policy 29, 113, 192n1
European Area of Freedom, Security and Prosperity (EFSP) 173
European Citizenship 108, 110–11
European Commission
  access to 34, 38–44, 45
  citizenship 98
  comitology committees 42–44
  infringements 17, 20–21, 69
  Internal Market Scoreboard 27
  intra-EFTA collaboration 48–49
  monitoring compliance 25
  social policy 181n10
European Council 44–46, 160, 172, 173–74, 181n10, 193n7
European Court of Justice 99
European Economic and Social Committee (EESC) 37, 181n10
European Economic Area (EEA) Agreement
  awareness of 43–44
  challenges in 162–68
  disputes *see* Article 102
  end of? 170–72
  expansion of 111, 172–78
  formation of 3–4
  future of 168–78
  history of 3–4
  impact of 5–6
  intra-EFTA collaboration 48–50
  Joint Committee 50, 64, 66, 68
  Joint Parliamentary Committee 47–48, 143
  legislation 5–6
  overview 1–2
  purpose of 101
  reviews of 160–62
  two member scenario 169–70
  two-pillar system 70–71, 165–66, 168, 181n2
  unanimity 66, 105
  vs an evolving European Union (EU) 165–67
European Economic Community (EEC) 3
European Employment Strategy (EES) 45
European External Action Service (EEAS) 50, 61, 66, 165
European Food Safety Authority (EFSA) 131, 134, 138

European Free Trade Association (EFTA)
  dependence 26
  dwindling numbers 167–68
  establishment of 179n3
  infringements 69–71
  intra-EFTA collaboration 48–50, 177
  legislation 5
  members of 1, 3, 4, 5
  Parliamentary Committee 47
  populations 27
  Standing Committee 50
  working groups 40, 43, 48, 50, 83–84, 187n18
European Neighbourhood Policy (ENP) 1, 8, 26, 176–77, 180n11
European Parliament, role of 46–48
European Union (EU)
  compliance 21–22
  decision-making process 21
  enlargement 167–68
  European Citizenship 108, 110–11
  Europeanization 20–22
  members of 4, *4*, 5, 185n23
  sovereignty 8, 164
  two-speed development 172–73
  uploading 20–22
  vs a static EEA 165–67
Europeanization
  definition of 1, 11–13, 179n1, 180n2
  EU member states 20–22
  impact of 147–48
  interactive nature of 6, 12–13, 148
  measuring 27–32
  new institutionalism 15–20
  non-member states 22–27
  variables 14–15, 148
exclusion 155
exemptions and adaptations
  Article 102 50
  Electricity Directive 83–87
  Emissions Trading Scheme (ETS) 119–20, 125, 153
  Food Law Package 153–54, 157
  increase in 165
  limitations of 152–53
  overview 50–53, 159, 163
expert groups 38–43

family members 101, 104, 110
Farmers Association 141
Federation of Trade and Services (SVTH) 144
financial crisis 2, 139

financial penalties 17, 20–21
Finland 3, 46, 61, 79
fisheries products 133, 135–36
fishmeal case 37–38, 44, 46, 136–37, 145, 196n19
food crises 133–34
food law 29
Food Law Package
  adoption at national level 137–40
  exemptions and adaptations 153–54, 157
  incorporation 135–37
  inertia 155–56
  infringements 157
  mismatch 132–35, 150
  national debate 140–45
  overview 30, 131–32, 145–46
Foreign Service 35–36
four freedoms 6, 96, 101
France 35, 59, 79–80
free movement, citizenship and 97–101
Free Movement Directive
  see Citizenship Directive
The Future of Europe (Piris) 172

Gas Directive 73
Germany 21–22, 59, 62, 79
Gislason, Atli 142
GMO Directive 67
'Governance Matters' (World Bank) 59
government effectiveness 59–60
Greece 59, 84
green-house gases
  see Emissions Trading Scheme (ETS)
Gudjonsdottir, Anna Margret 142–43
Gunnarsson, Jon 142

historical institutionalism 16, 18–20, 28, 32
Hitaveita Sudurnesja (HS) 82, 83, 87, 91, 92
Hulten, Michael van 172–73
human rights 98
Hungary 23, 25

Iceland
  accession 167, 168, 169–70
  administrative capacity 58–60
  compliance 26–27
  EU membership application 2–3
  European Economic Area (EEA) Agreement and 5–6
  financial crisis 2
  Foreign Service 35, 53

  membership negotiations 161
  population 15, 27
  small administration 34–38
  trade 65–66
Icelandic Competition Authority 93
Icelandic Electricity Act 89, 90, 94
immigration policy 103, 108
imported goods
  aviation sector 121
  ban on animal products 134, 136–37, 140–41, 144, 145, 157
inertia 31, 146, 151, 155–56
infringements
  exclusion 155
  member states 17, 20–21
  non-member states 24
  phases of 180n6
  procedures 69–71
institutionalism 15–20
Integrated Maritime Policy 45
interest groups 37–38, 62–64, 83
Internal Market Scoreboard 27, 71
international agreements 30, 113–14, 117, 118, 129, 152, 156
Italy, government effectiveness 59

Johannsson, Sigurdur Ingi 142

Kyoto Protocol 30, 114, 115, 117–18, 120, 128, 129, 150

Landsnet 90, 92, 95
Landsvirkjun 82–83, 87, 90, 91–92, 93
legislation
  adoption of 5–6, 137–39
  binding 17, 20–21
  intra-EFTA collaboration 48–49
Liechtenstein
  in EEA 3
  Citizenship Directive 29–30, 97, 105–6, 108
  derogations 51, 52
  Electricity Directive 86
  ETS 117, 119, 129
  Food Law Package 133
  future of 170, 172
  government effectiveness 59
  legislation study 160
  Money Laundering Directive 67
  monitoring 72–73
  population 27, 164
  report on EEA 161
  two member scenario 169–70
Lisbon Treaty 39, 42, 46, 98–99, 165

Index

live animal imports 136–37
lobbying 44–46, 153
Luxembourg
   diplomatic missions 36
   Electricity Directives 84, 85
   Foreign Service 35–36
   government effectiveness 59
   uploading 43

Maastricht Treaty 98, 99
Malta 36, 87, 124
Maritime Strategy 54
Members of the European Parliament (MEPs) 47
Ministry of Foreign Affairs 53, 161, 163
Ministry of Industry 83–84, 87, 89
Ministry of Justice 102
mismatch
   Citizenship Directive 150
   Electricity Directive 29–30, 81–83, 94, 150
   ETS 30, 126–27
   Food Law Package 132–35, 150
   measuring 28–29
   overview 149–50, 158
   as trigger 13–14, 20
Mission to the European Union (EU) 36
Monaco 175
Money Laundering Directive 67
monitoring *see also* EFTA Surveillance Authority (ESA)
   candidate countries 69
   CEECs 25
   effectiveness 71–76
   overview 76–77
   self-monitoring 155, 167

National Allocation Plans (NAPs) 115–16
National Energy Authority 88, 91
Natura Directives 192n1
Neighbourhood Policy 154
Netherlands, Electricity Directive 79
New Approach 63, 185n21
New Legal Framework (NLF) 49
Nice Treaty 99
Nordal, Olof 141–42
Nordic Council 46, 182n34
Nordic countries, compliance 59–62
Norway
   Citizenship Directive 97, 105–7
   complaints 72
   democratic deficit 162
   diplomatic missions 36

   in EFTA 3
   Electricity Directive 84–85
   ETS 117, 129
   EU membership application 179n2
   Europeanization 5–6
   expert groups 40–41
   Food Law Package 132–33, 136, 138, 143–44
   Foreign Service 35
   future of 170–72
   government effectiveness 59–60
   law-abidance 61
   lobbying 46
   monitoring 75–76
   pollution 73
   population 27
   Postal Services Directive 67–68, 104, 109, 111, 158–59, 163
   report on EEA 160, 161, 173
   two member scenario 169–70

observer status 42, 43
oil searching 73
oil tankers 49
Open Method of Coordination (OMC) 21, 25, 180n3, 180n7
Orkuveita Reykjavikur (OR) 82, 83, 91, 92, 93

Packaging Directive 62
phytosanitary measures 131, 133
policies/politics/polity 14
population 27, 35
Portugal, Electricity Directive 93
Postal Services Directive 67–68, 104, 109, 111, 158–59, 163
Presidency 45
projection 12

Qualified Majority Voting (QMV) 35, 44, 99
qualitative studies 28, 32
quantitative studies 27–28
quasi-membership 20

RARIK 82, 92
rational choice institutionalism 16–17, 19, 148–49
REACH Regulation 46, 49–50, 60, 113
reception 12
regulations 180n3
residence rights 98, 99, 100–101, 103–4, 110
Romania 24

Samorka 88, 91
San Marino 175
Schengen Convention 25, 99, 190n9
Sejersted, Fredrik 169
Sigfusson, Steingrimur J. 145
Skarphedinsson, Ossur 163
Slovakia 24, 25
Slovenia 25
small administrations
   democratic deficit 7, 162–64
   limitations of 34–38, 148, 154
   prioritization 40–41
social policy 103, 181n10
socialization 64–65, 149
sociological institutionalism 16, 17–18, 21
sovereignty
   EU member states 8, 164
   international agreements 113, 166
   non-member states 66, 96
   supranationalism 8, 163, 173
Spain 22, 84, 93
Store, Jonas Gahr 171
structure/agency 16
supranationalism 8, 163, 173
suspension 66–69, 145–46
Sveinbjornsdottir, Erla Maria 186n50
Sweden 3, 46, 59–60, 61, 79
Switzerland 3, 133, 172, 173–74, 179n5

Taxation 5
trade 65–66
transformation 31, 151, 155
transitional regimes 83, 188n33

Treaty Establishing the European Community (TEC) 99
Treaty on European Union (TEU) 179n1
Treaty on the Functioning of the European Union (TFEU) 179n1
two-pillar system 69, 70–71, 125, 163, 165–66, 168

Ukraine 26
ultra-peripheral regions 153
United kingdom
   compliance 22
   Electricity Directives 79
   government effectiveness 59
   return to EFTA 174–75
   uploading 20
United Nations Framework Convention on Climate Change (UNFCC) 193n5
uploading
   adeptness 20–22
   Commission 34–38
   exemptions and adaptations 50–53
   interactive nature of 12
   overview 6–8, 33–34, 53–55
   small administrations 34–38, 148, 154
   success of 30–31, 151–54
veterinary issues 131, 132–33, 136–37, 138–39, 144

veto points 62–64, 158–59, 163
voting rights 98, 101–2

Water Directive 67
World Trade Organization (WTO) 133

Printed in Great Britain
by Amazon